Managing Innovation in the Arts

Making Art Work

Marian Fitzgibbon

Q

QUORUM BOOKS
Westport, Connecticut • London

Library of Congress Cataloging-in-Publication Data

Fitzgibbon, Marian.
    Managing innovation in the arts : making art work / Marian Fitzgibbon.
       p. cm.
    Includes bibliographical references and index.
    ISBN 1-56720-434-1 (alk. paper)
    1. Arts—Management. 2. Creation (Literary, artistic, etc.)—Economic
aspects—Case studies. 3. Performing arts—Ireland—History—20th century.
I. Title.

NX760.F582001
700′.68′8—dc21   2001019183

British Library Cataloguing in Publication Data is available.

Library of Congress Catalog Card Number: 2001019183
ISBN: 1-56720-434-1

First published in 2001

Quorum Books, 88 Post Road West, Westport, CT 06881
An imprint of Greenwood Publishing Group, Inc.
www.quorumbooks.com

Printed in the United States of America

The paper used in this book complies with the
Permanent Paper Standard issued by the National
Information Standards Organization (Z39.48-1984).

10 9 8 7 6 5 4 3 2 1

Contents

Illustrations

FIGURES

Acknowledgments

This study was made possible by the cooperation of members and associates of Druid Theater Company, Opera Theater Company, and Macnas. My very sincere thanks to them all and in particular to Páraic Breathnach, James Conway, and Garry Hynes who graciously acceded to my request to quote them by name. The good counsel of Professor Bill Roche of University College, Dublin, is also gratefully acknowledged as is the affable assistance of Eric Valentine of Quorum Books.

Introduction: Managing Arts Innovation

Take almost any arts policy statement—an Arts Council report, a government arts plan, a mission statement for a national theater company, a metropolitan cultural center, or a local arts organization—anywhere in the Western world, and you can be sure to find an allusion to innovation. Why is this? First, trivial though it may seem, there is the trendiness of innovation in whatever field. In the organizational world as in all others, fashions come and go. A quick survey of the jobs section of a newspaper is ample illustration of the desirablity of this elusive and ill-defined quality: "Innovation is our password," or, "We are looking for an executive with an innovative approach." Even when an organization might need to consolidate, they look for innovative flair. This trend is reflected too in the volumes of business and management books on the subject. In short, innovation is to the organizational world today what reliability was in the 1950s. The arts world is no exception. Indeed, here the subject has added intensity derived from the notion that innovation is the very *raison d'être* of the arts sector, itself regarded as the crucible of creativity. Organizations that in other ways are very successful—high production values, good audiences, solvent accounts—are decried as boring if they fail on the innovative front. Conversely, those that are perpetually in the red, have eccentric management arrangements, and five lonely souls sitting in the echoing auditorium, may well be hailed as path-breaking and innovative and enjoy the patronage, at least in terms of verbal support, of the *cognoscenti*. Though a bit of a caricature, the readiness with which one can call up examples gives a degree of validity to this characterization. True artistic success is identified with innovation and arts organizations ignore this at their peril.

This holds for both the private and public sectors. In the world of the cultural industries, affected as all others by the numbing wave of globalization, the insatiable appetite for innovation is particularly in evidence. This is increasingly true given an abundance of prefabricated cultural "product," propagated by increasingly futuristic means of diffusion, as well as an audience whose senses and sensibilities are relentlessly bombarded by banality and sated by sameness.

As the logic—at least of the funded sector—has it, the solution to the *massification* of culture is germinated in the protected environment of the subsidized arts. The argument (advanced by Adizes, 1975) goes that protected from the "blasted heath" of the marketplace and absolved of the necessity to delve into "the greasy till" of commerce, the individual or organization cushioned by public funding has the freedom to experiment and to be creative. Thus innovation is the most frequent argument in favor and justification of public funding.

Why this book and what does it offer? The initial impulse came from personal experience of what seemed to be a gap in knowledge, first at the policy level. As somebody who worked for the Arts Council in Ireland (the national funding body for the arts) in the 1980s and 1990s and who observed and participated in grant decisions, the abstract dilemma of supporting innovation took on very concrete and practical expression for me. Apart at all from the mesh of objectives that had to be met by public funding (support for high standards and excellence, education, support for artists, increased availability of and participation in artistic activity, etc.) and that inevitably complicated the decision-making process, how could one determine the relative innovativeness of one company or organization over another? In the absence of criteria, personal influence and opinion often swayed decision making particularly within the *realpolitik* of funding decisions, most frequently in straitened circumstances. The lack of any research on the subject of innovation in the arts; the frequently cursory nature of routine evaluations of policy in this area; the level of compromise which can tend to discourage rigorous examination of the facts; and the absence of explicit and informed discussion all meant that a frequent outcome was a somewhat embarrassed lapse into surrogate criteria and a rather feeble acknowledgment of the subjectivity of the whole thing. This was all the more easy to justify given the benediction of mystery, which, albeit anachronistic, is still endemic in discussion of the artistic:[1] how can one possibly legislate for artistic innovation?

The knowledge deficit at policy or regulatory level, described above, extends to companies working in the sector. The issue in itself is pressing: for subsidized arts organizations,[2] the requirement to innovate is intensified by increasing pressure on limited public funds. The many changes in the arts-funding environment (shrinking public budgets worldwide, calls for greater efficiency, transparency and accountability demands, etc.), combined with an exponential growth of interest in organization science, point inevitably to an increasing emphasis on management as a means of optimizing scarce public funding. But what do we actually know about how innovative arts organizations are run?

We can call up at least two diametrically opposed images of such organizations, both of them recognizable and current in the world at large. In one there flowers a creative environment where, by virtue of a supportive climate and a people-centered approach, organizational members are engaged in the excitement associated with producing new and valuable works of art. The antithesis of mechanistic or bureau-cratic-type firms, participants in such companies reputedly have the opportunity to explore and realize their own creativity. The other image presents these same arts organizations as disorganized, inefficient, wasteful, incapable of planning, with an excessively inward focus, and contemptuous of audiences.

How can we reconcile these two perceptions? Organization theorists might well suspect a number of misapprehensions in the former. There is evidence, for example, of a confusion between the management of creativity and creative management; a positive bias towards both the nature of artistic work and the management of innovation; and a range of unproven assumptions such as the relationship between job satisfac-tion and organizational output. The second image is contradicted by the sometimes spectacular achievement of small arts organizations, even with minimal resources. But this characterization only points up the cracks: it does not answer the questions as to what makes for innovation and how it is managed. Which image best corresponds with the reality of the innovative arts organization? The frequent allusions in business success books to the techniques and modus operandi of creative arts organizations are based more on preconception or heresay and casual observation than any close examination. In fact no work at all directly addresses this subject in the existing body of research, whether in the field of arts management or of business. Therefore policy makers, funding agencies, and arts organizations are singularly inca-pacitated in what is for the reasons already outlined, an area of signal and central importance.

What then are the questions? For our purposes here, they arise at two levels. First, for the arts policy/funding body there are two main issues:

- how does one decide on what is an innovative arts organization?
- can one intervene in some way to encourage innovation?

Flowing from these are a host of subordinate issues: is it possible to set objective or at least verifiable standards that have general application; how does innovation relate to effectiveness or success or recognition; what should be the margin of indulgence or tolerance of failure; and how does one justify this in terms of public funding. On a second level, there are questions for the arts organization:

- how does innovation work?
- are there ways of being more innovative?
- can skilful management convert innovation into success?

To state the problem more fully, how can innovative arts organizations manage to deliver high-quality, path-breaking work within notable resource constraints in a particularly visible context? How can they meet specific deadlines, while supposedly conforming at the same time to few of the characteristics frequently attributed to other categories of high-performing organizations—such as clearly communicated aims, objectives and standards of efficiency, a monitored control system, performance-related incentives and rewards, and often minimal regard for worker self-realization? Thus posited, their achievement constitutes in management terms a notable dilemma.

And in this field, dilemmas abound. Before we go on to say what this book does and does not offer and how it can benefit arts organizations at different levels, it is important to map briefly the minefield which confronts anyone who would investigate innovation in general and innovation in the arts in particular. Without an appreciation of the very real problems and pitfalls, one may deliver a flawed analysis and encourage unreal expectations. We refer here to three main problems. First, and most importantly, at a philosophical level, though acknowledging that in the real world decisions have to be taken, we must nevertheless recognize the impossibility of truly evaluating innovative achievement. This may be termed (borrowing from Robert Frost) "the-road-not-taken" syndrome. Simply put, how can one know in retrospect, in relation to any course of action or cycle of events, that another decision or alternative route might not have been more innovative than the one actually taken at a particular point in time? The exigencies of the moment can never be fully recaptured. Nor can the consequences of a hypothetical alternative action. This problem is exacerbated in practical terms by the positive bias of memory, and the fact that alternative possibilities are not reflected in files, even if files exist! The conflation of innovation with success further compounds this issue. As an organization emerges crowned with awards for innovative achievement, who will dare to quibble about whether a decision was sufficiently daring or imaginative. The researcher may have to accept the impossibility of disentangling these factors in any definitive way. Second, there are concrete problems of definition and meaning—innovation is inherently controversial, one man's meat is another man's poison—and here too one must accept a certain level of ambiguity and perhaps look to a usage in the field that may be less than philosophically watertight. Finally in the arts sector, creation or innovation is heavily wreathed in a mythology that has long proved resistant to investigation—whether from the superstitious, atavistic fear that exploration will break the spell, or as a consequence of those myths surrounding organizations which are conjured, instinctively or deliberately, by people whose very trade and currency is the manipulation of the image. It would be nice to be able to claim that all these problems are resolved in this book, but such dilemmas, by their nature, evade definitive resolution.

So what then can the study presented here offer? Far from suggesting that innovation is an intractable issue, immune to the peering and poking of the researcher, we show that a systematic and detailed examination into how innovative organizations in the arts actually function can offer real insights to arts managers and policy makers. The abovementioned issues are an acknowledgment of the contingency of innovation as well as a necessary qualification. Lets state it clearly: there is no recipe for innovation in the arts or in any other sector. Books which have claimed to offer such solutions have been embarrassingly discredited by the subsequent decline or even the untimely demise of their star cases. But it is possible to lift the veil, to distill common features and processes, and to help both policy makers and practitioners alike towards a better understanding and even a conceptual reframing of the innovation issue. The reader will find that the account offered here—what might be termed a warts-'n'-all description—departs to some considerable extent from the received view both of arts organizations and the innovation process. In addition the framework we put forward provides arts managers and policy makers with the tools and the language to handle, manage, and evaluate a process which up to now, for want of a vocabulary, has proved resistant and at times even suspect.

The shape of this book is straightforward: first, with a succinct survey of what is already known about the innovation process in the organizational world and in the arts sector, we set the platform for the investigation which is its core; second, we describe the research that constitutes the meat of our enquiry; and third, we mold the conceptual reformulation that derives from a marrying of the previous two parts.

Chapter 2, drawing on what has been written about innovation and about arts organizations, mainly by North American and European researchers and theorists, develops a profile of what one might expect to find in an innovative arts company. The dominance and pervasiveness of the Romantic paradigm or notion of creativity is noted and dealt with, as are distinctions between innovation and creativity. We discuss the organicism which is commonly associated with innovative organizations. A theoretical framework to facilitate discussion of the topic is advanced and a schema of models is proposed in order to present credible alternative accounts or explanations of innovation in the sector. (No such review of existing knowledge has been previously undertaken and this chapter will hopefully be of considerable use to arts management and administration students, as well as other researchers. Those more interested in the story of innovation in practice can move quickly on to the three chapters which follow.)

Chapters 3 to 5 describe, in what might be termed full color, the operation of Druid Theater Company, Opera Theater Company, and Macnas, three companies from the performing arts sector in Ireland. Each company, though small, has won considerable international acclaim and a reputation in Europe and, notably in the case of Druid, in North America, for high innovative achievement. Their operation is examined under headings cognate with the framework presented at the outset to give coherence and clarity to the book and its arguments and to facilitate interorganizational comparison. Distinct pictures emerge of the operation of each company, the essence of which is characterized as manifestations, respectively, of "primitive," "managerial," and "opportunistic" innovation. The features of these are described in full. This investigation constitutes the empirical core of the book. Based on a study conducted in 1997–1998, it is emphasized that the data on the companies refers to this period (although for reasons of style we do not repeat this fact throughout the text). Furthermore, that the analysis presented here may be regarded as evidence at times of poor governance or management practice is beside the point—the aim is to tell it as it was.

Chapter 6 assesses the results of the investigation, reflects rigorously on the import of its findings and distills its added value for understanding and achieving innovation. In so doing, it first highlights four aspects of the process which are either at odds with or would seem to merit a richer account than has been the case to date. As such, in effect a restatement of the innovation framework adopted at the outset of the study is offered. A reprise of the character of innovation found in each of the three companies prefaces the identification of its main drivers, allowing the adoption of a model which seems most likely to fit innovation in arts organizations The extent to which the findings of this study are consonant with arts organizations in general is discussed as well as an assessment both of the contribution of this study and the likely directions for further work.

Briefly to end, two questions may suggest themselves immediately to the reader: first why all performing arts companies and second why all Irish? In answer to the first, we have opted for arts organizations where innovation may be said to happen *within* the company itself, as opposed to being bought in, the result of an alliance, or otherwise introduced—as might be the case with an arts center or a publishing house, for instance.[3] The use of Irish cases is in part the result of practical research considerations and has the advantage of offering a single environment as a backdrop to organizational innovation. However (and at the risk of proving Brendan Behan's sardonic *bon mot* about the Irish that "we are very popular among ourselves!") the international reputation of the country for creativity, whether in the fields of literature, traditional music, and recent success stories in film and traditional dance, makes it at least interesting to explore the interstices and workings of this creativity by telling the story told here.

NOTES

1. See Denis Donoghue (1983) *The Arts without Mystery*.

2. It is worth recalling here that the lion's share of public arts funding goes to organizations—as opposed to individual artists.

3. Further reference is made to the selection process in Chapter 2.

2

The Theory of Innovation

What drives innovation in the arts sector? What are the features of innovative arts organizations? Are they all highly individual in their operation or do they share any common traits? Is the process an idiosyncractic one or can it be analyzed in a way that might prove helpful in understanding or encouraging innovative arts practice?

This chapter, as a first step towards answering these questions, provides the reader with as succinct a summary as possible of what is already known about the management of innovation. Though not wishing to expound on questions of definition, we realize that for some of our audience the difference between innovation and creativity will be an issue, given the particular connotations and quasi-emotive resonance of these words in the arts sector. Here no real distinction is made between the two and we explain briefly why. The frequent identification of the management of creativity with creative management is also touched on as a prelude to the presentation of previous research on this topic.

Despite the vast amounts that have been written on the subject, innovation theory can be described as exploratory and speculative rather than provided with developed theory and models. As a means of framing our inquiry, we therefore turn to the general model devised by Van de Ven (1986) as one we have found useful in representing central concepts of the reseach literature. We describe this and explain how to operationalize it for the purposes of drawing the innovation literature together in a coherent manner and as a matrix for the case descriptions in the following chapters.

We go on to outine the main thrust and findings of research work to date, drawing widely from North American and British writing on business and arts innovation, to fill out the theoretical picture of what makes for an innovative organization.

In the final section of the chapter, drawing on Van de Ven, we propose a theoretical framework as an outline response to our opening question and an approach to the field research which follows. The chapter ends by introducing the three cases that constitute the core contribution of this book.

CREATIVITY, INNOVATION, AND MANAGEMENT

In general in the arts sector, creativity is seen as a discrete process, the domain of the individual creative artist, and innovation has more to do with the organizational context. Table 2.1 summarizes the main points of difference. Taking these distinctions one by one the gap may be narrowed. First, creativity is the grander of the two concepts—the stuff of great artists, scientists, and Nobel Prize winners. Innovation is more mundane and can happen in the most humble and banal of widget-producing organizations. The difference lies in part in the degree of originality attained. Yet in the same breath experts readily acknowledge that nothing is truly original and that creativity results from a combination of different ideas or disciplines, a harnessing of tradition or knowledge in a way that is illuminating.[1] N. Nicholson (1990) succinctly demonstrates the relativity of creativity in his account of the range of reactions of a number of people to a piece of jazz music.[2] So new only means new to someone[3] (see also Van de Ven and Rogers 1988). This is not to deny that some opinions are not more expert or well-informed than others. As is evident from the vexed nature of aesthetic discussion and opinion, there are no absolutes. And this is true not just in the world of the arts: "In the domain of mathematics, originality is attributed by social processes that are relative and fallible and that sometimes are reversed by posterity." (Csikszentmihalyi 1988, 328)

Usage or function matters too. Can ideation be easily separated from implementation, as the second distinction in Table 2.1 implies?

A painting by Patrick Collins does not fulfill its function until it is seen nor a poem by Séamus Heaney until read or heard. Our experience of the painting may be non-aesthetic in all sorts of ways such as my use of it merely as a firescreen or as an investment stored away in a vault. While remaining an artwork in these cases it does not function as one. "Execution consists of making a work," argues Goodman, "implementation of making it work." (Benson 1989, 19; Goodman 1982, 282.)

TABLE 2.1
Contrasting Dimensions of Creativity and Innovation

Creativity	Innovation
Involves genuine originality	Need only be new to the innovating organization
Equated with ideation or invention	Includes implementation
Individual or small group process, needing protection	Social process involving many people and diverse functional specialisms
Mysterious, black box phenomenon, not amenable to management	May be broken down into distinct phases which can be managed

Thus the realization of creativity *includes* the idea of implementation hitherto considered the domain of innovation and supposes some level of management, however rudimentary.

The distinctions between the individual and the social are equally arbitrary: it is worth quoting R. K. Merton (1965) in full on this (noting that he uses the word "innovative" as a direct synonym of "creative").

> The notion of successive contexts makes it clear that the concept of the innovative act or the innovative man is a very high abstraction from concrete reality. It abstracts from the milieu, the organization and the organizational environment. It treats the innovative man as though he were entirely exempt from the social and interpersonal conditions under which he lives and works and so expresses his capacities, no matter how much these conditions vary. The abstraction is of course justified if it is deliberately and temporarily instituted. But it should be recognized as an assumption, not taken as a fact. It is by no means self-evident that Newton, Darwin, or Kelvin would have made significant scientific contributions had they lived in *any* kind of social environment. Had they been born into Bantu culture, they might still have been innovative but the character of their innovations would surely have been different. (1965, 52)

Although the notion of creativity as an individual process has wide currency in the arts sector, Janet Wolff (1981) has comprehensively addressed a convincing philosophical rationale for the social basis of the production of art. Stating that the idea of the artist "as an individual creative worker, engaged in some supra-human creative task, emerged from the period of the Renaissance" (1981,17), she demonstrates the historical contingency of the image of creativity as blighted genius, encased in his (always masculine) ivory isolation, an image which reached its apogee in the Romantic period. She goes on to justify her belief that artistic creation must be sited in a social, economic and therefore, a political context. Wolff's thesis explodes the basis for an ontology of creativity that is anything other than social in the fullest sense and, far from mysterious or mystical, well within both the range of sociological inquiry and the sphere of environmental and management influence. Thus there is a further *rapprochement* of the two sides of Table 2.1.

To turn to the final distinction, the stage models,[4] which are frequently invoked in relation to the innovation process (Kanter 1988; Kimberly 1981; King 1990; Schroeder, Van de Ven et al. 1986) typically segment this into anything from three to five different stages. While these are intended to be useful to managers and may be a handy artifice for discussion purposes, they are often far removed from the reality of innovation. If one considers the progress of a theater production, for instance, the value of schematic model is but a dim reflection of the multiple iterations of the process. The truth is that creativity tends to bleed into the different stages of the production; it is intimately connected with what would usually be termed the idea realization, implementation, and diffusion stages and is not confined to the idea generation stage. To limit it in this way is unduly restrictive and in conflict with the usage of the term in the arts sector.[5]

To conclude, it is clear that the basis for the distinction between creativity and innovation on the dimensions offered by the literature (as represented by the axes of Table 2.1) is rather fragile. The collapse of the two concepts is reflected in Van de Ven's (1986) definition of innovation: "An innovation is a new idea, which may be a recombination of old ideas, a scheme that challenges the present order, a formula, or a unique approach which is perceived as new by the individuals involved" (1986, 591), which fits equally well as a definition of creativity. The unpacking of both concepts here constitutes a redefinition that is justified both by ontology and common usage, and the distinctions that have fallen away in the face of the above analysis add nothing useful in the context of the arts sector.

At this point it is apposite to comment on a further confusion: the frequent identification of creativity management with creative management. These are two distinct processes; the first being the management of interactions for the purpose of developing a creative output of some sort, and the second having to do with style of management or administration that is associated with organic structures, a participative approach, low formality, and so forth.

Some questions arise. Does the management of creativity require creative management, as it is commonly understood? The purpose of creative management is to render organizations more productive or innovative than traditional hierarchical styles of management, the idea being that if one espouses a more organic type of organization structure, if systems allow for bottom-up instead of top-down communication of

ideas, if teamwork and more unconventional methods for the generation and growth of ideas are encouraged, one will free up organizational
members to be more creative and then one will benefit in terms of
competitive edge. H. Guetzkow (1965) explains the sclerosis associated
in the popular mind with more traditional styles of management and
its essential paradox. "In the very heart of the organization . . . are
important built-in forces for regularizing—for conformity. One then
manages organizations by reducing the uncertainties, by discouraging
originalities, by ridding the organization of the unexpected. In the very
process of becoming a surviving, thriving organization, the creative
innovations of the members are inhibited." (1965, 36)[6]

However, it might be naive to assume that for an organization to have
a creative output, it follows that its style of management should be that
which is usually termed creative. For one thing, such a thesis takes
insufficient account of the influence of the environment—generally
acknowledged as important in determining levels of innovation. "As
contingency theory would predict, when one examines these relationships empirically, the data neither support assumptions of isomor-
phism nor of opposition between . . . product and climate." (Nicholson
1990, 195)

Following up on this it is apparent that although the type of management widely advocated in the literature as maximizing organizational
creativity or innovation would seem to resemble what is commonly
known as creative management (in the sense of invoking participative
style, bottom up strategy making, etc.), this is not necessarily the case
and it is preferable to keep an open mind on the matter, waiting to see
the outcome of the investigation of what is involved in making the art
work—in both senses!

VAN DE VEN'S FRAMEWORK

As a means of approaching and shaping the vast body of innovation
research, a general model or framework is immensely useful. Van de
Ven (1986) identified a core set of issues to guide longitudinal study of
the innovation process: "the human problem of managing attention . . . the
process problem in managing ideas into good currency . . . the structural
problem of managing part-whole relationships . . . and the strategic problem of institutional leadership" (1986, 91), otherwise summarized as people, ideas, transactions and context.[7] The elements of the model as detailed
by Van de Ven are outlined in Table 2.2 (next page).

As illustrated by Table 2.2, each of Van de Ven's four elements—people, ideas, transactions, and context—are linked with *strategic issues*
which he sees as central to the innovation project. In turn, he offers a

TABLE 2.2
Components of the Van de Ven (1986) Conceptual Framework

Elements	Strategic issue	Managerial responses
People	Managing attention	Focus on most demanding customer Direct personal confrontation with problem sources Double-loop learning
Ideas	Managing ideas into good currency	Social-political process
Transactions	Managing part-whole relationships	Autonomous units Redundant functions* Requisite variety Temporal linkage
Context	Institutional leadership	Negative feedback Double-loop learning Preservation of uncertainty

*By "redundant functions" is meant an overall (as opposed to a partial) understanding of the enterprise, engendered by "training, socialization, and inclusion in the innovation process." (Van de Ven 1986, 600).

number of managerial responses that he identifies as typifying what happens in the innovative organization. For Van de Ven the most vital aspect of innovation management and one which includes all the responses outlined in Table 2.2 is the presence of *institutional leadership or context*. This underpins and has a determining influence on how ideas, people, and transactions are managed.

What is meant by institutional leadership? Van de Ven (1986) describes its purpose as fourfold: "Defining the institution's mission, embodying purpose into the organization's structure and systems, defending the institution's integrity, and ordering internal conflict." (1986, 602) Thus while institutional processes may be taken to include aspects of the external environment (or in context), they also encapsulate culture and climate, leadership, control, and reward systems etc. and are best represented by contrast with technical processes (Figure 2.1).

Figure 2.2 is an attempt to schematize Van de Ven's framework: here can be seen the pre-eminence of *institutional processes* which operate on *transactions* with the purpose of effecting the core task of the innovative organization: *managing attention*. As illustrated in Figure 2.2, institutional processes (also termed the management of context—Table 2.2) work by means of *negative feedback, double-loop learning,* and the *preservation of environmental uncertainty* on the management of transactions

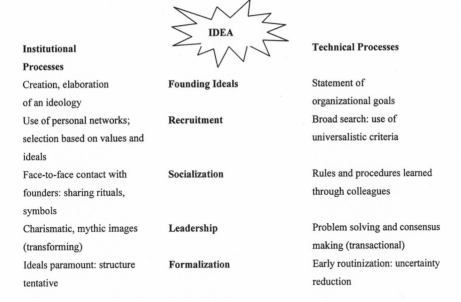

Institutional Processes		Technical Processes
Creation, elaboration of an ideology	**Founding Ideals**	Statement of organizational goals
Use of personal networks; selection based on values and ideals	**Recruitment**	Broad search: use of universalistic criteria
Face-to-face contact with founders: sharing rituals, symbols	**Socialization**	Rules and procedures learned through colleagues
Charismatic, mythic images (transforming)	**Leadership**	Problem solving and consensus making (transactional)
Ideals paramount: structure tentative	**Formalization**	Early routinization: uncertainty reduction

Figure 2.1 Institutional and Technical Processes
Source: Van de Ven (1986) after Lodahl and Mitchell (1980)

or part-whole relationships, which in turn are skewed towards the stimulation and management of attention as a key requirement for innovation.

The devices through which institutional processes operate require some explanation. Negative feedback is based on the cybernetic principle that goals are achieved by avoiding their non-achievement and re-

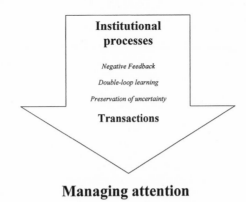

Managing attention

Figure 2.2 Management of Innovation [after Van de Ven (1986)]

quires the organization to have values and standards that determine the parameters of action (rather than tightly defined aims and objectives). Double-loop learning is differentiated from single-loop learning by its more fundamental questioning of "the relevance of operating norms" (Morgan 1986, 88) than is the case in the more simple adjustment associated with the former. The idea is that experience causes the organization to reflect on and adjust not only its current actions but in a more radical way its whole mode of operation. The preservation of environmental uncertainty is a process which contrasts with the more usual organizational strategy of uncertainty reduction vis-a-vis the external environment. Transactions or the "micro elements of macro organizational arrangements" (Van de Ven 1986, 598) are enacted in and through holographic units that in turn presuppose particular types of structure and management. The consonance of these concepts with the institutional processes delineated in Figure 2.1 is evident.

This is of necessity a summary description of the innovation process as outlined by Van de Ven. The high level of abstraction or generality of his framework is accepted—indeed, he does not claim to offer anything else. To flesh out this rather dense rendering, it helps to consider what it may mean in real terms; that is, how does it translate to the real world of innovative arts organizations. Therefore, Table 2.3 is a speculative exercise on what one might expect to find, *after* Van de Ven, in more and less innovative arts organizations. The table refers back one by one to the mechanisms or managerial responses described in Table 2.2 and describes their possible manifestations in the real world, in terms of positive and negative indicators. The indicative character of

TABLE 2.3

Indicative Positive and Negative Effects in Arts Organizations of Responses to Strategic Innovation Issues as Identified by Van de Ven

Strategic issue	Managerial response — highly developed attributes	Positive indicators —poorly developed attributes	Negative indicators
Management of attention	Focus on most demanding customer	Artists and critics as a primary target audience Search for new, challenging work Searching out of and interest in informed audience comment Arresting presentation / experimental approach to winning audiences	Low environmental scanning Weak and general audience focus Poor marketing Weak segmentation Repetitive work Low-risk strategy

TABLE 2.3 (continued)

Strategic issue	Managerial response — highly developed attributes	Positive indicators —poorly developed attributes	Negative indicators
Management of attention	Direct personal confrontation with problem sources	Sense of personal responsibility and engagement among staff Problem-solving approach Idea generation and filtering systems Flat structures Innovative input at several levels Mutual adjustment	Harvesting of past successes Low commitment and motivation Bureaucratic approach Buffering devices Role bound jobs Insularity
	Double-loop learning	Flow of new ideas Major organizational shifts and changes Environmental ripple-effect in terms of policy	Low organizational reflectiveness Impoverished levels of debate/habitual avoidance of conflict Minimal and usually conventional corrective response Quick-fix solutions Little effect on sectoral policy
Management of context	Negative feedback	Strong mission Notable commitment to art form Active approach to establishment of an integrative organizational culture Expansive and open approach to task Scope for new orientations	Narrow focus on objectives Routinized planning arrangements Reductive approach to enterprise or project Low tolerance of ambiguity Distrust of incongruent ideas or information
Management of context	Preservation of environmental uncertainty	Experimental approach Embrace of diversity Minimal fluid structures Flexibility in response to the unexpected even to the point of frequent turnarounds	Narrow interpretation of problems Editing out of environmental dissonance Uncertainty reduction strategies Early closure of debate or decision-making process

this illustration is emphasized. These indicators may still in some cases hold to a level of abstraction and at this point the reader is advised that these will be given more definition through the description of the actual operation of arts organizations in the field.

Having outlined the features of the Van de Ven model and suggested what this may mean in terms of real-life arts organizations, the next step is a consideration of the general wisdom in the innovation research literature. Aligning this simply and pragmatically along the issues identified by Van de Ven as shown in Figure 2.3, it is possible to reach some conclusions about the information available in advance of the examination of actual arts organizations. The sub-topics below will serve as headings that correspond both with Van de Ven's issues and the more usual discussion in the research literature, and for clarity will guide both the discussion of this and later, of the organizations chosen for investigation here.

RESEARCH ON THE MANAGEMENT OF INNOVATION

This section brings together two broad bodies of research: business innovation and the arts, to develop a profile of the innovative arts organization. However some preliminary caveats are entered. In general, business innovation research is based on studies of larger firms or companies and has a technological orientation. This and the commercial context of much of the work offers a poor fit with the world of

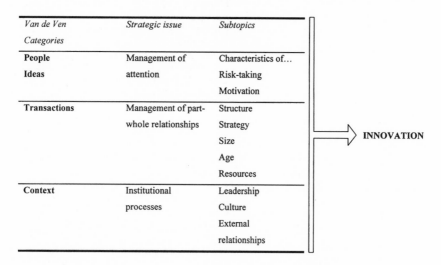

Van de Ven Categories	Strategic issue	Subtopics	
People	Management of	Characteristics of...	
Ideas	attention	Risk-taking	
		Motivation	
Transactions	Management of part-whole relationships	Structure	
		Strategy	
		Size	INNOVATION
		Age	
		Resources	
Context	Institutional processes	Leadership	
		Culture	
		External relationships	

Figure 2.3 Operationalization of Van de Ven (1986) Categories in Review of Literature

subsidized arts organizations.[8] As for the arts research work, discussion on innovation in general may be characterized as rather shy, hitting the topic in spots rather than examining it as a central issue. In fact there is virtually no work addressed specifically to this subject. Therefore, general business research that refers in an incidental way to arts organizations and whatever arts research that might form the basis for reasonable assumptions or throw some light on innovation in the arts is drawn upon, as well as that of other bodies of relevant literature (e.g., the management of professionals).

But first a word on why, if it is so important, so little research has been undertaken on arts innovation. For an explanation the prevailing image of innovation in the arts as a "black box" activity, inherently arcane and mysterious, is relevant. This conception not only places artistic work outside the bounds of what can be reached by management practices, but also beyond investigation and resistant to sociological inquiry,[9] shrouded as it were in a veil of mystery which is supported and legitimized by a web of myths. To boot, there is the intimation that any such inquiry, as if by disturbing the surface, risks violating the essence of artistic work (Bourdieu 1984; Wolff 1981). E. Chiapello (1994), in a very complete analysis that also demonstrates the contingent nature of common definitions of art and artists, traces the origin of this phenomenon to the Romantic concept of the arts, which exalted the discipline above scientific knowledge.[10] Allied to these notions and within the Romantic paradigm is the singular importance and status attributed to innovation itself. Perceived as a major justification of public funding and presented as the primary aim of arts organizations and "genuine" artists, artistic innovation is regarded as a discrete process, occurring in the upper regions of the ether; one which relates and is judged according to a somewhat mysterious and self-referential set of criteria, and which also is above and beyond the reaches of any type of management. Thus the dominance of the Romantic paradigm has clouded and discouraged investigations of the innovation process and accounts substantially for the scantiness of the research work on this topic to date.

The categories in Figure 2.3 are now considered in turn to establish the collective wisdom on arts innovation as it currently stands.

Managing People and Ideas

The discussion on managing people and ideas in previous research focuses generally on the necessity for and difficulties of getting attention, given both human limitations and organizational constraints in the face of uncertainty and risk in organizational life. Accepting the infinite human propensity for lethargy, innovative organizations must actively endeavor to motivate their members by encouraging risk taking and tolerating failure as a necessary trade-off in the innovation process. Attention is crucial (Amabile 1983, 1985; Cohen and Levinthal 1990; Simon 1967). T. M. Amabile (1979) in particular has researched motivation, concluding on the negative effects of extrinsic motivation and of the expectation of evaluation on artistic creativity, a finding which has been influential for thinking on innovation management (Woodman et al. 1993). However, she does not rule out the influence of managerial action in this regard, insofar as she allows refinements of her theory: recognizing people's needs for the extrinsics of life; the fact that intrinsic motivation is crucial "only in the response generation stage of the creative process" (1988, 145); that extrinsic and intrinsic motivation can go together; and allowing for individual difference in terms of motivation level—the motivation of certain people being relatively unaffected by external circumstances. Traditional depictions of artists as well as the Romantic paradigm, which both polarizes artistic and managerial discourses and alienates the artist from the organizational world, have obscured aspects of the reality of artistic work and made artists in general seem resistant to managerial processes.[11] However, attention remains central. Bo Gyllenpalm (1995) in his account of how Ingmar Bergman created peak performances in the theater refers repeatedly to this dimension, quoting Csikszentmihalyi (1988): "Because attention determines what will or will not appear in consciousness, and because it is also required to make any other mental events—such as remembering, thinking, feeling and making decisions—happen there . . . hence attention is our most important tool in the task of improving the quality of experience." (Gyllenpalm 1995, 33) Attention matters not just for the actors: "To create this peak experience, the actors have to 'peak perform' e.g. create a situation where everything is flowing and catching the full and undivided attention of everyone present." (1995, 10) To achieve this Bergman has techniques of bringing focus and concentration to the work of the company, as for instance, finding what he terms the "magic point" of the stage as a way "to focus the attention and energy" (1995, 56) of the performers and audience alike. However, in general, because of a dearth of actual descriptions of how attention is managed in arts organizations, a certain stripping away of the mythology surrounding artistic work will be necessary to an examination of how some of these succeed in achieving high levels of innovation.

Given the repetitiveness intrinsic to organization life, and of itself destructive of "attention," research also suggests that innovation is more likely in organizations which are less institutionalized (Guetzkow 1965; Van de Ven 1986). Van de Ven's recipe for directing attention for the purposes of innovation has already been outlined. That such mechanisms have consequences for the implementing organizations will become apparent later from the empirical work. Issues of size and institutionalization will be dealt with in the discussion that follows.

Management of Transactions: Structure

The nature of transactions in an organization is determined substantially by organizational structure. Here innovation research centers on the "bureaucratic versus organic" debate and the "innovation dilemma" which arises from this. Much of what has been written supports the view that organizations either give added value to the process of innovation or can smother it at birth. Structure shapes to a significant degree the mode of communication in any organization. Every form of organization design has implications for the way ideas are handled. At one end of the spectrum, bureaucracies—centralized and decentralized—operate through rules and formal procedures which standardize work, skills or outputs and where the flow of ideas is in the main unidirectional. At the other, what Mintzberg (1979) has called adhocracies operate through mutual adjustment and are more usually associated with innovative work, executed through project structures (Mintzberg 1979). It is widely posited that formal hierarchical structures tend to limit and stifle ideas by being intrinsically unreceptive and by predominantly allowing them to travel one way only—from the top down (Daft 1982; Damanpour 1991; Kanter 1983, 1988). The early research literature on innovation, which has "a strong anti-bureaucratic theme" (Nicholson 1990, 189) highlighted the problems inherent in the traditional bureaucratic model of the organization as a setting for innovation (Cummings 1965; Nystrom 1979; Thompson 1965; Zaltman, Duncan and Holbeck 1973). The alternative put forward as being conducive to innovation is based on the organic model (Burns and Stalker 1961) that is characterized among other factors by a "network structure of control, authority, and communication" (1961, 121). It accentuates mutual adjustment over hierarchies; exhibits extensive commitment and a value orientation as typical features; and emphasizes integration.

However, this debate has been complicated by what is known as the "innovation dilemma," which posits the need for different structures within the same organization to accommodate the requirements of the different phases said to be typical of the innovation process (as described in the stage models). Simply put, it seems to be widely accepted that while ideation thrives in the context furnished by loose, informal organic structures, a more bureaucratic design makes for greater implementation effectiveness.[12] Lack of formality would seem at least in the early stages of innovation to facilitate boundary crossing and the cross-fertilization of ideas or different disciplines—A. Koestler's (1967) "bisociation" theory—which is regarded as the source of innovation.

Much management thinking therefore has been expended on how to overcome the problem of idea generation in more hierarchical structures by introducing diversity—to allow good ideas from those working at the "coal-face" to make their way up to the decision-making levels; to allow ideas from those outside the organization, such as customers, to get through; to find ways of bringing together different functional units to spark off ideas; to establish linkages which contribute to creative ferment (Kanter 1988; Tushman and Nadler 1986). Often too, the thrust in bigger organizations to find ways of replicating the characteristics of small or new organizations—lack of formality, a familial atmosphere, a spirit of enterprise—derives from this same objective. In addition, the establishment of a climate conducive to ideas supposes that the organization allows a certain freedom to play: an atmosphere where it is possible to cordon off certain areas where organizational and performance stress is limited at least for the initial or idea-generation stages of a project—what Amabile terms a "creativity oasis" (1988, 161). From the mid-1980s however, research reflects an undercurrent of dissatisfaction with stage models, regarding them as overly schematized and not a helpful reflection of the innovation process[13] (Kanter 1988; King 1992; Van de Ven 1986).

Overall, there is a consensus view (King 1990; Pierce and Delbecq 1977) that a flat organizational structure is more conducive to innovation. Finding that innovation is "uncertain, fragile, political, and imperialistic (reaching out to embrace other territories)," R. M. Kanter (1988) emphasizes the importance of integration: "[Innovation] is most likely to flourish where conditions allow flexibility, quick action and intensive care, coalition formation, and connectedness. It is most likely to grow in organizations that have integrative structures and cultures emphasizing diversity, multiple structural linkages both inside and outside the organization, intersecting territories, collective pride and faith in people's talents, collaboration, and teamwork." (1988, 172) This recalls Van de Ven's "holographic" organization.

The notion of the "creativity oasis" (Amabile 1988) or "skunkworks" as it is sometimes termed, referred to above, presents yet another possible solution: the possibility that innovation is best encouraged by allowing it to develop in separate units—a special R&D section, for instance. Kanter (1988) sees such structural isolation as "a liability for idea generation or innovation activation" but "an asset for idea completion or innovative production" (1988, 191).[14] The issue then becomes one of effective boundary management. However it is worth invoking V. A. Thompson's dictum (echoed by Damanpour 1991) that "The innovative organization is innovative throughout." (1965, 19)

There is one organizational type that seems to be an exception in that though it is hierarchical or monocratic, it is also innovative. Thompson

(1965) in showing how monocratic structure is inimical to innovation describes this variant: "New organizations are sometimes begun by highly creative individuals who attract like-minded people, maintain an atmosphere conducive to innovation, build up a powerful *esprit de corps* and achieve a very high level of organizational creativity . . . . The organization is new and small and not yet bureaucratized. Many able young people may be attracted to it because of the opportunity provided for professional growth." (1965, 10) Such organizations are short-lived: "As [they] grow larger and particularly after the charismatic originator is no longer there, the monocratic stereotype reasserts itself and they become bureaucratized. This phenomenon is an old one, discussed by M. Weber (1956) as the "institutionalization of charisma" (1956, 10). This type of organization recalls H. Mintzberg's "simple structure" (1983) or C. Handy's "power culture" (1985), all of which combine an organic operating core and a high degree of mutual adjustment with strong centralized supervision from the strategic apex of the organization.[15] The resonance of the above with the typical configuration of small arts organizations is clear.

Mintzberg and A. McHugh (1985) have carried out one extensive case study on the structure and strategy of a large innovative cultural organization. Their examination of the National Film Board of Canada reveals a classic adhocratic structure operating in response to a dynamic and complex environment. The organization comprises highly trained experts configured in multidisciplinary teams, under a matrix structure. Coordination is by mutual adjustment and semiformal committees (as opposed to direct supervision and standardization) and the organizational structure is characterized by selective decentralization. In the beginning the organization was "organic in the extreme" (1985, 76) with a simple structure and an entrepreneurial strategy. As time passed it moved through alternative periods of diversity and concentration into an adhocracy. It cannot be taken from this however that adhocracy is the most prevalent structural form to be found in the arts sector. J. M. Guiot (1987) identified "at least three structural configurations of permanent systems and four configurations of temporary systems. . . . Therefore viewing these organizations as adhocracies is clearly invalid and has no other grounds than a perceived idea." (1987, 189) One can equally well point to examples of arts organizations that are professional bureaucracies, entrepreneurial, and so on. However Mintzberg and McHugh (1985) argue for structures which allow skilled individuals as much freedom as possible since "the obsession with control found in machine bureaucracy is anathema to the exercise of expertise." (1985, 92) In this case, "Diversity, emergent strategy, a virtual absence of planning, and a steady weakening of direct managerial authority over operations were all associated with excellence and creativity." (1985, 182)

The issue of structure as communication and control receives some consideration in arts research. P. DiMaggio and P. M. Hirsch (1976) have observed that "cultural production systems are characterized by a constant and pervasive tension between innovation and control." (1976, 741) Chiapello (1994) regards organizational structure as integral to her discussion of control mechanisms in cultural organizations and finds that a more organic structure is typical of innovative arts organizations. In her dissertation, she addresses the traditional belief that the application of control is hostile to the production of art and even risks killing it. While there will be further discussion of her work in the coverage of the treatment of culture and climate in arts organizations, here her description of the inadequacies of the classic cybernetic control model when applied to the arts context is noted. She shows that the traditional polarization of the Romantic concept of art and the mechanistic image of control is excessively reductive, and goes on to develop a contingent theory of the operation of control in arts organizations which transcends this. Her model combines motivational factors, the operation of personalized interaction and relationships,[16] and organizational culture and structure as an alternative that is more appropriate to the development of innovative work.

Our discussion of organization structure as a feature of "transaction" management has focused on the preference for organicism as more conducive to innovation in the business literature. However sufficient caveats—whether with stage models or the causal direction of the relationship—have been entered to raise a query about whether a pure form of organic structure will always fit best (King and Anderson 1995). While a similar preference is discernible in research on arts organizations, Guiot's (1987) work suggests a wider range of structural types and thus of communication and control devices, and opens the possibility that aspects of organizational life which are commonplace outside the arts sector, whether problems or solutions, may also have a place within it. In general the importance of integration and integrative devices echoes Van de Ven's holographic organization as well as pointing to the advantages of small organizations (with simple or entrepreneurial structures) in this respect.

Management of Transactions: Job Design

Frequent discussion arises in the innovation debate about the degree to which the presence of professionals in an organization, sometimes termed organizational diversity, would seem to impact on innovation levels (Pierce and Delbecq 1977; Wilson, J. Q. 1966). "To the extent that professionals bring long training as well as outside reference groups to the organization, they contribute to organizational diversity and, hence, to the potential for innovation in organizations."[17] (Aiken and Hage 1971, 71) As J. Hage and R. Dewar (1973) see it, "a diversity of tasks means a diversity of perspectives, a variety, which, in turn, produces a creative dialectic that results in the development of innovative products and services." (1973, 279–80)

It is possible to consider artists as professionals. Such a casting allows us to regard their behavior within organizations with a colder eye than is usually afforded by their popular characterization as outsiders who are congenitally intractable when it comes to the management processes. The principal debate in the research literature on professionals in organizations for almost the past four decades centers around the difference in organizational commitment between organization members who are characterized either as "locals" or "cosmopolitans" (Gouldner 1958), and the tensions and conflicts which arise therefrom— between an organization's bureaucratic needs for expertise and social needs for loyalty. The debate was advanced somewhat by D. W. Organ and C. N. Greene (1981) who in their examination of the effects of formalization on professional involvement found that the presumed conflict between and negative effects of these two forces were "neither omnipresent nor inevitable." (1981, 251)[18] J. E. Wallace's (1995) treatment of organizational and professional commitment treats these two as separate rather than zero-sum. Her study of lawyers in nonprofessional organizations found that structural characteristics did not explain differences in commitment levels and she advised a general shift in approach: "We should avoid adopting a mythical approach to professionals and their work, refrain from taking an overly critical view of bureaucracy and nonprofessional organizations, and not assume that the relationships between professionals and their employing organizations are inherently conflicting." (1995, 252) DiMaggio (1991), differentiating between *intra-* and *inter-*organizational work and drawing an example from the cultural sector, shows how professionals can contribute to sectoral innovation (and the structuration of new fields) and bring about radical change in the organizations in which they work while remaining loyal to those same organizations: " Professional activism and organizational work were compartmentalized roles that evoked distinctive forms of rationality, forms of discourse and orientations toward action." (1991, 285–86) While in A. W. Gouldner's (1958) terms artists might be represented as archetypal "outsiders" (1958, 449), this may not be true of all; the issue may be one of degree, and in addition, mitigating factors such as the necessity to earn a living or the power balance which generally leaves the freelance artist in the weaker position undoubtedly colors the interplay between artists and arts organizations. Thus while a degree of conflict may be endemic, it rarely achieves the volcanic proportions suggested by the mythology and, as

Wallace's (1995) comments might suggest, peaceful cohabitation of artists and administrators within the organizational context is certainly achievable.

The remainder of the discussion on this aspect focuses on the preference for broad job design (Kanter, 1988) and the degree of supervision appropriate to creative people and projects (Amabile and Gryskiewicz 1991; Glassman 1986; Kets de Vries 1994). Overall it would seem that the type of competences suited to innovative organizations is broadly congruent with the organic ideal which allows for loosely defined jobs, flexible work roles, a shifting locus of power, and a high degree of mutual adjustment.

Management of Transactions: Strategy

The strategic stance of the innovative organization is generally characterized as entrepreneurial, with consequences for organizational behavior and processes, and in probable conflict with the demands for efficiency (Acar, Melcher, and Aupperle 1989). Similarly, the strategy process (1983, 1996) in Mintzberg's simple structure or his entrepreneurial organization is "highly intuitive and nonanalytical" (1983, 158) and closely related to the vision of the organization's leader, to the extent that it is "often an extrapolation of his or her own personality" (1996, 615). The centralized approach of this organization type makes for a high degree of flexibility and adaptability, essential in a dynamic environment. Strategy making in Mintzberg's ideal innovative structure—the adhocracy—is typically unconventional: "Any process that separates thinking from action—planning from execution, formalization from implementation—would impede the flexibility of the organization to respond creatively to its dynamic environment." (1996, 687) Thus strategies are emergent, evolving continuously and "each leaving its imprint . . . by creating a precedent or reinforcing an existing one" (1996, 688). Nevertheless Mintzberg regards this approach as a strategy rather than a nonstrategy. "This habit of cycling in and out of focus is quite unlike what takes place in other configurations. . . . The innovative organization, in contrast, seems not only able to function at times without strategic focus, but positively to thrive on it. Perhaps that is the way it keeps itself innovative—by periodically cleansing itself of some of its existing strategic baggage." (1996, 688)

DiMaggio (1987) in a discussion of the preeminence of the nonprofit form within the arts sector in the United States points to the issues and implications for strategy arising from the nature and impact of goals on the operation of such organizations. He reviews the type of goals typically present in arts organizations: quality, audience size, survival and legitimacy, budget maximization and growth, and participant rewards, and notes their heterogeneous nature, their instability over time, and their ambiguity. This, he says, gives rise to a set of tensions between administrative and professional staffs and between executives and trustees as well as causing evaluation difficulties. Although he acknowledges the need for further research, his study points clearly to tensions, conflicts, the necessity for frequent and difficult trade-offs between quality and quantity or different types of quality, and difficulties in planning and evaluation as being endemic within the sector. Discussing uncertainty of funding, for instance, he points out: "The often-decried lack of systematic planning[19] in nonprofit cultural organizations may be a realistic response. The multiplicity of goals ... provides protective coloration for the administrator, who will find that nearly anything that he or she does will appear to further at least some of them. . . . At the same time, goal ambiguity ensures that any course of action will be inconsistent with some participants' favored objectives." (1987, 214) In terms of goals and appropriate strategies, DiMaggio (1987) differentiates between innovation and quality and realistically, based on an assessment of their outcomes, queries the assumption that all arts organizations are committed to innovation. In addition he refers to the potentially positive effects of goal ambiguity in arts organizations in affording "flexibility and slack" (1987, 214), conditions generally regarded as conducive to innovation.[20]

Despite the preference in the innovation research literature for entrepreneurial-type strategy, the empirical work undertaken by N. Nicholson, A. Rees and A. Brooks-Rooney (1990) in textile factories discourages any simplistic conclusions about the relationship between strategy, innovation, and performance (as suggested or implied by the "excellence" literature). Instead they underline the close relationship between strategy and culture which they see as "inextricably entwined:" "Strategic orientation, and whatever consequences it brings, is dependent upon strategic self-awareness. By this is meant the extent and kind of attention key organizational agents give to their strategy and how it is supported internally." (1990, 527) Thus no prescriptive one-best-way is possible. Instead, continuing innovation depends on the capacity of the organization to renew itself; a process (analogous in many respects to personal growth and development) which requires an ability to reflect critically on its operation and a culture which supports such reflection.

Management of Transactions: Size, Age, Resources

Despite the seeming desirability of small size for innovation purposes (making communication and integration easier), research is not only inconclusive but contradictory on this matter (Aiken and Hage 1971;

Pierce and Delbecq 1977). As always much depends on what is meant by innovation; adoption of expensive innovations, for instance, being more feasible in bigger, better resourced organizations (Kimberly and Evanisko 1981). N. King (1990) reflects the division of opinion in his review, pointing out after E. M. Rogers (1983) that size may not be a variable of theoretical interest or importance in itself, but rather "a surrogate measure of several dimensions that lead to innovation." (1990, 32)

In the same way as with size, research on the relationship of organization age and level of innovation is also inconclusive. King (1990) accounts for these divergences by the different ways in which organizational age was operationalized—the absolute age of the organization or the length of tenure of key organizational members. In addition issues of the stage of institutionalization or organizational life cycle (Gainer 1997) may have an impact.

Finally on the impact of resourcing there is also division among researchers (King 1990) and this may depend too on the type of innovation under discussion. Thompson (1965) proclaims the need for "uncommitted money, time, skills, and good will" (1965, 10)[21] as resources for innovation, while R. Payne (1990) reported on studies which generated "no evidence that more resources and better facilities led to necessarily better performance" (1990, 114) in research teams. Some writers proclaim the value of hunger or poverty, what Kanter (1988) terms "tin-cupping" for innovative purposes, a rationale which is familiar in the arts sector. G. W. Downs and L. B. Mohr (1976) sensibly conclude: "There would be no point in trying to generalize about the impact of a variable like wealth on innovativeness because wealth would not have a constant impact. It is no doubt a determinant of the adoption of high-cost innovations but may have no bearing at all upon the adoption of low-cost innovations." (1976, 700) On the whole, Kanter's (1988) contention that innovation is rendered easier by adequate and even dedicated funding seems credible: "Since innovations generally require resources beyond those identified in operating budgets for reasons that are logical—the exact nature and timing of innovation is often unpredictable—the existence of multiple sources of loosely committed funds at local levels makes it easier for potential innovators to find the money, the staff, the materials, or the space to proceed with an entrepreneurial idea." (1988, 181)

In the arts sector, issues of resourcing and in particular financial resourcing (Lyon 1974) are endemic and conflictual (Jeffri 1980; Powell and Friedkin 1983). Not only the amount but also the type and source of funding have an impact. DiMaggio (1987) in his discussion of nonprofit organizations, alludes to studies in both the United States and Britain which "find higher percentages of subsidy and lower levels of dependence on earned income associated with more innovative or highbrow programming" (1987, 207). Resourcing has an impact too on the degree of freedom accorded to managers. Chiapello (1994) points out the relative power of the manager in non-trading organizations because of the weakness of the two main types of control which apply in private enterprise, that is that of the owners and that of the consumers, control which she characterizes as "uphill" or "downhill," respectively. Weaker owner control (uphill) means vague objectives, strong asymmetry of information, little pressure to reduce this, and a scarcity of inexpensive evaluation methods. Weaker consumer control (downhill) means low economic power of consumers, relative autonomy of the nonprofit organization, and low emphasis on control. In her view, the relaxation of "uphill" and "downhill" control mechanisms also seems a condition necessary to the development of a certain organizational creativity. (1994, 77) The reinforced role of the manager may therefore have a particular impact on innovation. It may be too that the nonprofit form, offering such relative freedom from constraint, may attract managers or artists with an interest in the development of innovative projects.

At the same time it is likely that certain limits operate. D. C. Wilson (1992) points out that while slack makes change easier to implement, "It simultaneously lowers the motivation of individuals to undertake the change, largely because they are happy as they are. Thus, slack can, in time, alter the sensitivity of an organization in recognizing problems and in responding to environmental changes." (1992, 78)

To summarize, no easy correlation is possible when one considers the relationship of size, age, or resourcing to innovation levels. In all cases a range of intervening factors prevent any simple conclusion.

Management of Context: Leadership

As apparent from Figure 2.3, Van de Ven's (1986) management of context, central to his framework for organizational innovation, is operationalized first under the concept of leadership, without which "structures and systems focus the attention of organizational members to routine, not innovative activities." (1986, 596) Though he does not discuss it in great detail, Van de Ven's concept of leadership tends to the charismatic: goals become ideology; recruitment is personalized rather than universalistic; and rituals and symbols replace rules and procedures. He quotes N. Roberts (1984) to describe the "special kind of supportive leadership" (Van de Ven 1986, 601) which he sees as necessary to innovation: "This type of leadership offers a vision of what could be and gives a sense of purpose and meaning to those who would share that vision. It builds commitment, enthusiasm, and excitement. It creates a hope in the future and a belief that the world is knowable, understandable, and manageable. The collective energy that transforming leadership generates empowers those who participate in the process. There is hope, there is optimism, there is energy." (Roberts 1984, 3) In the research literature, discussion of leadership covers three general aspects: values and ideals of leaders, their personal characteristics, and their management style (King 1990). Despite a debate about the greater usefulness of structural factors to explain organizational innovation (Perrow 1970), most writers underline the significance of leadership and the particular added value it brings to the management of innovation (Amabile 1988; Hage and Dewar 1973; Kimberly 1980; Kimberly and Evanisko 1981; Pierce and Delbecq 1977). There seems to be a consensus that a participative and collaborative leadership style is more conducive to innovation[22] (Kanter 1983, 1988; Kets de Vries 1994; King and Anderson 1995; Kolb 1992; West 1990).

The discussion of leadership in the arts sector takes up various themes: the sectoral shift from impresarial to administrative leadership (Peterson 1986); crisis and leader succession (Gainer 1997; Zeigler 1991); leadership without formal controls (Mintzberg and McHugh 1985); and tensions in artistic/managerial leadership (Castaner 1997). J. K. Murnighan and D. E. Conlon (1991) discuss a basic paradox of leadership, which would seem to have resonance beyond the arts sector. Examining the dynamics of intense work groups in a study of British string quartets, they explore the leadership/democracy paradox. This is contained in the seeming contradiction that players in such groups regard the first violin as "leader," while at the same time the other musicians join such a group in order to have a say in how they play (in contrast with the situation that generally pertains in other musical groupings, such as orchestras). Murnighan and Conlon (1991) find that this paradox is reflected in and recognized by all the top quartets examined in their study, and that it is difficult to establish a clear line on the actual location of power and control. They conclude:

> The more successful British quartets provided clear evidence that they recognized and managed the inherent paradoxes they faced. All of the groups except one espoused democracy. First violinists in the successful groups, however, recognized the need for a directive leader more than first violinists in the less successful groups. They took active control of many of the group's activities and acknowledged this in their interviews. They did not advertise their leadership, however, within their group. Instead they advocated democratic action and, it appears, did so sincerely. Thus, they preserved the leadership-democracy paradox by acting as a leader while simultaneously advocating democracy. . . . In the less successful groups, members felt that democracy ruled too much: everyone but the

first violinist looked for more leadership and authoritative action. (1991, 181)

It is unusual for an account of leadership to give such detailed regard to the perspective of "followers" and to recognize the paradoxes inherent in this relationship, particularly in a situation that requires creative input from organizational members,[23] and is a theme which will recur.

Overall, the research literature on the arts sector provides some insights but includes no comprehensive study of leadership in innovative arts organizations. Yet the mythology of the sector places a strong emphasis on leadership and the identification of (usually charismatic) leaders with organization and innovation. This is a factor of the small size of organizations and the relative power of leaders as well as the dominant Romantic paradigm of individualism.

Management of Context: Culture and Climate

Management of context in Van de Ven's usage is close to the concept of organizational culture. In general research on this aspect is scanty (King 1990) and what literature there is is dominated by a preference for the type of culture commonly associated with the organic organization where, "The emptying out of significance from the hierarchic command system . . . is countered by the development of shared beliefs about the values and goals of the organization." (Burns and Stalker 1961, 122)[24] Kanter (1958) points to a "Pygmalion effect" which influences "whether the organization's culture pushes 'tradition' or 'change'" (1988, 182–83). But this has little empirical basis and is roundly criticized by D. C. Wilson (1992) as being based on a number of unproven assumptions about the link between culture and performance.

A number of writers refer, directly and indirectly, to the culture of arts organizations. E. Lyon's (1974) examination of a small avant-garde theater company places an emphasis on relationships which are analogous to those in a family or a marriage where "the relationship between intimacy and commitment" (1974, 81) is fundamental to an understanding of the operation of the organization. Their theater work was a continuation of the lives of the individual company members and as such had to fulfill "a variety of shared needs" (1974, 84) including that of having fun. Murnighan and Conlon's (1991) account of intense work groups demonstrates how such intensity was successfully maintained through techniques that are in their essence cultural. The relationships within string quartets, which were both intense in their interdependence (the necessity for a high level of coordination and the close interlocking of diverse talents and roles), and demanding in terms of what was required from the individual members—"The best quartets ask each player to have a soloist's skills but not a soloist's temperament" (1991, 167)—cannot be maintained and managed through the straightforward exercise of authority. Rather the internal dilemmas and inevitable conflicts of the groups were handled through a mode of behavior to which the members adhered. Conflict was managed not through compromise but by the avoidance of confrontation. " Direct confrontation of these unsolvable contradictions appeared infrequently among the successful groups. Instead, paradoxes were managed implicitly." (1991, 182) Group members also acknowledged the added weight of friendship, given the internal orientation of these groups, referred to above—"We play more and more to each other." (1991, 179)

Chiapello (1994) offers the most complete exploration of the culture of arts organizations and its implications, particularly in relation to control systems. Interpersonal relationships are of primary importance and are characterized by informality, friendship and even what she terms *la logique de l'amour*. Such relationships mean that a vital element of the control system in arts organizations is based on the notion of the *don* or gift. Showing the compatibility of this approach with the Romantic notion of art, she notes how the concept of gift, while encapsulating a subtle form of control (gifts engender debts: the donor controls the receiver), at the same time permits a safe atmosphere for critical comment and an "affective atmosphere which is conducive to creation" (1994, 397). In fact, Chiapello regards the operation of control through organizational culture, deriving from professionalism and sectoral characteristics, as more important than other forms of control. In her opinion, the closer the organization to the innovative end of the spectrum, the more its integrative mechanisms take on the character of friendship and family relationships (1994, 517).

In general there is agreement as to the impact of rituals, symbols and ideology on innovation in organizations.[25] However, once again, as Nicholson (1990) demonstrates from his research which turned up various combinations of climate and innovativeness, "the relationship between product and climate is less straightforward than might be assumed" (1990, 196). It is of interest too that the arts management literature makes frequent reference to work relationships by calling on the concept of family or friendship or even love, dimensions on which the bulk of management literature is relatively silent.

Managing Context: The External Environment

Research on the impact of the wider organizational environment and external climate on innovation, though the literature recognizes the importance of this dimension, is primarily speculative (Kimberly 1981; King 1990) and imprecise. Commentaries have tended towards the generalized, for example receptivity of the environment (Kanter 1988). The discussion generally hinges on the notion of environmental uncertainty by which is meant the levels and predictability of change in the external world. J. L. Pierce and A. L. Delbecq (1977) (as well as Daft 1982; Ettlie 1983) speculate that "environmental uncertainty will be positively related with organizational innovation" (1977, 32) in that turbulence stimulates innovation. The institutional processes advocated by Van de Ven (1986) serve to maintain the complexity, diversity, and uncertainty of the environment within the organization—as per the holographic model: "Although technical processes of formalization press to reduce uncertainty, institutional processes attempt to preserve it. Just as necessity is the mother of invention, preserving the same degrees of uncertainty, diversity, or turbulence within an organization that is present in the environment are major sources of creativity and long-run viability for an organization." (1986, 603) Other issues which arise in the discussion of the influence of the environment on innovation include the "absorptive capacity" of the organization in relation to environmental complexity (Cohen and Levinthal 1990), the impact of competition (King 1990), and interdependence (Pierce and Delbecq 1977; Wievel and Hunter 1985).

Discussions on the external environment in the arts sector have been for the most part incidental. Those which seem to have implications for innovation are rehearsed here. The gradual professionalization of the sector and the displacement of impresarial by administrative management constitute major features of the arts world since the early '60s. The phenomenon of institutionalization in the sector is explored by DiMaggio (1991) who, contrary to popular understandings of this as a bureaucratizing, negative trend, sees in it the seeds of innovation. Describing the development of the museum field in the United States and noting the parallel rise of professionalism in that discipline, DiMaggio elaborates on "the contradictory tendency of successful institutionalization projects to legitimize not just new organizational forms, but also new categories of authorized actors whose interests diverge from those of the groups controlling the organizations, and new resources such actors can use in their efforts to effect organizational change" (1991, 272). Professionals began to redefine the museum through their legitimate associational activities, " the professionalized environment [having] offered sites for the development of critical alternatives to existing organizational arrangements" (1991, 286). This ultimately brought about the radical reinterpretation of the role of the museum and the establishment of a new organizational form. Thus he shows how, in a very practical way, "institutionalization bears, if not the seeds of its own destruction, at least openings for substantial change" (1991, 287).

DiMaggio (1992) also shows how uncertainty in the environment can stimulate change. The business of organizing in a complex and dynamic environment renders networking important in the quest for organizational legitimacy since "under conditions of uncertainty or resource scarcity, organizers are forced beyond their immediate networks" (1992, 125). DiMaggio explores in detail the processes involved in the recruitment of a founding board for New York's Museum of Modern Art and shows both the importance of the process, influencing as it does the likely strategic direction of the organization and its ultimate effectiveness, and the role of such imponderables as "sympathy" in the formation of this board. He proposes that the position of an organization in "relational networks" will be the primary factor in determining its potential to "mobilize" (1992, 133) and thus the organizational outcomes.

Audiences represent a key element of the environment for arts organizations. However, this relationship is far from straightforward. DiMaggio (1987) notes the "complex and often ambivalent attitude" which most decision makers in nonprofit arts organizations have toward audiences, and finds that, contrary to what might be expected, "their objectives have more to do with audience quality than with size or social composition" (1987, 208), with evident implications for marketing. This corresponds with Murnighan and Conlon's (1991) observations on the internal focus of successful string quartets and accords too with the weak client power, typical of public sector organizations. "Their primary audience was each other. They played to please themselves individually and collectively before they played to please an audience. Consideration of what an audience desired rarely, if ever, entered into their determination of how to interpret and present a composition." (1991, 179) As the authors point out, "this internal orientation is in direct opposition to common organizational wisdom that espouses organization-environment fit" (1991,184).

D. Crane (1976) has discussed the influence, at environmental level, of reward systems in shaping production and innovation in the arts. A key variable here is "the extent to which innovators control the system" (1976, 720). She identifies four types of reward systems: independent, semi-independent, subcultural, and heterocultural, based on the "cohesiveness of the relationships between innovators" and their "control over resources for producing, displaying and distributing innovations" (1976, 725). The subsidized arts would ideally seem to operate for the most part in independent and semi-independent reward systems where in the case of the first, innovations are produced for an audience of fellow innovators, while in semi-independent systems, symbolic rewards are allocated by innovators and material rewards by "consumers, entrepreneurs or bureaucrats" (1976, 721). These reward systems have implications for variety and continuity of innovation within the system, depending on the availability of material resources and the relative balance in terms of importance, of symbolic and material rewards.

To summarize, the environment is taken to be dynamic and uncertain, and in contrast with the usual organizational response of uncertainty reduction, the innovative organization tends instead towards uncertainty preservation (Van de Ven 1986). Thus research work on the external environment in the arts world to some extent charts the influence of this on changes and innovation in the sector—through increased professionalism or reward systems—and points to the significance of networking as a mobilizing device. While it reflects the ambiguity of attitudes toward audiences it does not consider the implications of this for innovation.

THEORETICAL FRAMEWORK AND CASE SELECTION

Summary: The State of Theory

What does the survey of the previous research work on innovation amount to? The generalized, normative, and speculative nature of this work has already been remarked on as has the dearth of models that attempt to relate or link the organizational features that are deemed to have a relationship with innovation in the business world. Despite the menu of variables left by previous research, there is a poor apprehension of what actually drives innovation in organizations, and only an imagistic grasp (i.e., the hologram) of how these variables interrelate. At the outset of this chapter the dominance of the Romantic paradigm, which places a high value on individualism and as a discourse stands in opposition to the managerial mode, was noted. This gives rise to tensions and an antipathy which is often taken as endemic between the artistic and the managerial, as well as clouding aspects of the operation of arts organizations.

Nevertheless there is a picture of what one might expect to find in an innovative organization. The structure will be predominantly organic, characterized by intense communications and interactions, mutual adjustment, flexibility, informality, and integration. The organization will have a high commitment and value orientation, loosely defined jobs, and a soft (predominantly cultural) control system. Leadership is of pivotal importance and is most likely to be of the supportive, participative, and collaborative type, allowing for the expression and exploration of a range of ideas as being the core of innovation, and taking due account of the personal investment in and affective dimension of artistic work and the resulting importance of motivational issues. It is expected too that the leadership will have charismatic dimensions with the capacity to exert a certain transformational power. Leaders will be able to absorb and mediate the uncertainties and ambiguities associated with the environment interface. Innovative organizations will have high environment awareness and focus, and this environment will typically be complex and dynamic. The likely effects of the age of the organization on innovation seem to be linked to the leadership dimension, which determines crucial transition points. Age may have positive or negative effects. The resourcing of the innovative arts organization is likely to be problematic and conflictual, coming from its uncertainty and its link with aesthetic concerns.

However there are problems with research to date. A central strategic challenge for innovation in organizations and one which is at the core of both the holographic model and the "innovation dilemma" is that of integration: without it effective delivery is impossible and the innovation (successful, new initiative) becomes simply a failure or a mistake (Van de Ven et al. 1984). The biological nature of the organic metaphor provides in theory for such integration though this should not suggest that its achievement is easy or flows naturally in some way.[26] A number of writers note the positive bias in the literature (Kimberly 1981; Kimberly and Evanisko 1981; King and Anderson 1990; Nicholson 1990). This is apparent in two ways: first innovation is almost always regarded as "a good thing" and assumed to be beneficial; and the fact that many actions or events, initially labeled innovations, might ultimately prove detrimental to or even disastrous for an organization is conveniently forgotten.[27] The positive bias is also evident in an idealism or a rather optimistic notion of work practices which may have contaminated thinking on the subject, "a presumed identity between the organizational culture and its outputs. Creative organizations generate innovative products." (Nicholson 1990, 189) This is most apparent if note is taken of the typical opposition between the bureaucratic and innovative (usually organic) types of organization that is pervasive in the literature. Table 2.4 summarizes the dichotomy which underlies much of the thinking on this subject and which, while it may well have some basis in reality, may also, by virtue of its polarization, overlook or obscure other aspects of innovative organizations.

Thinking on leadership within innovation studies tends to lag behind contemporary management research on organizational leadership. Despite the importance attached in general to the influence of culture and the environment on innovation, research work on these dimensions is both scanty and imprecise. Finally the contradictory nature of findings of research on many variables has been commented upon. In addition to the lacunae mentioned above, certain aspects of organizational life like control and discipline, which might be expected to figure in relation

TABLE 2.4
Typical Polarizations of Bureaucratic and Innovative Organizational Characteristics

	Bureaucratic	*Innovative*
Structure	Centralized	Integrative
	Stratified	Fluid
Control	Governed by rules	Characterized by freedom
	Control-oriented	Dispersed power
	Formal appraisal	Peer evaluation
Processes	Efficient	Slack
	Non-conflictual	Open and engaging
Climate	Conservative	Adventurous
Environment	Stable	Dynamic

to high innovative output, or the side effects of processes regarded as conducive to innovation, do not emerge strongly in the research literature.[28] The picture of innovative organizations that emerges constitutes almost a ready-made description of the perception or received image of arts organizations. This may be taken equally as an indicator of the validity of the formula (provided it is accepted that arts organizations are by definition innovative), or point to a double positive bias.

All of the above contributes to the difficulty in establishing a satisfactory theoretical framework for innovation in arts organizations. The general framework proposed by Van de Ven (1986), unique in its attempt to relate the variables—albeit in a generalized way—has already been outlined. Having said that, however, his model holds to a fairly high level of abstraction and does not delineate the precise components of innovation nor say if or whether elements of the framework are dispensable. It edits out or chooses to ignore other approaches to achieving its desired ends[29] and does not address such practical problems or issues as: the effects of control or reward systems on the management of attention; the implications for job design and recruitment policies of the concept of "redundant functions;" or the differences between the use of matrix structures, commonly promulgated in the literature, and his preferred holographic model for the coordination of autonomous units. Allusions to issues such as resourcing are vague and although Van de Ven recognizes the importance of the external environment, its relevant features remain imprecise. These comments are not intended as criticisms of the framework since it does not pretend to offer anything other than "an interdependent set of critical concepts and problems for studying innovation management" (1986, 604). The resonance of his approach with the organicism described by T. Burns and G. M. Stalker (1961) has already been noted, though Van de Ven adds to this a strong awareness of human limitations. The above observations form the agenda for researchers interested in undertaking work on innovation: first, there is a need to cut through the positive bias with a view to refining or extending the literature; second, it is important to contribute to the effort of modelbuilding in order to provide a useful guide to practice.

Three Models

As a way forward and taking Van de Ven as a starting point, there is a range of possible variations to allow for diversity in the profile and character of different innovative organizations. The location of the research described here in actual practice should allow us to cut through the aforementioned positive bias and help to refine as well as to introduce greater realism in terms of the operationalization of the framework. Three alternative theoretical models that constitute an advance on the current state of theory in this domain are proposed. These three models are similar in that they are all drawn from the same conceptual seedbed and comprise the range of variables encapsulated in the extended Van de Ven framework; they differ however in how they interrelate and integrate these variables.

1. *The Integral Model.* Taking Van de Ven's as the most developed conceptual framework available at this stage, there is a need to consider as a first option whether this represents an integrated, essential, and comprehensive approach accounting for innovation in organizations. The question then arises as to whether the absence of any single element would render this same innovation out of reach or somehow deficient. The primary motor of the Van de Ven framework—in that it affects the management of attention and transactions—is the concept of institutional leadership. An integral model supposes for instance that were an organization to tend towards a bureaucratic or hierarchical or "technical"[30] mode of operation as opposed to the holographic model described by Van de Ven, and were any one of the strategies of negative feedback, double-loop learning, and uncertainty preservation (all explained above) to be replaced, respectively, by the narrower identification of goals, single-loop learning, which merely corrects deviations from accepted values and norms, and the more usual organizational approach of uncertainty reduction, then the organization would be insufficiently geared to achieve innovation.

2. *The Accented Model.* A second possibility is that organizational innovation will require that most if not all of the attributes as-

cribed by Van de Ven will be found present in the innovative organization to some degree, but that some of these will be more pronounced than others leading to different emphases or types of innovation shaped by the dominant influences. Thus while institutional processes may operate in a company on a threshold level sufficient to support or sustain innovation, it may be that leadership or strategy vis-à-vis the environment or structural arrangements will constitute a primary or predominant influence and therefore give a particular flavor to the type of innovation in operation. This is termed an accented approach in that while the basic recipe remains the same, one or another feature will be preeminent by virtue of local organizational or environmental conditions or circumstances.

3. *The Componential Model.* Finally a third possibility presents itself: that while Van de Ven's (1986) model outlines the general requirements for organizational innovation, not all of these are essential. The thoroughgoing nature of Van de Ven's framework has already been illustrated. It may be that the literature has exaggerated the number of attributes necessary to innovation and that simple subsets will suffice to arrive at an innovative result. Thus an organization may show little or no evidence of double-loop learning, may engage in uncertainty reduction by opportunistic or entrepreneurial pursuit of a single idea, and yet may be deemed innovative simply as a consequence of its leadership strategy or the effectiveness of its negotiation and management of transactions. This is termed a componential approach to the theory.

These three models represented schematically in Table 2.5 indicate a range of support for the Van de Ven model from full through to partial

TABLE 2.5
Three Theoretical Models of Innovation Derived from Extended Van de Ven (1986) Framework

Integral	◆ Essential requirement of all elements (of Van de Ven model)
	Management of attention
	Management of transactions (part-whole relationships)
	Institutional processes
Accented	◆ Comprising all elements to a 'threshold' level.
	◆ One or several dimensions are dominant drivers and shape character or type of innovation
Componential	◆ Adequacy of a subset of elements shaping different types of innovation

and as such offer a theoretical explanation for the variability of findings of innovation studies. They also provide a basis for the empirical inquiries.

The selection of the companies that will form the basis of the examination of innovation-in-practice is now described.

Case Selection

Case selection for the purposes of examining innovation is a problematic issue in any field but particularly in one where innovation is mythologized to the extent that it is claimed by virtually every organization. Innovation is held almost as a badge of honor in the arts sector. As a manageable case set for investigation purposes, three organizations were selected for detailed examination. These were all chosen from the subsidized arts sector in Ireland. While the reasons for selecting Irish cases were practical, there were also some advantages to be gained from such a focus. The arts in Ireland enjoy a strong reputation for innovation in the Western world, certainly one which outstrips its small size and population base. Whether this derives from the worldwide renown of the Abbey theater, the fact that the country has produced four Nobel prizewinners in literature, the seminal text in contemporary English literature, the pervasive influence on a world scale of Irish traditional music, or most recently, the worldwide antics of Riverdance, matters little. The fact of this reputation makes further exploration worthy of interest. In addition, choosing from one population base/country hopefully allows for a gain in terms of depth over what one might lose by not having the possibilities of comparing with examples from other countries. It also enabled us to take fully on board the contextual factors which have an important bearing on the operation of arts organizations.

An exercise (Coopers and Lybrand 1994) which mapped and quantified the cultural sector in Ireland identified a population of almost 400 organizations comprising enterprises in the the five categories of performing arts, heritage and libraries, combined arts, visual arts and design and media, employing 33,800 people. The economic value of the sector was placed at £441 million calculated on the basis of combined turnover of which 88 percent was earned by way of direct trading activity and just 12 percent provided by way of grants. While many grant-giving agencies were listed, grant aid from the Arts Council, an arms-length body appointed by the Government, accounted for 46 percent of the total. The performing arts subsector was largest in terms of employment—41.9 percent of total employment in the cultural industries. In spite of notable increases in funding in recent years, the absolute level of total arts funding in Ireland is low by comparison with other

Western European countries. In 1997, the year of this study, the figure of £20.8 million (the Arts Council's budget) addressed decisions in relation to the fields of literature, visual arts and architecture, film, drama, dance, opera, music, and multidisciplinary arts, representing more than 800 arts organizations and individual artists.[31] Since direct support for the individual artist averages at around 10 percent of the total, it is clear that the bulk of Arts Council funding is distributed through organizations. The organizations that were chosen were publicly subsidized and involved in the direct production of artistic work (as opposed to promotional, educational, artist-support, or other activities), and this within the organization itself. Importantly too there was a consensus as to their innovative achievement within the sector. This latter was established by an opinion survey of active people in the arts field in Ireland, an account of which is given in Appendix 1. Of particular interest here is the breadth of meaning subsumed in the designation "innovative." This breadth was respected as reflecting common expert usage within the sector.

A creaming off of the organizations delivered by these filtering processes, based in the main on longevity, left three companies: Druid Theater Company, Opera Theater Company, and Macnas. While there is a detailed description of these in the following chapters, it is important to note at this point that the companies selected are not exceptional in any way that would seem to explain their high level of innovation: there is no obvious explanation. Druid is the fourth oldest theater company in Ireland and also receives the third highest grant from the Arts Council's theater budget.[32] Its staffing levels are closer to those of the smaller Irish companies. There is no clearly discernible or easily calculable pattern in the ratio of grant aid to total income over the population of theater companies. Similarly, only crude generalizations may be made in relation to company output (number of productions), dependent as this is on a range of factors. Opera Theater Company, in 1997 one of three Arts Council-funded opera companies in Ireland, is notably younger than its sister opera companies with a higher ratio of grant aid to total income than these. Macnas is a community arts and theater company engaged in street spectacles as well as indoor theater and was for a long time the major player in this field in Ireland.

Chapters 2–4 report both the history and the operation of the three chosen companies[33] as an account of the working of an innovative arts company. This is placed in a theoretical context through the use of the extended Van de Ven framework and, in each case, the analytical approach is focused on identifying the main drivers of the innovation process.

Our reporting in the following three chapters gives primary emphasis to a narrative rendering of the activities of each company in its full richness and complexity. This does not preclude systematic analytical reflection on the drivers and character of innovation in each case narrative (undertaken mainly in an analytical section at the end of each chapter).

In the final chapter this discussion will be completed with a thematic review of the empirical material, marshalling evidence from across the organizations to assess the bearing of the three cases on the alternative theoretical understanding proposed here.

NOTES

1. See T.S. Eliot's (1932) essay, "Tradition and the Individual Talent."
2. Five different people react to the same piece of jazz music. Their reactions range from one who considers it highly original to one who regards it as extremely derivative.
3. Csikszentmihalyi (1988, 327) calls this "social agreement."
4. Many of the theoretical or empirical studies are either explicit about or assume a stage model of innovation (Cummings and O'Connell 1978; Daft 1982; Kanter 1988; Pierce and Delbecq 1977).
5. Appendix 1 describes how innovation is perceived and interpreted by practising arts managers, and how they see it manifested in the contemporary arts world in Ireland.
6. The descriptions offered by Amabile (1988) of the type of organizational climate which removes the barriers to creativity also correspond closely with what is commonly understood by creative management.
7. He later added a fifth dimension—outcomes (Van de Ven and Angle 1989).
8. King (1990) has also noted a "diffusion bias" in the business research literature deriving from the fact that it deals with bought-in as opposed to internally generated innovation.
9. Zolberg (1990) explains the dearth of sociological inquiry in this field in terms of the noncompatibility of the arts with the dominant positivist science tradition of American sociologists up to the end of World War II. She also discusses the real dangers of sociological reductionism or the commodification of art, arguing the merits of bridging the gap between the humanistic and the social scientific study of art.
10. Romanticism associates creativity with inspiration, as opposed to work; with the individual, as opposed to a collective endeavor; with liberty as opposed to the constraints of an organizational context. Its pervasiveness can be traced in a number of central features of the arts world:

- through the criteria which determine what art is (the importance of authorship and the signature, of artistic reputation and of authenticity, both attributive and subjective);
- through the image of artists, often clichéd;
- through the artistic life—the vocation effect and the extreme engagement of artists with their work, which has both an affective (the self-exposure and

commitment which this work involves) and a temporal dimension (the fluid boundaries between work and leisure); and

- through the means by which one attains the title of artist (Thesis by Chiapello 1994, 123)

11. For instance the notion that innovative artistic achievement may involve such banal ingredients as hard work, persistence, patience, determination, professionalism, good management; that success in the arts field may be attributed as much to networking or reputation management or media manipulation or even good luck as to innate creative ability; that artistic creation may be a social rather than an individual activity; that its planning/organizing component may be as essential as its inspirational dimension; that commitment to virtuosity among artists may be less than absolute—all these factors may well be recognized by artists as part of their experience but they somehow do not surface in the common preconceptions and images of what it is to be an artist.

12. Goodman and Goodman's (1976) investigation of temporary systems in theater organizations suggests a two-phased structure for the management of temporary systems: a blurred-role team-building stage followed by reversion to more traditional occupational roles. This finding echoes the innovation dilemma's solution of different configurations at different stages of the process.

13. King (1990) discusses the evidence for differing effects of centralization, formalization, and complexity at different stages of the innovation process (the 'innovation dilemma') but finds it inconclusive and necessitating "longitudinal studies . . . which can effectively monitor " (1990, 33) these influences over time.

14. Staw (1990) agrees, characterizing innovative behavior as in its essence deviant and positing the need for "protection" against "domain-relevant practices" (1990, 299).

15. Mintzberg (1996) claims this type of structure is suited to simple and dynamic environments and will deliver simple as opposed to sophisticated innovation.

16. The importance of personalized relationships is also demonstrated by Faulkner (1983) who examines communication and authority in an orchestra and finds that the system of authority is more than a question of "static" role and status as might be the case in a hierarchy. A two-way process, the necessity for "respect, reciprocity and trust" was seen to underlie the exercise of authority by conductors in symphony orchestras (1983, 73).

17. Interestingly, Aiken and Hage (1971) found that the continuing extra-organizational activities of professionals mattered more in this regard than their actual level of professional training.

18. This conclusion is borne out by Raelin (1985) who identified mitigating factors at individual, job and organizational level.

19. See Mintzberg and McHugh (1985) discussion.

20. Other studies bear out DiMaggio's (1987) observations on goals—see Powell and Friedkin (1983).

21. This is echoed by Aiken and Hage (1971) and Farr and Ford (1990).

22. This conclusion parallels that of findings from many descriptive case studies of effective managers. However it is in sharp contrast to the conclusions of thirty-five years of research on participative leadership which finds that "it sometimes results in higher satisfaction and performance, and at other times does not" (Yukl 1989, 259).

23. See Grint's (1997) concept of "deep leadership."

24. See also Amabile and Gryskiewicz 1991, Cummings 1965; Nystrom 1990; Tushman and Nadler 1986.

25. Castaner's (1997) account of the Barcelona Symphony Orchestra points to deficiencies that are primarily "cultural"—its closed and clanic as opposed to professional ethos and the inhibiting effect of the the images used by the organization to represent itself.

26. Morgan's (1986) discussion on the strengths and limitations of the organismic metaphor bears this out. The limitations include "an over concrete perception which de-emphasizes the constructivist nature of organizations and their environments," an "assumption of 'functional unity' which may be a feature of organisms but is not the case in organizations riven by power and other political issues" and "the danger of the metaphor becoming an ideology" (1986, 71–6).

27. A longer time perspective shows many "innovations" in a new light. One has only to recall the effect of certain drugs, initially hailed as "pathbreaking."

28. This is part of the blurring effect of romanticism as well as a mythic tone in many of the more popular writings about innovation and innovators in what is known as the "excellence" literature.

29. For instance, the management of attention may arguably be achieved by means other than those suggested by Van de Ven (e.g., via incentives, coercive, or through the exercise of sanctions).

30. We use the word "technical" here as a description of processes that are in opposition to the institutional processes described by Van de Ven (1986) as fundamental to innovation (see Figure 2.1).

31. Art Matters, 25 May 1997.

32. And this even though Druid does not have to manage a large building.

33. Appendix 2 lists data collection and information sources.

3

"Primitive" Innovation: Druid Theater Company

The first part of this chapter outlines the innovative achievement of Druid Theater Company. A brief history gives the reader a perspective on its position at the time of our investigation, showing the various stages through which Druid has passed. From this summary emerges a style of operation which seems integral to the company and to its innovative performance.

Then, we endeavor to account for the innovation level of the company by interpreting its operation and highlighting those dimensions that seem to have most explanatory power. We follow the A. H. Van de Ven (1986) framework as elaborated in Chapter 2 (Figure 2.3) and draw in detail on the case study material to support the understanding that is proposed.

The conclusion picks up the major themes illustrated by the case to point to the main features of Druid's brand of innovation.

DRUID—INNOVATIVE ACHIEVEMENT AND HISTORY

Druid: The Innovative Dimension

Sometimes you don't even know what you have been craving until the real thing comes along. Watching the Druid Theater Company's production of *The Beauty Queen of Leenane* . . . is like sitting down to a square meal after a long diet of salads and hors d'oeuvres.

The New York Times, 1998.

She [Garry Hynes] is an alchemist who can conjure drama from thin air, drape characters in the detail of their parts and, most precious of all, stir emotions.

The Guardian, 1998.

The Druids have lived up to their name: they are indeed priests of an ancient magic.

Sydney Morning Herald, 1994.

The emergence of Druid Theater Company is probably the single most important development in Irish theater in the last ten years.

The Irish Times, 1982.

Based in Galway in the west of Ireland, Druid's longevity as an innovative company renders it exceptional—and for our purposes particularly interesting—among all those nominated as highly innovative.[1] While most commentators acknowledge peaks and troughs in its artistic output, it is generally agreed that overall, the company has a remarkable record. Druid more than meets the usual criteria for high achievement: awards, invitations to perform as part of prestigious overseas events, critical acclaim, audience response. Most notably in recent times (1998), Druid swept the boards with six awards at the prestigious Tony ceremony in New York with its production of "The Beauty Queen of Leenane," the author of which (Martin McDonagh) was "discovered" by Druid though its script-reading service. The company director, Garry Hynes, had the distinction of being the first woman in the history of the awards to win the Tony for Best Director. An institution in Irish theater, its legacy has been widely acclaimed. "The distinctive contribution of Druid lies in moments of magical imagery that have existed on the stage, in the unique sensations of performances shared between actors and the audience." (O'Toole 1985) F. O'Toole (1985) refers to "that primacy of performance, the quality that makes it difficult to sum up Druid's contribution", stating that it "does not lie in its repertoire, but in its style of performance and the vision contained in the style." Aspects of Druid's repertoire (Appendix 3) may nevertheless be classed as innovative. Its work with—and sometimes, discovery of—new contemporary writers has been a notable feature of the company's output. This may be traced to a deliberate management policy of environmental scanning in that, since the 1980s, the company has provided a script-reading service. Over the years Druid has reclaimed and reinterpreted the Irish repertoire, giving new life to the major works of John Millington Synge, as well as revivifying forgotten plays and transforming some of these from their status as fairly inconsequential pieces of work into major events in Irish theater.[2]

Apart from style, vision and the distinctiveness of its staging, the work of the company has been especially important in an Irish context, fulfilling the social role of the contemporary arts as a critique of society, challenging and subverting the images which this projects of itself in a language to which the audience can relate: "Garry Hynes has been subverting [the Canon Sheehan] notion of the West,[3] subverting it from within the traditional theatrical representations of rural western life." (O'Toole 1985). Overall it is generally acknowledged that Druid has been successful in developing a corpus of work which has been influential in artistic terms.

In terms of its modus operandi too, the company broke new ground by its establishment of an unconventional touring network in Ireland, following on its realization that the existing network, largely established through the Arts Council's investment in arts infrastructure around the country, wasn't working, at least for Druid. This gave rise to the Unusual Rural Tour (URT) through which the company brought productions to small venues following on the model of the legendary touring fit-ups of Anew McMaster[4] in the 1950s. This approach earned Druid a unique relationship with audiences, and was instrumental in weaving an elaborately textured mythology and a national reputation fed by a rich and colorful store of accounts of packed venues in rural villages like Lisdoonvarna, visits to school halls in the windswept Aran Islands, as well as a listing of places visited which puckishly gives equal value to the international and the local—"Swinford, Sydney, Thurles, Toronto."

This summary assessment of innovation in Druid focuses on a dimension that may be cast as purely artistic (its handling of repertoire) as well as one that more clearly falls within the managerial/marketing domain (the development of URTs). As the story of the company unfolds, the linkages between these two dimensions—often characterized in the arts as being at opposite and even opposing poles—and even their inextricability in any meaningful sense, becomes apparent. Furthermore, as the company ages, its central dilemma may be said to lie in the continuous effort to achieve unison and balance in this relationship: to refind today in a more complex environment the harmony which enabled the high innovative output of the company's beginnings.

History of Druid

One of a number of theater companies funded by the Irish Arts Council, Druid was for many years the first regional company to be so subsidized. In receipt in 1997 of a core grant of £275,000 plus additional funding for touring, this ranks the company third in theater funding in Ireland after the Abbey and the Gate Theaters, making it one of the major clients of the Arts Council. Table 3.1 details Arts Council funding to Druid since its beginnings in 1975 to the period of this research, 1997. Its grant is far ahead of its sister regional companies, all of which, it should be said, are considerably younger.

Since 1975 Druid has undertaken 130 productions, never less than three per annum and a maximum of ten in 1976 (Table 3.2), most of which have been directed by Garry Hynes (see table in Notes,[5] p. 85). These productions have been presented in 70 places including London, Edinburgh, New York, Sydney and Toronto.

A company limited by shares and incorporated in 1981, Druid's operation was overseen by a small, four-member board of trustees, membership of which has been virtually static since the inception of a formal Board structure. Since then too (1989)[6] the Board has been chaired by Donagh O'Donoghue, a prominent Galway businessman who in 1978 provided the space in Chapel Lane, Galway that was to become the theater, home, and symbolic heart of the company. The company's main source of income is its Arts Council grant, on which it is heavily dependent. Receipts from the box office have at best repre-sented no more than one third of the Druid's total annual income, mainly because of the limited capacity of its main venue, while spon-sorship from private sources is negligible (Table 3.3, p. 50).

Since its formation, Druid has had two different artistic directors (over three periods of Artistic Directorship): Garry Hynes (1975–1991), Maeliosa Stafford (1991–1994), and Garry Hynes from 1994 to the pres-ent. The company has had four Administrators/General Managers— Deirdre Murphy (1980–1981), Jerome Hynes (1981–1989), Jane Daly

TABLE 3.1
Arts Council Funding of Druid, 1976–1997

Year	Amount in £s	Year	Amount in £s
1976	1,500	1987	253,000
1977	3,000	1988	192,000
1978	6,000	1989	237,500
1979	16,000	1990	270,000
1980	24,750	1991	279,000
1981	32,000	1992	274,800
1982	56,300	1993	295,000
1983	82,000	1994	312,500
1984	114,000	1995	318,000
1985	147,000	1996	337,000
1986	192,400	1997	345,000

Source: Arts Council records.

TABLE 3.2
Number of Druid Productions Per Annum, 1975–1997

Year	Number	Year	Number
1975	8	1987	7
1976	10	1988	4
1977	8	1989	4
1978	8	1990	4
1979	6	1991	5
1980	6	1992	6
1981	7	1993	6
1982	5	1994	4
1983	6	1995	5
1984	5	1996	4
1985	5	1997	3
1986			

Source: Druid, 21 Years.

(1989–1996), and Louise Donlon (1996–present). In addition Druid currently employs an Administrator and an Administrative Assistant.

Context of Company Formation. In the J. M. Richards (1976) report on provision for the arts in Ireland, Druid Repertory Company is mentioned along with a number of "amateur drama groups" as providing theater in County Galway. Like the rest of the country outside of Dublin, Galway had then no professional theater companies. In terms of its planning for the arts, the Arts Council had singled out the Everyman Playhouse in Cork as the only regional project for special development.

On the national arts front too the Arts Council had recently appointed a new Director, Colm O Briain, whose artistic background and experience in contrast with that of his predecessors, had been in the Dublin *avant-garde* of the day, who held strong ambitions to effect major changes in arts provision and funding, and who was acutely aware of the necessity to widen the remit of the Council outside of the metropolitan centers. This wind of change was to prove opportune for Druid.

Beginnings and First Home. The early days of Druid have an inescapable mythical ring about them with all the unfailing appeal of lore (unsullied by any actual records of the period) and infused with a contagious excitement—a small group of students/drama lovers emerging from the Drama Society in University College, Galway (UCG), and Taibhdhearc,[7] all sharing a house for a time, fired with a mission to bring exciting, challenging theater to Galway, and putting

TABLE 3.3
Income of Druid Theater Company, 1987–1995

Year	1987	1988	1989	1990	1991	1992	1993	1994	1995
Total Income	£443,551	£340,777	£409,762	£436,924	£424,500	£438,164	£486,969	£526,923	£469,245
Arts Council–core and touring	£253,000	£192,220	£237,500	£270,000	£279,000	£274,800	£295,000	£312,500	336,595
	57%	56%	60%	62%	66%	63%	61%	59%	72%
Box office	£149,856	£119,986	£139,297	£125,002	£106,339	£103,952	£151,344	£170,884	£121,290
	34%	35%	34%	29%	25%	24%	31%	32%	26%
Other – Local Authority, shop receipts, sponsorship etc.	£40,695	£28,571	£32,965	£41,922	£39,161	£59,412	£40,625	£43,539	£11,360
	9%	9%	6%	9%	9%	13%	8%	9%	2%

Source: Druid Arts Council Records.

on plays in the Jesuit Hall. As a student Garry Hynes had directed three productions with UCG Players. The first Druid production (3 July 1975) and one which was to develop iconic significance for the company was Synge's "Playboy of the Western World," directed by Garry Hynes and featuring actors Mick Lally and Marie Mullen, names that are associated with Druid up to the present.

The company received a small grant of £350 for their first season from Bord Fáilte (the Irish Tourist Board) and played to audiences of 100 to 200. Otherwise its activities were funded by a bank loan. Though operating on a shoestring, their aspirations from the beginning were professional: wages were low but guaranteed. Quickly frustrated with the facilities of the Jesuit Hall in 1976, they leased a pub—the Fo'castle—as a small 47-seat theater to serve as a rehearsal and performance area, a workshop, and an office. "The dressing room was built by the simple expedient of putting a door at the end of a narrow corridor and the box office was—naturally—under the stairs, but it was here the style and substance of Druid Theater Company took firm root and flourished."[8] At this time the company had a distinctly homemade feel: programs credited the cast with set construction, costumes, lights, design, and so on:

> The company doing everything necessary to get a show on the road, from set building and technical work to administration and publicity. The work, however, was assigned on the basis of individual responsibilities, which continued from production to production so standards of quality evolved. Artistic liveliness was maintained by a policy of presenting only plays that interested the members of the company to rehearse and perform. This led to catholicity in repertoire and methods of presentation.[9]

Thus commitment was forged in classic style, heightened by the precariousness of their existence. Arts Council recognition came with a first grant of £1,500 in 1976 during which year Druid brought their first production to Dublin's Project Arts Centre.[10] Gradually other actors who were to form the solid core of Druid joined the founder members—Séan McGinley in 1977, Maeliosa Stafford in 1978, and Ray McBride in 1979—and the company's second production of "Playboy" (1977) won them national press coverage.

Chapel Lane. By 1978 Druid needed a bigger theater than the Fo'castle. Their search unearthed an old grainstore owned by McDonagh Milling and Trading Co. Ltd. in Chapel Lane, then a rundown part of the city. Acquiring this after persistent negotiations the company set about its physical conversion, all while rehearsing. Five thousand pounds was raised through a fund-raising campaign. The official opening on 19 May

1979 was followed by a production of Brecht's "Threepenny Opera" in the new 110-seat theater. The increasing of their Arts Council grant from £8,000 to £15,000 on the opening night represented a vote of confidence in the company. In early 1980 the company appointed its first administrator.

Druid in the 1980s. By a twist of fate or a form of subversion, which has come to seem typical of Druid, their national stature followed on their overseas success. Having struggled to gain recognition in the national press since their inception, Druid achieved this in spectacular fashion through their triumph in the Edinburgh Festival in 1980. With £5,000 from the Department of Foreign Affairs, the company, first in the person of Jerome Hynes (brother of the Artistic Director) as publicity officer, set off to embark on the "conquest of Edinburgh—or at least of the Irish media" (Burke 1985). Like many things about Druid, this expedition has entered into the company lore and was described by one Scottish commentator as "the most extraordinary public relations assault the Fringe may ever have known" (Dudley Edwards 1985). With two devised plays, "Island Surrounded by a Bridge of Glass" (written by Garry Hynes), and, "The Pursuit of Pleasure," the company was awarded a Fringe First, presented to Garry Hynes by Dame Peggy Ashcroft. The ecstatic reaction in the Irish media was compounded by Druid's nonparticipation in the Dublin Theater Festival despite increased inducements by the Festival[11]—"This piece of 'bad publicity' was worth more to the company than any number of performances in Dublin." (Burke 1985) The message was clear—Druid as a regional company disdained the Irish metropolis and establishment. The classic image of the "West-of-Ireland-as-underdog," which had its basis in long periods of neglect in what is the most highly centralized country in Western Europe, was something that Druid and other arts companies in the west were able to turn to their advantage. The company could hold its own in an international field: subsequently the Dublin audiences would have to come to Galway to see Druid—and they did!

In the following decade the company continued to present its varied repertoire, directed for the most part by Garry Hynes. From 1981, Jerome Hynes took over as Administrator of Druid. Key points of the decade were the company's award-winning production in 1982 of "The Playboy of the Western World" which toured to Edinburgh and the Aran Islands, "Wood of the Whispering" by M.J. Molloy in 1983 which won a Harvey's Award[12] for actor Ray McBride, and the phenomenal collaboration with the acclaimed Irish playwright Tom Murphy beginning with "Famine" in 1984. In 1983 the company undertook its first URT, accounts of which have entered the realms of legend. The success of these tours necessitated sensitivity on the part of the company to the changing needs of venues and audiences, a challenge that they met handsomely. In 1984 a number of appointments were made—Associate Designer, Production Manager, Stage Manager, Administrative Assistant, and Assistant Stage Manager—putting the company on a more firm footing.[13] The following year, Druid brought "Playboy" to the Donmar Warehouse theater in London and was offered a West End contract. This they declined, instead returning to Galway to rehearse Tom Murphy's "Conversations on a Homecoming," also to great acclaim. In 1986 "Playboy" was presented in New York.

However by the end of the decade the company was encountering its first serious artistic slump. Jerome Hynes left to become Chief Executive of the Wexford Opera Festival in 1988. Garry Hynes was working with the Royal Shakespeare Company (RSC) in Britain where she was joined by some core Druid actors. Finally in 1991, Garry Hynes left to take up the prime theater job in Ireland—Artistic Director of the National Theater—the Abbey. Arts Council reports of the 1980s reflect the successes of the company but focus in addition on two related issues: its insecure financial base and its limited earning capacity due to the small size of the Chapel Lane theater, its home venue. Itself severely strapped for funds at the time, the Council remarked as early as 1980 that the company "may have reached the limit of its capacity to earn."[14] This was reiterated frequently:

> Some concern is felt about the future growth and development of Druid in view of the absence of adequate space in their present premises and the absence of significant local financial support.[15]

> There still remains a substantial gap between the company's real needs and the Council's ability to meet them. The absence of a theater in Galway with adequate seating capacity is an ever-growing problem for this dynamic company and it is hoped that a remedy for this situation can be found in the near future.[16]

> The problems arising from the absence of an adequate theater space in Galway city for this company have become acute.[17]

> The Council recognizes that it is imperative that a new theater be provided in Galway to provide a base for Druid and also a viable venue for professional touring companies.[18]

The end of the 1980s sounded a note of anxiety: "Druid Theater Company experienced a difficult year in 1988, largely arising from the box office potential of their small Galway-based theater, combined with the Council's inability to provide a touring grant to the company this year. [This] threatened the continued viability and the very existence of the company, and imposed constraints that effectively deprived the company of any flexibility for experiment or scope to absorb failures."[19] Finally in 1989 the company became embroiled in a public controversy with Galway Corporation, the Galway city authorities. Unhappy with the physical configuration of the long-awaited new theater in that city, Druid issued a statement that it felt obliged to withdraw from any association with the project so as "to protect its integrity,"[20] this in spite of considerable Arts Council pressure, given that the theater would furnish Druid with a new home and a greater earning capacity. The company came to believe that the burden of venue management would be a millstone around its neck, seriously encroaching on the flexibility which was vital to its operation: in Garry Hynes words to the *Irish Times,* "the plans would have seriously compromised the essence of Druid and we had to shout stop."[21] The end of the 1980s was a definite trough in the fortunes and the reputation of Druid, attributed by the Irish Times to events in the life of the Artistic Director:

> The latter part of the decade has not been an altogether happy time for the director. Druid's productions have grown fewer and some of them have been disappointing. The promise of developing new Irish writing has only been fulfilled sporadically. Frequent touring abroad, coupled with Hynes' recent work for the RSC . . . have loosened her roots from her home city . . . the impression remains that Druid has been suffering from lack of artistic direction for some time. Hynes has seemed unable either to let go of the company or to give it her full commitment.[22]

Second Artistic Director. Jane Daly became the new General Manager of Druid in 1988, an appointment which was heralded by the *Irish Times* as "perhaps the most positive indication of the company's future."[23] From 1989 the Board of the company began to keep proper records of meetings and to constitute itself more formally, resolving to put structures and policies in place for the future.[24] While the funding situation was by now cutting deeply within Druid, Garry Hynes initiated a script-reading service in an effort to encourage new writing. Maeliosa Stafford who had been an actor with Druid and had directed a number of productions took up the position of Artistic Director of the company in 1991, a position he was to hold until 1994. His agenda for his directorship included: the development of a core company, the future of the Chapel Lane venue; the question of Druid's relationship with the Municipal Theater; the development and commissioning of new work; and the winning of sponsorship for particular projects.[25] Of the twenty productions presented by Druid during this period, eleven were directed by Maeliosa Stafford (one in conjunction with John Crowley) and the remainder by invited directors. This period saw a relationship develop with playwright Vincent Woods whose work, "At the Black Pigs Dyke," proved a major success for the company, winning two Belfast Telegraph Awards and touring to London in 1993 and the Sydney Festival in 1995. Also, 1993 saw the beginnings of Druid's relationship with playwright, Billy Roche. In this year the Arts Council Drama Officer professed the Council to be "enormously encouraged by the vitality and creativity of Druid,"[26] although later the same year the same officer expressed "major reservations about the [current] artistic thinking"[27] of the company. In spite of these mixed messages, the company's grant for 1994 showed an increase that the Drama Officer declared to be " a strong vote of confidence and support on the part of the Arts Council for the work of the company and in particular at this significant point in time for the company."[28] Minutes of meetings indicate that during this financially turbulent period, the Board took an altogether more active role in the artistic decision making of Druid given the serious implications of this for company finances. Likewise, the manager was under constant pressure to reduce costs.[29] The Board minutes underlined the need for planning,[30] discussed problems with publicity,[31] and the necessity to inquire into the reasons for poor touring audiences.[32]

Return of Garry Hynes. Upon Maeliosa Stafford's departure in 1993 the company continued without an Artistic Director for about a year (from October 1993 to November 1994) during which time Jane Daly continued as General Manager and the Board interviewed a number of possible candidates for Artistic Director. In July 1994, Garry Hynes returned to direct Antoine O Flathartha's "Silverlands," and by November of that year had agreed to accept the role of Consultant Artistic Director, the arrangement being that she would devote about 50 percent of her time to Druid.

This was to prove a critical point and to precipitate a major crisis in the history of Druid. In her new capacity the Artistic Director presented a proposal for a review of the company's operations to the Board and outlined a formidable agenda of objectives/problem areas which she felt needed to be addressed:[33] review of policy, structures, and effectiveness of the company; the drawing up of job specifications for staff; the need to address the absence of public relations resources within the company; problems with revenue and the level of subsidy per seat; the lack of sponsorship income; the need for real commitment to new writing and script development; a proposal that the imminent twentieth anniversary of the company be shelved and the celebrations moved to the twenty-first anniversary; and the desirability of setting up a pool of artistic associates. This agenda was at the very least implicitly critical of current artistic and managerial policy in the company.

changed a great deal over the last three years and that Druid has changed greatly also."[48] In her unique relationship to the company, not in awe of its "sacred cow status in Irish cultural life,"[49] it may be that she was in a better position to rout the embedded myths which may indicate that the company was looking more to the past than to the future, or which distorted its take on the changing environment in Galway. She was quite explicit about this: "As the company approaches its 20th birthday, it's important that it finds new directions and in some ways it's easier for me to let go of the past than it would be for someone new, because it's not that sentimental for me."[50]

Resisting institutionalization. Séan McGinley, leading actor and long-term member of Druid, expressed the view that "we must avoid at all costs propping up the institution for its own sake."[51] A striking dimension of the history of Druid, and a point that will be taken up again in relation to its management, is the fact that at a number of key points in its development the company has opted for directions which might be deemed unexpected and even at times, from the perspective of others, somewhat cussed. In the initial stages the creative direction of the company deliberately eschewed the obvious and familiar repertoire available to theater companies at the time. Its route to national success was one not previously taken by any theater company in Ireland: almost seeming to scorn Dublin, the company set its sights on Edinburgh; in this way winning the Irish media. At a time in the early 1980s when the Arts Council was establishing a circuit of professionally managed touring venues in the major centers of population around the country, Druid, having experienced problems with audience numbers on some tours, set its face against this policy by setting up instead its URTs and fighting for the right to use its touring grants to service these small local venues (a more expensive option than multiple nights in "established" venues). In 1985 when the company had a chance to transfer its production of "The Playboy of the Western World" to a West End theater in London, it declined what would have been a dream opportunity for any Irish company, preferring to return to Galway to begin rehearsals for their next production. A staff member noted: "We did negotiate the possibility of a West End deal and . . . for any manager that's the dream—to actually achieve something like that and to move it onto a plane like that. But we turned it down in the end because we felt that it wasn't the right deal and I have no regrets about that. The only thing I wonder is what direction might we have gone . . . you just wonder . . . two roads divided, what would have happened if we had taken which one or whatever. . . . We didn't take the obvious route."[52]

Most controversially, the company rejected what might well be re-garded—and what was regarded by the Arts Council at the time—as the answer to their dream: a home of their own in the new municipal theater being proposed for Galway. In the light of the financial problems that bedeviled the company by virtue of the limited box office capacity of their small theater, the development by Galway Corporation of a new purpose-built theater space might understandably be regarded as the answer to the company's prayer. Yet again Druid took a surprising stance, rejecting the role of resident company and the "establishment" implications of such a role, and taking up a position against their main sponsors and holding on determinedly to their marginalism. "Suddenly Druid began to realize that there would be a creative straitjacket put on it and . . . it would have to write off a lot of the kind of work that it did."[53] Their rejection was regarded, in the words of the Drama Officer of the Arts Council as "very serious and of grave concern to the Arts Council."[54] It can be argued that these decisions were impractical, costly, uncompromising, made little sense from a managerial perspective, and furthermore risked alienating their main source of funding.[55] However, the net effect of these choices was described glowingly on the occasion of the company's twenty-first birthday (1996): "One of the great things about Druid, indeed, is how little, as an institution, it has to show for twenty-one years. The company has accumulated only the bare necessities of its art. There is no vast building, no great organizational infrastructure. The legacy of twenty-one years is invaluable but intangible. . . . Druid has existed much more as an idea, a spirit, than as a set of fixed assets."[56] Rather than being by virtue of happenstance, this resistance to anything which would make of it an institution is a feature of the company, almost a credo of the Artistic Director:

> I think that is really deep within the company from the very beginning—to kick against the obvious. . . . The obvious when we started off was to do things like John B. Keane[57] and so on, to get in our audience and I remember very consciously . . . (deciding) two things we're not going to do. We are not going to do just whatever they are doing in Dublin just because . . . they are doing it. Because we are not Dublin. We're Galway. Which was really strong. And we are also not going to do the obvious because we are doing all this for the . . . bread and beans and drinking money. And if we are not enjoying it, what's the point in doing it in the first place? We are doing this for ourselves in a kind of a way. I think that's kind of been built in to the company. Whatever the ongoing definitions are . . . we question them at least. Just to keep it vital. I mean I think it is just so important you throw the balls up in the air.[58]

"Druid is a company involved in making theater. We don't want to have a shape or a form imposed on us."[59] This constant questioning of the accepted mores and the rejection of institutionalism makes Druid what it is today and will be shown to have consequences for the management of the company. It is worth noting that this modus ope-randi—sailing close to or even against the wind—is stressful and high-risk and has personal implications for those involved. Speaking of the municipal theater decision, Garry Hynes explains: "We've had to con-tinue the argument of not going in all through those years and it has felt scary at times—there has been always the question 'Are we going to miss out here? What's going to happen to us?'"[60] The capacity to cope with this uncertainty, to tolerate and even to hold on to ambiguity in the face of establishment opposition (in the form of the Arts Council and Galway Corporation—its two main funders), is a striking feature of the history of the company. "So, you know, it has been a continued fight for insecurity, if you like . . . there hasn't been [just] one major watershed point."[61]

APPLICATION OF RESEARCH FRAMEWORK

Management of Transactions: Structure

Whatever the phases Druid theater company has gone through since its inception, the structure of the company has not changed notably since the 1980s. It is a very small organization comprising a four-mem-ber Board of Trustees, two directors (an Artistic Director and a General Manager), and a small-core administrative/artistic staff (four full-time staff members). Classically organic in its origins and in the evolution of roles within the organization, the company has been substantially shaped around the vision and ambitions of its founder and current Artistic Director and corresponds in detail with the simple structure described by H. Mintzberg (1983). If one might expect that the radical reconceptualization of the company occasioned by the return of the founding Artistic Director would have engendered notable structural shifts, this has not been the case. Each of the elements of structure will be examined in turn.

Incorporated somewhat unusually as a company limited by shares rather than by guarantee, the Board of management of Druid began to record its meetings formally in 1989, fourteen years after the establish-ment of the company and a time when it was going through a major trough. In the beginning, "the Board comprised the company for many years so . . . the people who were working together were the Board and therefore it was very informal."[62] Since its formation the board has changed little and the question of a turnover of membership has not arisen formally at any meeting of the company. The Board is made up of the Chairman, two academics from University College, Galway, and Jerome Hynes, Manager of the company from 1981 to 1988 and brother of the Artistic Director.[63] The Chairman of Druid has a strong belief and pride in the company: "Obviously we want to be the premier theater company in this country and we set out to do that."[64] He shows an active interest in its financial management and the reporting systems associated with this. The composition of the Board evolved directly from and reflects the contacts necessary and useful to the company as it began to formalize its operation—Galway business life and the university from which it sprung. Membership cannot be said to be representative of any sector in particular—the population of Galway, for instance, or the theater world in Ireland—and does not accord with the current characterization of Druid by its Consultant Artistic Director as a national theater company based in Galway.[65] There is a somewhat belated recognition of this as a possible deficiency. In the early years, the issue, as expressed by a Board member, was one of control.

Druid was trying to establish and find a structure and I think structure was probably the least important thing. We didn't want to create some sort of an animal that would become difficult to service and all of that. We wanted to get on with the core work and, I suppose, if there is one regret that I would have from the period, [it] would be that maybe we didn't reach out far enough to establish contact with people outside of the company. I suppose in a way we were probably afraid of losing control of the company; we wanted to run the Company in our own way and this was the great freedom that Druid had.[66]

The company endeavors to hold meetings on a quarterly basis but this is not always possible. The record shows considerable fluctuation in the number of meetings per annum (Table 3.4) but monthly meetings between the Chairman and the General Manager and a degree of informal contact between the Chairman and the Artistic Director supplement these.

In contrast with other companies in receipt of public funding the Board of Druid has never had an Arts Council nominee and there is no record of any Arts Council officer in attendance at any Board meeting as an observer.[67] It is quite likely that attendance at board meetings was not deemed necessary in the light of the good relations that existed at the Board and executive level between the two organizations. (Indeed,

Table 3.4
Board Meetings of Druid Theater Company, 1989–1996

Year	1989	1990	1991	1992	1993	1994	1995	1996
No. of Meetings	3	2	8	5	6	6	9	2

Source: Druid board minutes.

as shown, the company was able to call on these friendships at crucial moments in its history and always received a sympathetic response.)

While preoccupied with the financial state of the company, the Board has no record worthy of mention in respect to fund-raising, in spite of their dangerous level of dependence on Arts Council funding. It would seem too that its capacity in this regard may have been somewhat compromised by the position adopted by the company in relation to the Municipal Theater—the flow of municipal funding, and the corporate funding which might be expected to accompany this, more likely tending towards the new building rather than to Druid. The question of fund-raising arises on a regular basis at board meetings but has engendered little or no action to date. Records of meetings show that the Board takes a lively interest in the artistic operation of the company, and especially how this relates to its financial situation. It became increasingly involved in this aspect of Druid's operation during Maeliosa Stafford's period as Artistic Director, possibly because of his lack of experience in this role and also because of the financial problems which began to bite at that time. The role of the Board in respect to the staffing of the company seems to be primarily in relation to the selection and appointment of key personnel and the fixing of remuneration levels. There is no evidence of any interest in other aspects of staffing—formalized conditions of employment, staff training and development and so forth—and no effort to formally evaluate the operation of the company in its entirety other than in respect of its financial situation and its public profile. While there is a recognition that the board needs "to evolve," opinions of key company members differ as to what this may mean:

> I think it does change . . . the Board has evolved the way the organization has. And I don't think there is any doubt that the Board needs to continue evolving. For instance the Board needs to be small. I think that's undoubtedly true.[68]

> If anything the Board needs to be extended even further, even wider.[69]

> I would prefer it to be bigger . . . it's only four members and I would prefer if there were . . . the full seven and, you know, I think it would help us be more strict, really, in many ways, in the whole meeting process.[70]

In summary, it must be said that the Druid Board is ill-fitted to the national aspiration of its mission and poorly constituted in respect of its significant public funding and the accountability that this should entail. The implicit acquiescence of the Arts Council in this is noted. Indeed both the legal status of the company and the key benefactor and family relationships give the management of transactions in the company something of the character of a private rather than a public arts organization. The explanation offered above for the small size of the Board in previous years—greater control and flexibility—must be deemed to still hold true.

Management of Transactions: Staffing and Systems

The record of the company in relation to staffing is broadly to periods of relative stability followed by periods of turbulence, the latter most notably in 1996 with the return of the founding Artistic Director. The administrative core is small with a sense that the current staffing level is inadequate, although the company has not chosen to dedicate funding to this area. While the Artistic Director and the General Manager have equal status on paper, it is clear that in practice the symbolic power and authority of the founder Artistic Director is difficult to supersede.

The staff of the organization was and remains quite generalist and no administrative specialisms are defined by role-title. The work undertaken by staff members tended in the past to follow the abilities, interests, or preferences of personnel, and opportunities to try out different tasks or roles have been offered to staff members over the years. Coordination is by a combination of direct supervision and mutual adjustment (Mintzberg 1983) and depends on intensive communication. So, as matters transpire, even functions that are regarded as highly important, for example, marketing, tend to be carried generally by the staff rather than being the responsibility of one staff member, or else, on occasion, these services are bought in. Again it would seem that this is a situation that has evolved. A possible consequence of this style of operation is that those areas for which nobody has an aptitude may become somewhat neglected and suffer from a certain expertise lag within the company. Furthermore there is less internal development of skills than in a situation where functions become the particular responsibility of a designated staff member. There is some evidence that the marketing and fund-raising functions of the company have suffered as a result of this lack of definition or analysis.

The staffing pattern of the organization has followed generally the different phases associated with the three periods of artistic direction, moving from the family relationship that applied in the first and most "instinctive" phase of the company when structure as such was not an issue, to the more "professional" nature of the relationship of current management: "In the beginning and up to 1995 the staff and company members operated substantially as a team. . . . I think everybody had their own responsibilities but, as I say, the good thing was there was always a team spirit. And if there was a particular problem you could always talk to each other about it."[71] In the opinion of the Artistic Director, the early days of the company approached the ideal: "I'd say by 1985 we were a fully professional organization, in all respects ... we had this enviable mix of professional skills and aspirations but a real sense of community both amongst ourselves and with the people within the community in which we were working."[72] This dynamic carried Druid into the second half of the 1980s but slumped towards the end of the decade. The appointment of a new General Manager and Artistic Director restored or gave the illusion of restoring elements of this earlier dynamic and despite serious financial problems, this period is recalled by the staff as very happy. It would seem from accounts that the structure and style of the company during this time was highly organic in the sense of participative, lacking the drivenness of its earlier and later phases.

The financial difficulties did not provoke any radical reexamination of structures or staffing until the return of Garry Hynes. Her analysis diagnosed a poor fit between Druid and its environment with consequences for every aspect of the operation of the company, a drift which, if allowed to persist, would lead in her opinion to the demise of Druid. The task then in her view became that of "applying structures onto something that was instinctively formed in the first place. And things don't happen in a graded kind of way: certain things shoot forward in a period of time and fall back."[73] The appointment of a manager with both an arts administration qualification and experience in theater management was an important first step in effecting the necessary overhaul of structures and staffing. There is a recognition that contracts and job descriptions are needed and that it is high time that these were in place:

> There is a very strong awareness that there needs to be job descriptions. There needs to be clarity of relationships between people and clarity of reporting structures and communication. . . . Whatever is not there, it is not not there as a result of any belief that it shouldn't be there. . . . That's the direction we're moving. . . . We are aware of the fact that people need clear job definitions, that they need clearer reporting structures. And as a result of that, those things will come in and I think it is well above time.[74]

Systems within the organization were and still are kept to a minimum along the lines typical of an organic structure or of the "institutional processes" described by Van de Ven (1986). Control, evaluation, appraisal, and so forth are very much part of the ongoing operation of the company and have no discrete procedures. In recent times staff meetings have been introduced and there is a strong awareness of the necessity for a deliberate effort to ensure effectiveness of communication:

> There is a problem in an organization . . . like Druid where, because every-
> body meets everybody else every day and . . . tends to be friends outside
> of it and drink together and be very sociable and family-like and every-
> thing like that. There is then a presumption that everybody knows every-
> thing. There have been huge problems within Druid of communication.
> There have been huge problems of "I found out on the street that this is
> happening and I hadn't been told" and I have constantly reiterated the
> notion that because we're so small and informal, [this] is actually the
> reason why we need to be really [careful]. Because when you're big, like
> when you are in the Abbey and you have a hundred employees, you know
> you have to send out a memo. When you're small you think "Ah well,
> everybody knows." But, in fact, they don't.[75]

(As this statement indicates, holographic organizations of the type
outlined by Van de Ven [1986] are by no means easy to achieve.) Minutes
of staff meetings are not filed and thus were not available for examination. However, one has the impression from verbal accounts that they
generally take the form of a more or less unidirectional checklist of
activities and duties, rather than any form of substantial discussion of
ideas or policy. While the company operated for some time under
structures which were quite loose, there is now a sense of a general
tightening up and professionalization of operation although the
company's style of management still remains friendly and informal.

Staffing and internal communication systems in Druid extend beyond the core staff relations. Since the organization, like all other Irish
theater companies, continually expands and contracts in size, its approach to communication with artists is a vital aspect of its overall
operation. Druid has been remarkable for the close relationship it has
maintained over a long period with a number of key actors who were
all around at its formation and who still maintain total loyalty to the
company. The founding core group was involved in every aspect of its
operation—artistic and administrative—and members have expressed
their relationship to the company in terms of it being a family: "literally
speaking, theater company is somewhat of a misnomer when applied
to Druid. It is more, I think, a sisterhood and a brotherhood" (Lally
1985). (In the consideration of organizational culture, this will be discussed in greater detail.) As in a family, the company members continually leave and return, and their basic experience with Druid would
seem to have colored their overall attitude to theater and to their
profession. It is clear that the company at all times sought to make
artists feel valued and welcome: "They were embraced. . . . It was something people wanted to be part of and when they came to Galway, they
were made at home. They were looked after . . . making the actor happy
was very important to ensure that nothing was distracting them
from their work."[76] The Artistic Director puts a conscious effort into

maintaining a company spirit; "Garry is desperate for organizing drinks parties. Like, before we begin rehearsal. . . . The social side is a big thing. . . . Just for company morale . . . everybody going out for a drink together"[77] even if this may prove tiresome for some of the staff since it can involve travel and may eat into their personal free time. "Everybody would join up together and have cocktail sausages and sambos. . . . It is very important, but I certainly think there is too much of an emphasis on it."[78] This effort is born of the value which the Artistic Director personally places on her interaction with other artists, the need to foster good relationships and a company spirit, and how this intimately affects the company's output in terms of the depth and level of performance which can be achieved.

Management of Transactions: Strategy

For most of its history, strategy in Druid may be described as emergent and highly instinctive. By their own admission, the company had no major game plan, and operated as one organic unit. "The focus was the next production and doing the best possible work and being able to look back proudly on the record of achievement, be it artistic or managerial or touring or whatever. . . . Before that and certainly for the first couple of years that I was there it was very much [that]. Yes, we did some great shows but there wasn't a coherent policy or artistic policy or long-term policies."[79] Different members of Druid describe the progress of the company as something unplanned, though informed by their vision and high ambitions. That these ambitions were realized is never attributed to any kind of premeditated planning or strategy, and even the business of making major decisions is acknowledged as a process with all the twists and turns of uncertainty: "It was a process we had to go through to realize exactly where we were. . . . I can't pretend that it was anything but a realization as we went through the process."[80] Thus for quite a long period, the company's planning horizon was short-term; the only evidence of a longer-term approach, which involves a conscious positioning of the company, is quite recent and comes from a sense that the conditions which existed at the time of the formation of the company no longer apply.

Two major principles underpin the change effort on the return of the founding Director, signposted in the "Towards 2001" policy document prepared jointly by her and the then newly appointed General Manager. First, this evidences a keen wish to reestablish the strong integration that was a feature of the company during its earlier years while recognizing that this probably cannot be achieved in quite the same way as before. Physical proximity is important to this integration: "Because I think that all the elements of the company have to stay within day-to-day contact with each other. It's extremely important. And we now have a possibility of getting the building beside Chapel Lane, which would be offices, and there would be a link. In effect, we would reintegrate the various activities of the company once again . . . almost under one roof and that's absolutely to be wished for."[81] This integration is a reflection of the Artisitc Directors belief in the interrelatedness of financial or administrative or any other management decisions and artistic decisions:

> It seems to me that the two are so interlinked. So, for instance, to me, artistic policy is the price you charge for your tickets. Unquestionably it's a fundamental building block of artistic policy. . . . I think that the most successful organizations are the organizations where the artistic and the management are integrated to the degree that one is the other and the other is the one. And that whatever the debate that happens between money and creativity will happen vitally and passionately within the walls of the organization and . . . that a split would never be seen on stages or outside of them.[82]

Second, and linked to this integration, is the flexibility of operation that has always been a basic tenet in Druid: "We wanted to run the company in our own way and this was the great freedom that Druid had. . . . What we wanted to do was to control our own destiny. . . . The freedom to do what we wanted, when we wanted, how we wanted."[83] This underpins many of the decisions of strategic import taken by the company. We have already accounted for their decision to decline the offer of a permanent home in the new city theater in this light. "Well, we would have lost what it is we have. What the company has is a unique flexibility at this point. It is the third highest funded theater in the state and yet at the same time it does not have the awful responsibility which has to drive the other two theaters, which is—a building and keeping it open."[84]

The Artistic Director recognizes that the company has deliberately chosen insecurity. Instead of the stability that would come from an association with the municipality, it has retained its "fringiness" seeing it as essential to the spirit of Druid—"a continued fight for insecurity."[85] This ability to tack and jib is vital to the talents and ambitions of the Artistic Director and she rejects any suggestion that there might be a dilemma or a conflict between the effort to retain this flexibility and the structures necessary to sound planning.

> If it is a downside, and if it has from time to time been a downside for Druid, it doesn't need to be. I don't think there is a relationship between staying flexible and not properly planning. So you have to have a kind of a flexibility but then again . . . that flexibility cannot be an excuse for poor

management and poor structures. . . . So, I mean, that flexibility has been key, and to me coming back to the company and being here where I am now, [it] is key.[86]

Nevertheless a dominant feeling still is that the company's choices, what we have termed its consistent resistance of institutionalization and its tendency to sail close to the wind, has costs—at least in terms of stress levels: "We do seem to be constantly just running to stand still."[87]

While the return of the founding Artistic Director has occasioned the most sweeping changes in the company in the last decade, these changes have been primarily in terms of personnel. Although there is a live awareness of the need for a continuing evolution in the structures of the organization as well as a full appreciation of the difficulties of this task, as yet no significant structural changes are evident.

> Well, first of all I would say that the structure is and should be constantly changing because it should be adapting to circumstances all the time. I think that there has been a very strong awareness [of this] in the last five years—maybe five to seven years. And it's a debate that has continued to some degree. One of the weaknesses of the organization would be that a structure which was appropriate, (which came about because it was appropriate at the time when it came about, i.e., early 1980s) . . . continued to be used long after its appropriateness, its usefulness. And that the company still has not solved that fully. The thing is that it is aware of it. At least. And attempting to solve it. And attempting to find an appropriate structure for what it is now . . . I don't think there is any question [but] that the structure of the company is part of an ongoing assessment . . . it's from what was unconscious and informal to something that's conscious and formal. It's hard. It's hard but you have to do it.[88]

The underlying concern is that structure must always be subservient to the purpose of the organization; it must not be allowed to impose its own agenda on the organization. The battle is between stasis and the fluidity necessary to organizational flexibility.

> So you have to really work hard all the time at what you are. And you have to be able to have a sufficient set of structures that mean that you are operating in a financially and artistically efficient manner. And yet, at the same time, not having those structures determine what's coming out at the other end. So there has to be a real balance achieved. . . . I think of it as the great battle to have structures which are adequate reflections and adequate to the organization at the time.[89]

Despite this awareness, the board remains the same; neither the staff complement nor the deployment of tasks have altered significantly. This is not to underplay the importance of personnel changes both in signaling and in the delivery of a different approach. However, if this is not underpinned by appropriate structural arrangements, there is a constant risk of staff burnout and turnover, with costly implications for the organization. While there may be some disagreement as to the detail of what is now needed within Druid, there would seem to be general consensus that greater reflectiveness is required in regard to the internal operation of the company, and that problems have arisen from a deficiency in this area. "In a way that probably comes from the company not looking harshly enough at the structure it currently has and wondering whether it serves the organization, the company, as it now is or [what it] is going to be in the next two years, or whatever."[90] The need for constant change is a fact of life for Druid and a dilemma for any arts organization that wishes to survive beyond its first phase.

> And, again, it's part of the constant transition from an organization that worked brilliantly for a couple of years because simply the collection of people who came defined their roles, defined their jobs, and defined the organization. Now, what happens when those people move on because the structure they leave behind is chaos and confusion to anybody else, because it was always defined by the people and when you take it away there is nothing there. So you then have to go through the hard work of actually defining, of making specific definitions.[91]

In the view of the Artistic Director, this process is actually inherent in the nature of an arts organization:

> One of the images I have often used for an arts organization like Druid or any arts organization is, it's a bit like retooling an assembly line every three months because the product changes. So, as much as you would like to run it on a set of fixed certainties, as you can run a business (you know, like the profit and loss at the bottom is what dictates everything), the structure is back up there—you can't.[92]

To summarize, the structure and systems of Druid remain that of a simple organization. The main changes in these over the years are directly attributable to the intervention of leadership. The development of policies, structures, roles up to the mid-1990s seemed to flow from the history of the company, with the lag that this sometimes implies.[93] While structures evolved in an incremental way up to the mid-1980s, it seems that for the following decade there was little evidence at any level of a critical appraisal of the management of the company. It is surprising that the main programed change took place just three years ago, the company having maintained its operation in a broadly homogeneous mode for almost twenty years, a long period in the arts world. This is suggestive of a degree of environmental bolstering.

In spite of a very definite consciousness of the need for this change, its effects, three years into the contract of the current Artistic Director, are not yet clearly visible in terms of the structure and mode of operation of the company: the overall shape remains the same—size and composition of the board, absence of staff specialisms, mode of operation, and so on. As expressed by the Consultant Artistic Director, what is now in progress is a deliberate and conscious effort to recreate, almost artificially, what happened in the first instance by what appeared a natural process. In this endeavor, it would seem that a number of tensions and conflicts are being played out. While the Artistic Director may not accept that there is a degree of tension between the requirements for security and those for flexibility, this is belied both by the stress levels in the company and the perennial difficulties it experiences in planning. The wish to generate high levels of commitment through the agency of a professional staff (as opposed to a closely knit group of people with shared ambitions) supposes a range of incentives and an approach to staff development that are not in evidence in Druid. There may also be a degree of conflict between the desire to establish proper (and therefore autonomous) structures and the need to maintain tight controls—as evidenced for example by the absence of change at the Board level. Similarly while there is an expressed wish for a participative approach and an effort to avoid organizational schizophrenia (between the artistic and administrative sides of the company), there is wide consensus that the personal style of the Artistic Director is hierarchical: "I would say it was very hierarchical. . . . It was Garry's show."[94] "There is nobody in there strong enough to compete with Garry."[95] Thus while the analysis and aspirations in terms of the management of the company are convincing, they lack coherence—some pieces of the jigsaw are missing. The organization is still small enough to suppose that these conflicts may be a playing out of the dimensions of the personality of the Director herself (see Mintzberg 1996), her internal conflicts relating to autonomy and control for instance, as well as the very real management conundrums of running an organization where so much hinges on personal relationships and contributions.

Management of Context: Leadership

When one attempts to account for the innovation level of Druid, the key role played by the founding Artistic Director overshadows all other dimensions of the organization. The strong identification of the company and of key company members with Garry Hynes has endured to the present, surviving a number of comings and goings. There is no doubt that her vision and drive formed and gave impetus to the company and that she is the dominant and pervasive influence in Druid today. Varying reports of the style of her leadership proliferate, characterizing her in a range of roles from power-hungry martinet to exceptionally gifted and even visionary director. Accounts of charismatic leadership typically have two salient features: first, they attribute to such leaders a crystalline visionary capacity, and second, they pay little attention to the leader-follower dimension. Although the leadership of Druid would certainly fall within the charismatic category, the evidence points to rather different findings in relation to the above two dimensions. The tone of the director's first communication with the Arts Council in the mid-1970s certainly indicates a high degree of confidence: " I am aware of possible scepticism regarding a venture of this nature. However I am confident that with my experience and ability, and that of the company, the project can and will work ."[96] However it seems something of an overstatement to suggest that the Artistic Director or the company had from the outset a clear and sure vision of outcomes and an unequivocal approach to strategy and planning. There is ample evidence of the ups and downs, turnarounds, uncertainties and vagaries involved in achieving the artistic reputation of Druid. In relation to decisive moments in the history of the company, there is a sense that decisions were arrived at often slowly and over time rather than by unilateral decision of a single leader. Speaking of the Town Hall controversy, the Director acknowledges: "I would say that the issue of . . . not going for what is now the Town Hall, that argument has had to be had endlessly for about five to ten years."[97] In addition, the Artistic Director refers repeatedly to the collectivist nature of Druid's achievement: "Every single thing I've done here, I've only been able to do it because other people were involved as well and because I've related both to it and the people involved."[98] This is corroborated by the accounts of some actors: "Rehearsal is discovery, not just a means to an end and we are working *with* her." This collectivist approach was very much a feature of the company in its early years.

> So, really, the crucial relationship for the actual formation of Druid, in the sense that the formation takes a year to two years to achieve, was the relationship between myself, Mick, and Marie. And that relationship was very much a common aesthetic . . . the discovery of a commonness and a common set of attitudes and a very strong set of attitudes that really actually welded the bond between us in the early rehearsals in 1975 and created the bond that continued [in] the company through the first ten years.[99]

The director recognizes that this approach is not confined to the artistic side but needs to apply throughout the company as a whole: "I think it carries across because you can't make an organization schizophrenic. You can't actually have a collectivist approach within the rehearsal room and within the aesthetic of the company and then . . . something else outside of that."[100] The account of the first decade of the company delivers a strong sense of collective growth and learning which melded its members into a cohesive unit: "It was a very tightly knit group of people. And very responsive to each other. And very early on our instincts about each other and how we'd work and various situations were very finely tuned. . . . And, also, that was a time of real artistic growth as well and there was real learning going on and . . . I think the work was probably getting better and better."[101] This had implications for the way the company worked—an effort to achieve honesty and a high degree of openness: "either things were always worked out or would have to be worked out. . . . You couldn't let them fester because it affected literally every waking moment of the time that you actually spent in there."[102] However, the Artistic Director does not underplay the role of responsibility and leadership:

> Having said all that . . . I mean I do believe absolutely that it is a kind of a collectivist, but it is a collectivist with a leader. And there is no question that an Artistic Director has to set goals outside the rehearsal room as much as inside it. And set objectives and demonstrate things that can or should be achieved and help to persuade people to have a common view of things and to work towards the common objective.[103]

The second leadership phase of the company—under Maeliosa Stafford—was highly participative but in a qualitatively different way. The new Artistic Director was "not an authority person," rather "more a chairman/facilitator than a boss," and through his approach "created something akin to what Druid was in the early years—a family-type structure."[104] However, while staff describe this financially turbulent period as a very happy one and while it was characterized by notable artistic successes, it did not result in any substantial reshaping of Druid and the director's departure left the company rudderless and in drift, living on its past successes and reputation, and in serious financial difficulty.

We have already noted the shake-up that marked Garry Hynes' return to the company. This may be characterized as the return of a more defined type of leadership in that she attempted immediately to take stock of the environment and, quite determinedly, to bring a changed vision to bear on Druid. In her view the company was by now notably out of kilter with the changing environment in Galway to the extent that its very raison d'être had to be questioned: "Who wants it? Who needs it? And like with the Municipal Theater there now, all our original raison d'être, so-called, the raison d'être we were funded, that is to provide theater or entertainment to people in Galway and in the West—it's gone. They have it every week of the year. So therefore why are Druid still there?"[105] The trauma engendered by the root and branch surgery, which she deemed necessary, was widespread. "It was painful for everybody. And, I'm sure for Garry. I am sure for Garry."[106] While ex-staff members can recognize the validity of her analysis, they take issue with how the change was wrought—"as a result we all just left en masse."[107]

Although the Consultant Artistic Director has an intellectual appreciation of the necessity for involving people and bringing them along with her and for establishing close links between the artistic and management sides of the company, her personal style or character does not lend itself to this in any easy way. However this same style obviates the dangers of coziness which may have engendered a degree of groupthink and organizational drift in the years prior to her return. It would seem that the restlessness and lack of complacency that drive innovation in Druid come from the Artistic Director herself: "I think it is just so important you throw the balls up in the air . . . that you look at everything you are doing and say, 'That's working perfectly. Why are we still doing it?' You know what I mean? Never mind 'that's not working, why are we still doing it?' . . . The opposite is the big danger for Druid, for ten years, has been [that] they would become a repertory company."[108] This is borne out by her manner of briefing, which by their account, requires that staff members think things out for themselves and approach each task afresh.

> As Garry said, "You really can only do a good job when you are totally ignorant of what it really means to do it." . . . What Garry meant . . . was that . . . what happens when you are a long time in one job of any kind, you tend to do things the one way because they work and you never take risks or, certainly, not enough risks. . . . You know, there were no rules. . . . We just think . . . how should we do it. And that was great! Very exciting![109]

Although working in a consultant capacity, the Director has reshaped the vision and reoriented the direction of the company. Speaking on the occasion of Druid's twenty-first birthday she insisted: "The past is . . . *gone*. The central issue is that we must move on." This involves constant application and effort. "So you have to really work hard all the time at what you are and you have to be able to have a sufficient set of structures that mean that you are operating in a financially and artistically efficient manner."[110] This translates to the rehearsal room and to staff level, making Druid a highly driven organization. "I can't stress this enough. Garry was such an amazing person to work for that she did enthuse everybody and she got 100 percent from everybody, but she was also a hard taskmaster. She drove people very hard and it's not that they minded but they got tired very quickly."[111] This drivenness is cast in an unfavorable light by some informants who see it as running counter to the spirit of Druid. "The emphasis now . . . the motivation seems very, very much work-orientated and success-orientated and structure and formula and all those type of things. Whereas before, all of that was achieved, but the sense of pride and pleasure in what you were doing was there. And I think that that made Druid a unique organization to work for."[112]

Though no longer resident in Galway, the Consultant Artistic Director is on top of every detail of Druid's operation and in frequent contact by phone or fax, three or four times a day. Her need to be involved in all aspects of decision making tends to slow down the response rate of the company even on relatively routine matters. This may be logically attributed to the fact that she regards all decisions as having a bearing on the artistic output of the company, consistently refusing the notion of any clear line between the administrative and the artistic. It follows that this sense of the wide implications of even small decisions and the wide variety of pros and cons make it seem best to hold out on final decisions for as long as possible, and where one can, to try things one way and then another. In a task as uncertain and fragile as the production of theater pieces which have that ineffable "something" which makes them work, it may be expected that experimentation and reversals and the stress associated with these would be a fairly consistent operational feature. This is certainly true of Druid.

Thus, while leadership is crucial in Druid, it seems important to point to its collaborative and processual dimensions and to understand that the high risk involves a sometimes painful level of insecurity for the leader and her colleagues. This contrasts somewhat with the common image of such a leader, either as the person who sweeps in with a clear vision and whose charisma carries all before them or as a strategic expert with a strong orientation towards planning. The artistic leadership of Druid does not fit either of these molds. While there are elements of vision and strategic ability, the uncertainty of the task in question here requires of a leader the capacity to tolerate a high degree of ambiguity, relief being afforded in the main by the trust which develops from close personal or professional relationships.

Management of Context: Culture

A striking feature of the company, the Druid mythology, is embedded in and part of an overall romanticism associated widely with Galway and the west of Ireland. It is constructed from the same stories being recounted over and over, stories which though perhaps somewhat clichéd, have the appeal of moral fables—the shoestring beginnings of the company, their spunk and tenacity in the face of adversity, their propensity to go their own road rather than the trodden path, and so on. By and large the mythology was earned. Their classic origins, the construction of their first home in the tiny Fo'Castle venue, the do-it-yourself building of the Chapel Lane Theater, the lore associated with the company's URTs, their fairy-tale and meteoric success in Edinburgh enabling them to cock their snook at the Dublin theater world. All of these factors forged a set of relationships and a potent story which would sustain the company through leaner periods, constituting a vital personal identity for Druid. This aura or reputation affected everybody who came into contact with the company—staff, actors, audiences, and funders. "There is the kind of, in a sense, I suppose, a bit of an 'island' feel to it whereby there was a creative island called Druid onto which many many people came, participated, enjoyed, and benefited from or whatever."[113] The achievement of the company was built on an approach that was firmly focused on the future and driven by a strong ambition. Each of the participants had a strong stake in making the venture work. Mick Lally, a founder member attributes their success to "naiveté, allied with a strong tincture of tenacity" (Lally 1985). In addition:

> There was this independence and sense of purpose and sense of ambition. ... There would have been artistic ambitions and ... there were clear management ambitions that the company should tour internationally and that the reputation should be a national one and an international one ... with the bit between their teeth and ... the mutual shared ambition ... to establish a company in Galway and to do the best possible work and then to have an individual professional experience within that.[114]

Discipline, rather than being enforced from without through systems, was a vital dimension of the organizational culture. "I think the very fact that we are small and informal and that people will put more than they are asked for into something is the very reason why we should be starting at ten o'clock. Not any time anybody feels that any time of the day is convenient to stroll in. So, the answer to the question about discipline is an unequivocal yes."[115] It was and is still evident from the productions: one critic commented on: "The perfectionism to which the director clearly aspired. Garry Hynes quite clearly believed in training actors to a hair, in blocking and timing as precisely executed as Euclid might demand in a geometrical proposition, and in a spirit of conviction which saw theatrical performance in sacramental terms." (Dudley Edwards 1985) While it may have been necessary on occasion to impose discipline in an explicit way, the dedication of company members to the project meant that by and large, it came from within—a combination of trust and commitment:

> Some people think she must be strict, a disciplinarian. But it's more a process of trust than anything else . . . [discipline] comes from within. And, I suppose, it's a collective thing as well. You know, that people are very aware of their responsibilities whether they be as actors or whatever other way. I think people are aware that the standard of work in the place is of a fairly high order and that people do give of their best or as near as they can to their best. So, there is a responsibility on you to live up to that and to honor that. To respect it, really, in the best way you can—which is to give of your own best yourself. I mean, there are variations, of course, within that.[116]

This meant that company members and staff brought a high level of loyalty to their work: "Because of what the company was, people worked in that company extremely hard. Long hours and frequently, never ever complained about it because they had this sense of huge commitment and a loyalty to the company. . . . I think anybody who was ever associated with Druid, if they got a phone call asking them for something, we would always say 'absolutely.'"[117]

The concept of a home too was vital to the culture of Druid: the Chapel Lane venue gave the company cohesion. As their home, and more particularly, a home they had built themselves, their identity inhered in this little theater, which is still seen as the creative core or powerhouse. The Druid mythology extended to the point where some people believed there was actually something unique or special about the company; in some cases almost akin to the mystical and something that made it well nigh impossible to wrench oneself away from it.

> But I think Druid has a way of getting right into you, that you give everything you can to it and [leaving is] almost like breaking up in a relationship. . . . It's almost like you have to get it out of your system. You have to kind of completely remove it from your consciousness for a while until you can get back to it again. . . . There's a particular—I don't know—some kind of eccentricity to the company and I enjoyed nearly every minute of it.[118]

The strong identity of the company was also built around a sense of pride in its achievement: "I think if you ask anybody who was involved in the company up until 1994, 1995 maybe, they would say that there was a great sense of pride in working for and with Druid. There really was. It wasn't about kudos or prestige or power or anything like that. It was actually an incredible sense of pride."[119] The atmosphere of the early days continued by and large through Maeliosa Stafford's period as Artistic Director. However the comments of staff at that time are redolent of a certain nostalgia and there may have been a tendency to rest on the reputation of the company in the past. Speaking of a production which happened during Maeliosa Stafford's directorate, one informant demonstrates, albeit unconsciously, the dangers of this: "I picked up an article recently about X (an actress) in relation to making [a certain play] and she was talking about her career and she said one of the best memories she has is working for Druid. She did one show with us. It was a terrible show. It did nothing at the box office but there was a great atmosphere in the company."[120]

We have seen that this changed abruptly with Garry Hynes' return. While she appreciates the special atmosphere which prevailed in Druid during its first decade, she has less allegiance to it and little patience with the romanticism associated with the Galway origins of the company: the "rootedness" of the company was forged in the early relationships and intense effort which developed in the Fo'Castle and not by virtue of its Galway origins. "[The company] still contains, I think, the best of what the early Druid was in a sense that it has a very direct and specific relationship with Galway and yet, at the same time, it isn't tied by that. So, there is a rootedness to the company and to its work that continues regardless of the fact whether 50, 70, 80, or 90 percent of the people would be from Galway or not."[121] The trauma associated with the return of the founding Director may be characterized as deriving from the effort (felt by many of the staff as brutal) to establish a new organizational culture. "Now, there can always be a resistance to change and I am all for embracing change. I mean, I think it has to be positive. But I think it served to undermine a lot of people in Druid and unfortunately they were the key people who were so committed to the company; and they felt more like operatives than people who were genuinely contributing to the overall welfare of the company."[122] The viewpoint expressed by those staff members who were committed to Druid in an emotional way is in vivid contrast to that which obtains for the current Manager of the company who, though she undoubtedly came into the organization with an admiration and awe for the work of Druid and its Artistic Director, and though she recognizes that Druid had a special past, has a much more pragmatic approach:

Those working in Druid over the years have likened it to being "part of a family," whereas I came to it very much as just another job. I know it's a job in an industry which prides itself on having an alternative style to that of the public or private sector: it's not just about shuffling figures. However it can't be the be all and end all. At the end of the day it's another job. It has to be done and then you move on to the next thing.[123]

The notion of Druid as just another organization is tantamount to heresy for the earlier staff. While there is much that is familial about Druid—in an actual sense as well as a metaphoric one—the Artistic Director casts a cool eye on this representation: "But this family thing seems to me to have a danger of taking it outside of what it is. It's a family thing in the sense that in any artistic endeavor there has to be a set of relationships that are over and above the kind of formal relationships of other organizations."[124] She also believes it is possible to engage the commitment of actors to a similar extent without the trappings of history—speaking of an actor who recently played his first role with the company to great acclaim: "X came, by absolute accident, into the company a year and a half previously. In my mind and in the minds of everybody else involved in the company there is no day-to-day discernible difference in his commitment."[125]

In short, while the organizational culture is important in a number of ways to Druid—its reputation, marketing and so on—and exerts an influence on its daily operation as an element of systems—how things are done in the company—it is not so cultish that it be held to account in any unique or superordinate way for the company's level of innovation.

Managing of Context: the External Environment

In this section three key relationships are considered: audiences, the Arts Council, and other organizations. There will be further comment in the concluding chapter on a major dimension of the approach of the organization in Van de Ven's terms, that is, the preservation of environmental uncertainty.

The concept of reputation management encapsulates a major part of Druid's relationship with the outside world. This extends from the ability of the company to make work from whatever source (new or old) impinge in a real and fresh way on its audience to the more mundane concept of marketing which in the opinion of the Artistic Director, "is absolutely huge."[126] The reputation of the company has been helped too by the fact that for most of its history, Druid has had a very small audience space to fill—first the 37-seat Fo'Castle and then their 110-seat Chapel Lane venue. While this has posed severe problems in terms of the earning potential of the company, the difficulty of getting a seat for the many successes that the company presented in Galway, helped by adept image management, meant that tickets were highly prized. It became almost as if one had to earn a seat to a Druid show; the Dublin cognoscenti had to displace themselves to Galway for this prize, especially since the company frequently made a virtue of not touring to the capital.

It is notable too that one of the key innovative features of Druid might be termed a marketing rather than a strictly artistic dimension of their work. The Unusual Rural Tours (URTs) were introduced at a time when the Arts Council had begun to fund regional venues which were very much in need of touring "product" to program and keep their doors open on a full-time basis. As the only regionally based theater company, and since it was in receipt of specific touring grants, it was reasonable to assume that Druid would be a lynchpin of this policy . However the company opted instead for (more costly) one or two-night stands in small regional venues. These URTs quickly became legendary, part of the Druid "magic," packing houses, adding to the aura of the company, and winning new and loyal audiences in towns and villages around the country—"After Druid visited for the first time they couldn't wait for Druid to come back again."[127] As well as conferring added *cachet*, it became much more of an event for audiences to see "The Wood of the Whispering" or "Famine" in Lisdoonvarna or Skibbereen, where one had the sense that the happenings on stage bore a real relationship to the everyday life of the place, and where the audience itself became more truly a part of the production, than to see it in the conventional Dublin venues. The concept of theater as an event, still very evident in the work of Druid today, received its first major expression in the URTs.[128] The Artistic Director sees touring as part of the company's artistic policy, an aspect of Druid's dialogue with its audience, vital to the special dramatic depth or resonance of a production—"our touring experience has been crucial in shaping our artistic policy in the 1980s and continues to do so now."[129] Once again there is a close association between the administrative and the artistic: "If 'At the Black Pig's Dyke' had opened just there, on the Black Pig's Dyke, the border between north and south (Ireland) . . . how would that have informed the playing of it and thus the production itself?"[130] These tours were continued in spite of Arts Council and professional venue management pressure[131] and remain crucial to the artistic policy of the company. The approach adopted by Druid in this is indicative at base of an awareness of the audience, an openness to the environment, which is also exemplified by their script-reading service. Druid's early marketing successes were in the main a function of two primary factors: first, the competition for audiences in its environment (Galway and rural Ireland) was much less intense in the 1970s and 1980s than is the case today; second, the first General Manager of the company had an instinctive flair for marketing, an awareness of the importance of image management, and perception in respect to key relationships (with artists or the Arts Council, for instance), as well as in terms of box office receipts.

Reviews and national coverage were very important because actors wouldn't work in a company they didn't hear that much about and if they didn't hear much about it, they didn't think much of it. But, if they learned a lot about it, it became a place they wanted to work. That was extremely important. . . . In fairness to the Arts Council members, they can't attend absolutely everything and there are members in that Council who are interested, let's say, in poetry and music but don't attend theater. So, like it or not, their perception of the company has very often come from a media comment.[132]

The relationship with audiences was fostered from the very beginning within the company:

Druid's relationship with its Galway audience was very close as opposed to it being a kind of "out the front door," actors "out the back door" and never shall they meet. There was always a feedback in the town which it got, be it for good or bad, of the work and the way in which the company was going and what the company was doing . . . I think these were part of the unique factors that allowed Druid to grow. And that it was prepared to live in a community and listen to what the community was saying.[133]

The sense of identity with the Galway audience was actively encouraged:

So the link with the Galway audience is extremely important because you can't spend your life touring the world and you need an identity. You need an identity with an audience and be that in a hundred seater in Chapel Lane or in a three or four hundred seater in the Town Hall Theater, you need that kind of feedback and that working within the community. And I do believe, in fairness to Galway people, that the Druid idea could not have been parachuted...The audience felt: "This is our company."[134]

In the view of some informants this identity, which is tied in with the idea of Druid's home in Chapel Lane, has been eroded of late. This is part of the change registered by the Director on her return and an aspect of its operation that presents an ongoing challenge for the company: "The whole element of marketing, audience development, development generally, and so on and so forth has been an ongoing crux . . . I would say, to some extent, since Jerome[135] left, and continues to be an issue. There is a sense that it is done within the company and yet there are obviously people who come into the company who neither have the expertise nor the instinct for it."[136]

It is generally agreed that the intimacy of the early years has been lost and the company now does not know who or what its audience is. This has implications for box office revenue and corporate sponsorship. The current task is nothing less than to reforge relationships with a new audience in a considerably more competitive leisure environment than heretofore: this is part of the remaking of the company and the retooling of its professionalization which is currently under way: "Oh, we have to [do an audit of audiences] because they have to be part of our audience development. We'll have to do it consciously—again, this is the same thing: it's from what was unconscious and informal to something that's conscious and formal. It's hard. It's hard but you have to do it."[137]

The Arts Council represents a major dimension of the external environment for Druid. The initial act of faith by the Council in the company was a vital confidence-building gesture:

> It was the lowest point of the company. We were doing a play called "Mother Adam." At the time we had to close down the production, blah, blah, and so really it did feel very sort of Dickens-kind-of-poor-Christmas sort of thing. But, it was an imprimatur from the national organization dealing with the arts . . . and it also established us. . . . We were being given it for a year's work. Therefore, we ourselves saw ourselves in terms of a year's work if you like.[138]

That the birth of the company coincided with changes at a national level in the arts was also opportune. The truth was that the Arts Council needed Druid almost as much as Druid needed the Council—the company was to be an exemplary dimension of the regional thrust of Council policies:

> And the relationship with the Council always continued to be good. . . . I think the fact that Druid was founded the same time that Colm O Briain became Director of the Council was a major piece of serendipity and just at the time where they were beginning to assess their own policies and saying, "Hang on here. We need a regional policy." And then this little organization down in the West says, "Excuse me, can we have some money?" I think that was very useful for both.[139]

We have already noted the relatively laissez-faire approach of the Council in relation to Druid. While there is no evidence of any close scrutiny of Druid operations by the Council at a formal level, very good informal relations were maintained both at the board and executive levels.

In terms of more general networking, the company has tended to be rather closed. The composition of the Board of Trustees has already received comment. In spite of having done considerable international touring, the company has little experience of partnership and their most recent experience with the Royal Court in respect of the Leenane Trilogy proved difficult. "Now, obviously, they came up with their own money and all of that, but it was like we had very different ways of doing things and, for instance, we had huge problems with the actors and the way they were looked after in London . . . there was no sense of bending even slightly sideways . . . . At least, that's what I felt."[140] In terms of their relationship with venues around the country, Druid is regarded as being frustrating to work with insofar as they are considered slow to make even routine decisions. This is a factor of their decision-making structures and their tendency to hold their cards close to their chest until the last possible moment—"Garry will hold a decision right up to the very last minute and that's the way she operates."[141] While others associated with the company emphasize the sense of community in Galway and the close interaction between the different arts organizations, the perception of the Artistic Director casts the environment as competitive—one where Druid has to fight rather fiercely for audiences with other sources of entertainment and leisure.

CONCLUSION—"PRIMITIVE" INNOVATION

The title of this chapter characterizes the nature of innovation to be found in Druid as "primitive." At its best the company achieves a viscerality which undercuts the received version of much in Irish theater. This is the case both with new work and in its treatment of what many would have considered superannuated pieces, before they were reenergized by Druid. Thus its "primitivism" in terms of output inheres primarily in the depth and at times subversive nature of its inquiry into the basic impulses of the plays it has chosen and its capacity to upend the interpretations of tradition to give some of these works a life and vitality that they arguably never had in the first place. However it is primarily in relation to its method or approach that the description of the type of innovation found in Druid has been cast as "primitive," a way of working which, consistently starting from degree zero,[142] takes nothing as given and which frequently results in a rejection or reversal of norms in favor of what has become "the Druid way."

Paradoxically, though by now very much an institution in the true sense of being a valued entity, Druid's most striking feature, whether from its history or as exemplified in its day-to-day operation, is its resistance of institutionalization. As amply illustrated in this chapter, Druid has relentlessly pursued an uncompromising line in this regard, refusing over its lifetime anything which would make it an institution anywhere other than in people's minds. Equally it can be argued that the choices they have made—opting for new work, inventing the Unusual Rural Tours, refusing to saddle themselves with a venue which would limit the type of work they could do—are at the core of Druid's success and all, in the view of the Artistic Director, profoundly artistic. Since the company has scorned the security which institutional status implies, its route has not been easy but rather one that has engendered a continual precariousness of existence, staved off in the main only by Arts Council support.

Druid's resistance is born of the wish for maximum flexibility and total control of the company's destiny. This same resistance is discernible in the everyday operation of the company, most notably in the fluidity of its structural arrangements. Neither the board nor the core staffing can be regarded as solid scaffolding. Based on the beginnings of the company as a classic organic form, they have evolved little, in spite of the fact that many of the conditions of its early organicism (close personal relationships forged in the smithy of a shared dream) have long since evaporated. Despite the declared intent of the Director to recreate "artificially" what once occurred naturally, an ambivalence is readily discernible in this regard, if only because although she has now completed her most recent three-year contract with the company, few arrangements that would seem fundamental to this intent have been put in place. Thus, at the same time, there is an attempt by the company to remake itself, in parallel with a reluctance to do so, because of the losses that this would inevitably entail.

While the structure of Druid can be cast as flexible, it can also be cast as weak, a factor which locates the balance of power clearly with the leadership of the company in the person of the Artistic Director. Any change in this situation (reconstitution of the board, establishment of a proper staffing structure with a distribution of authority over different roles) would of necessity mean a diminution of that power.[143] Currently the company dances primarily to one tune. There is little evidence either today or throughout the history of the company of a managerial agenda to match or contest that of the artistic. Thus the artistic leadership of the organization very definitely drives the innovative achievement of Druid. The organization has been carried forward primarily by a hard spine of single-mindedness, ambition, and discipline. Much like an entrepreneurial organization (coordination by direct supervision, informal structure), control is direct, personalized, and at times autocratic in style, with little that is "soft," and in general is dependent on a significant differential between the leader and other organization members in terms of reputation, experience, and other power levers.

Paradoxically however, the achievement of Druid within both the artistic and administrative sides of the company, also requires a degree of autonomous input on the part of other organization participants. Although accounts of the artistic process within the company place considerable emphasis on the driven nature of its direction and the relentless pursuit of the perfection and precision demanded by the

Artistic Director, there is also an acknowledgment by both sides (the Director and the artistic personnel involved) of a deep and demanding level of collaboration which is vital to the process. On the administrative front, while the Director is clearly the main source of ideas and while her persuasiveness is acknowledged, there is not only room for input on the part of other organization participants, but this is emphatically and uncompromisingly demanded by the challenging nature of the leadership of the company.

A further effect of the pattern of power distribution is the unmistakably sulphurous smell of burnout at different periods throughout Druid's history. The altogether skeletal structure of the company has meant that its success has been achieved by continuous intensity of effort, and inevitably, at considerable human cost for all the parties involved. The stress and strain engendered by the company's constant "fight for insecurity,"[144] its closeness to and even embrace of the edge, and by the paradox of functioning as a continuous project organization—striving to build and sustain a reputation in the absence of a structure to maintain it properly—is everywhere evident.

The long survival of Druid as an innovative entity needs some explanation given the virtual absence of structure within the company. Its trajectory has led it from success to slump through change to drift to deep crisis and back to success. In order to buy the time and money necessary to live through the crisis, it had to call on the widely held perceptions of its symbolic value as well as the personal relationships developed over long years with Arts Council members. So again its survival, like its operation in general, had a strongly personalized dimension and draws significantly on reputational effects.

The interaction of the company with its environment is closely bound up with its internal stress levels. The current of uncertainty, which is a feature of the outside world, is conducted through the person of the Director who, rather than reducing it, radiates it within the company. This maintains a level of organizational anxiety—felt both within and without Druid—which keeps attention focused on the key task (though sometimes causing the company to keel over into near crisis), and has resulted in substantial reshaping both of itself and of that same environment. Thus while Druid may in some senses be described as entrepreneurial, the company manifests an underlying authenticity which is somehow absent from this concept. Its reverberation with an intrinsically uncertain process—the making of theater that says something new to a heterogeneous and ill-defined audience—makes of the company at its best a highly attuned instrument and explains perhaps more than other factors its capacity to remake itself and to reform its mission, and thus its longer innovative life than other organizations. Uncertainty, however painful, is, after all, the flip side of the discovery that motivates and drives Druid.

NOTES

1. Established in 1975, Druid at the time of this study was twenty-three years old. The other organizations described in this book are at least a decade younger.

2. Though it is no longer a feature of their output, the company in its early years devised two original plays, the second more conventionally authored by Garry Hynes, founder-member and current Consultant Artistic Director of Druid.

3. A conservative and romanticized version of Ireland, its history and culture.

4. Anew McMaster led a troupe of actors around towns and villages thus providing the only access to theater in rural Ireland in the 1950s and generating a store of legend and story.

5. Of the 130 different plays presented by the company, most have been directed by Garry Hynes. However over the years, 21 others have directed for the company.

Number of Plays/Number of Directors, Druid: 1975–1997

Number of plays	75	20	6	5	2	1
Directors	1	1	1	3	1	15

Source: Records of Druid Theater Company.

6. Minutes of board meetings are available only from 1989 onwards.

7. Irish language theater in Galway.

8. Druid program for Edinburgh Fringe, 1980.

9. Druid program for Edinburgh Fringe, 1980.

10. At the time, the home of the avant-garde in Ireland.

11. The company subsequently brought "Island Surrounded by a Bridge of Glass" and Geraldine Aron's "Bar and Ger" to the Peacock theater in Dublin, winning rave reviews.

12. Irish theater award.

13. In addition, Garry Hynes was appointed a member of the Arts Council by Government from 1984 to 1988.

14. Arts Council, Annual Report, 1980.

15. Arts Council, Annual Report, 1981.

16. Arts Council, Annual Report, 1983.

17. Arts Council, Annual Report, 1984.

18. Arts Council, Annual Report, 1986.

19. Arts Council, Annual Report, 1988.

20. Druid statement, 11/5/89.

21. Garry Hynes quoted by Paddy Woodworth, "Druid withdraws from £2.7m. municipal theater project," *The Irish Times,* 13/5/89.

22. Paddy Woodworth, "Bringing the Druid spirit to the stage of the Abbey," *The Irish Times,* 4/8/90.

23. Paddy Woodworth, "Druid: too soon for a wake," *The Irish Times,* 10/12/88.

24. Minutes of Board meeting, Druid Theater Company, 3/6/90.

25. Minutes of Board meeting, Druid Theater Company, 21/9/91.

26. Letter from the Drama Officer of the Arts Council to the General Manager of Druid, 22/2/93.

27. Internal memo to Druid file, The Arts Council, 17/7/93.

28. Letter from the Drama Officer of the Arts Council to the General Manager of Druid, 7/3/94.

29. Minutes of Board meeting, Druid Theater Company, 13/3/93.

30. Minutes of Board meeting, Druid Theater Company, 7/8/93.

31. Minutes of Board meeting, Druid Theater Company, 10/7/93.

32. Minutes of Board meeting, Druid Theater Company, 30/4/94.

33. Minutes of Board meeting, Druid Theater Company, 12/11/94.

34. Minutes of Board meeting, Druid Theater Company, 3/3/95. The report of the consultant proved unsatisfactory (board minutes, 12/8/95).

35. Minutes of Board meeting, Druid Theater Company, 12/8/95.

36. Minutes of Board meeting, Druid Theater Company, 13/5/95.

37. Minutes of Board meeting, Druid Theater Company, 12/8/95.

38. Minutes of Board meeting, Druid Theater Company, 16/6/95.

39. Minutes of EGM, Druid Theater Company, 9/9/95.

40. Minutes of EGM, Druid Theater Company, 9/9/95.

41. Minutes of EGM, Druid Theater Company, 9/9/95.

42. Minutes of EGM, Druid Theater Company, 9/9/95.

43. "Towards 2001," Policy document, Druid Theater Company, November, 1996.

44. Minutes of Board meeting, Druid Theater Company, 3/3/95.

45. "Towards 2001," Policy document, Druid Theater Company, November, 1996.

46. Minutes of Board meeting, Druid Theater Company, 23/11/96.

47. Paddy Woodworth, "URTs: A Druid tradition." *The Irish Times,* 15/11/90.

48. Garry Hynes quoted by Paddy Woodworth, "Hynes returns to Druid in consultative role," *The Irish Times,* 1/10/94.

49. Colette Sheridan, "Playgirl of the Western World," *The Sunday Tribune,* 11/6/89.

50. Garry Hynes quoted by Paddy Woodworth, "Hynes returns to Druid in consultative role," *The Irish Times,* 1/10/94.

51. Quoted by Paddy Woodworth, "Druid: too soon for a wake," *The Irish Times,* 10/12/88.

52. Staff member, Druid Theater Company, interview by author, tape recording, Galway, 24/11/97.

53. Staff member, Druid Theater Company, interview by author, tape recording, Galway, 24/11/97.

54. Phelim Donlon, quoted by Paddy Woodworth, "Druid withdraws from £2.7m. municipal theater project," *The Irish Times,* 13/5/89.

55. The pressure on Druid at the time to adhere to the existing touring network and to accept the offer of a Municipal Theater should not be underestimated. Their refusal of these options was the subject of long battles with the Arts Council and other agencies with potentially significant roles in terms of their current and future funding.

56. Fintan O'Toole (1996). "A Moveable Feast," *Druid, 21 Years*.

57. Well known Irish playwright whose work is widely performed, particularly on the amateur circuit.

58. Garry Hynes, interview by author, tape recording, Dublin, 1/12/97.

59. Garry Hynes quoted by Colette Sheridan, "Playgirl of the Western World," *The Sunday Tribune*, 11/6/89.

60. Garry Hynes, interview by author, tape recording, Dublin, 1/12/97.

61. Garry Hynes, interview by author, tape recording, Dublin, 1/12/97.

62. Staff member, Druid Theater Company, interview by author, tape recording, Galway, 21/11/97.

63. Two members of the company were included on the board for a number of years but because of work commitments were rarely in a position to attend meetings.

64. Chairman, Druid Theater Company, interview by author, tape recording, Galway, 2/12/97.

65. Consultant Artistic Director's report, 1995.

66. Board member, Druid Theater Company, interview by author, tape recording, Galway, 24/11/97.

67. The Arts Council has a right of nomination to the Board of any organization that receives a grant in excess of £10,000. While the company believes that this matter simply has never arisen, Arts Council records show that, following on comments made in 1993 by the Office of the Irish Comptroller and Auditor General, the Drama Officer of the Arts Council requested the Manager of Druid in a letter to bring up the question of Arts Council representation at Board meetings with the company Directors. There is no record of any response to this request or of any follow-up on the part of the Arts Council. (In reality, no request was necessary.)

68. Garry Hynes, interview by author, tape recording, Dublin, 1/12/97.

69. Board member, Druid Theater Company, interview by author, tape recording, Galway, 24/11/97.

70. Staff member, Druid Theater Company, interview by author, tape recording, Galway, 2/12/97.

71. Staff member, Druid Theater Company, interview by author, tape recording, Galway, 24/11/97.

72. Garry Hynes, interview by author, tape recording, Dublin, 1/12/97.

73. Garry Hynes, interview by author, tape recording, Dublin, 1/12/97.

74. Garry Hynes, interview by author, tape recording, Dublin, 1/12/97.

75. Garry Hynes, interview by author, tape recording, Dublin, 1/12/97.

76. Former staff member, Druid Theater Company, interview by author, tape recording, Galway, 21/11/97.

77. Staff member, Druid Theater Company, interview by author, tape recording, Galway, 2/12/97.

78. Staff member, Druid Theater Company, interview by author, tape recording, Galway, 2/12/97.

79. Former staff member, Druid Theater Company, interview by author, tape recording, Galway, 24/11/97.

80. Former staff member, Druid Theater Company, interview by author, tape recording, Galway, 24/11/97.

81. Garry Hynes, interview by author, tape recording, Dublin, 1/12/97.

82. Garry Hynes, interview by author, tape recording, Dublin, 1/12/97.

83. Former staff member, Druid Theater Company, interview by author, tape recording, Galway, 24/11/97.

84. Garry Hynes, interview by author, tape recording, Dublin, 1/12/97.

85. Garry Hynes, interview by author, tape recording, Dublin, 1/12/97.

86. Garry Hynes, interview by author, tape recording, Dublin, 1/12/97.

87. Staff member, Druid Theater Company, interview by author, tape recording, Galway, 2/12/97.

88. Garry Hynes, interview by author, tape recording, Dublin, 1/12/97.

89. Garry Hynes, interview by author, tape recording, Dublin, 1/12/97.

90. Garry Hynes, interview by author, tape recording, Dublin, 1/12/97.

91. Garry Hynes, interview by author, tape recording, Dublin, 1/12/97.

92. Garry Hynes, interview by author, tape recording, Dublin, 1/12/97.

93. Because the first General Manager had a particular aptitude for marketing, it was assumed that this would be part of the General Manager's role, even if subsequent managers had little interest or skill in this area; similarly the important function of fund-raising remained unaddressed for no clear reason.

94. Artistic associate, Druid Theater Company, interview by author, tape recording, Dublin, 22/12/97.

95. Former staff member, Druid Theater Company, interview by author, tape recording, Galway, 3/12/97.

96. Letter from Garry Hynes to the Director of the Arts Council, 13/5/75.

97. Garry Hynes, interview by author, tape recording, Dublin, 1/12/97.

98. Garry Hynes, interview by Ray Comisky, *The Irish Times*, 24/9/83.

99. Garry Hynes, interview by author, tape recording, Dublin, 1/12/97.

100. Garry Hynes, interview by author, tape recording, Dublin, 1/12/97.

101. Garry Hynes, interview by author, tape recording, Dublin, 1/12/97.

102. Former staff member, Druid Theater Company, interview by author, tape recording, Galway, 24/11/97.

103. Garry Hynes, interview by author, tape recording, Dublin, 1/12/97.

104. Former staff member, Druid Theater Company, interview by author, tape recording, Galway, 5/12/97.

105. Garry Hynes, interview by author, tape recording, Dublin, 1/12/97.

106. Former staff member, Druid Theater Company, interview by author, tape recording, Galway, 3/12/97.

107. Staff member, Druid Theater Company, interview by author, tape recording, Galway, 3/12/97.

108. Garry Hynes, interview by author, tape recording, Dublin, 1/12/97.

109. Former staff member, Druid Theater Company, interview by author, tape recording, Galway, 2/12/97.

110. Garry Hynes, interview by author, tape recording, Dublin, 1/12/97.

111. Former staff member, Druid Theater Company, interview by author, tape recording, Galway, 2/12/97.

112. Former staff member, Druid Theater Company, interview by author, tape recording, Galway, 21/12/97.

113. Former staff member, Druid Theater Company, interview by author, tape recording, Galway, 24/11/97.

114. Former staff member, Druid Theater Company, interview by author, tape recording, Galway, 24/11/97.

115. Garry Hynes, interview by author, tape recording, Dublin, 1/12/97.

116. Company member, Druid Theater Company, interview by author, tape recording, Galway, 4/12/97.

117. Former staff member, Druid Theater Company, interview by author, tape recording, Galway, 21/11/97.

118. Former staff member, Druid Theater Company, interview by author, tape recording, Galway, 21/11/97.

119. Former staff member, Druid Theater Company, interview by author, tape recording, Galway, 21/11/97.

120. Former staff member, Druid Theater Company, interview by author, tape recording, Galway, 21/11/97.

121. Garry Hynes, interview by author, tape recording, Dublin, 1/12/97.

122. Former staff member, Druid Theater Company, interview by author, tape recording, Galway, 21/11/97.

123. Manager, Druid Theater Company, interview by author, tape recording, Galway, 2/12/97.

124. Garry Hynes, interview by author, tape recording, Dublin, 1/12/97.

125. Garry Hynes, interview by author, tape recording, Dublin, 1/12/97.

126. Garry Hynes, interview by author, tape recording, Dublin, 1/12/97.

127. Former staff member, Druid Theater Company, interview by author, tape recording, Galway, 3/12/97.

128. This acronym has become part of the vocabulary of Druid, to the extent of delivering adjectives like "urtish"!

129. Garry Hynes, interview by author, tape recording, Dublin, 1/12/97.

130. Garry Hynes, interview by author, tape recording, Dublin, 1/12/97.

131. In a letter to Druid on 11/9/90, the Drama Officer of the Arts Council expressed "very considerable concern at the failure of production companies . . . to include the professionally managed regional venues in all of their touring circuits" and even threatened that they might make this a condition of funding in the future.

132. Former staff member, Druid Theater Company, interview by author, tape recording, Galway, 24/11/97.

133. Former staff member, Druid Theater Company, interview by author, tape recording, Galway, 24/11/97.

134. Former staff member, Druid Theater Company, interview by author, tape recording, Galway, 24/11/97.

135. Jerome Hynes, first General Manager of Druid.

136. Garry Hynes, interview by author, tape recording, Dublin, 1/12/97.

137. Garry Hynes, interview by author, tape recording, Dublin, 1/12/97.

138. Garry Hynes, interview by author, tape recording, Dublin, 1/12/97.

139. Garry Hynes, interview by author, tape recording, Dublin, 1/12/97.

140. Staff member, Druid Theater Company, interview by author, tape recording, Galway, 2/12/97.

141. Staff member, Druid Theater Company, interview by author, tape recording, Galway, 2/12/97.

142. Or "Starting from Scratch" as in the title of O'Toole's (1985) article.

143. This accords precisely with Mintzberg's (1996) entrepreneurial organization.

144. Garry Hynes, interview by author, tape recording, Dublin, 1/12/97.

4

"Managerial" Innovation: Opera Theater Company

The character of innovation that emerges in this account is notably distinct from that of Druid Theater Company (Chapter 3). We shall describe the operation of Opera Theater Company (OTC) in detail so as to be in a position to highlight its distinctive features and in order to determine the degree of correspondence both with the research literature on the topic and the extent to which it might share common features with the other cases.

We first summarize the record of OTC, justify its selection for investigation as a highly innovative arts organization, and outline the history of the company. Then we examine the company along the dimensions identified in the conceptual framework. The chapter concludes with an account of what drives and sustains innovation in OTC.

OTC—INNOVATIVE ACHIEVEMENT AND HISTORY

Innovation and OTC

The Four Note Opera—"Essential viewing for all opera lovers . . ."

Opera, 2000

I have tried to make a point of catching Opera Theater Company's work whenever possible, and have been rewarded with two of the best stagings of opera by Handel that I have seen anywhere in the world.

The Sunday Times, 1999.

Opera Theatre Company's trump card is an unerring understanding of how to handle its audience.

The Independent (U.K.), 1997.

Amadigi at the Covent Garden Festival—"It's a rewarding evening for the singing and playing gives a real sense of the work's quality . . . recommended."

The Guardian, 1996.

For eight years, the Dublin based Opera Theatre Company has been widening the operatic experience in Ireland, supplementing such predictable fixtures as Wexford and the Opera Ireland seasons with small-scale productions touring to the furthest corners of the republic. . . . Last Friday's guest visit to the Covent Garden Festival can only be described as a howling success.

The Times, London, 1994.

In innovation terms, OTC is notable for the number of "firsts" with which the company is credited—the generation of a respectable portfolio of new work, and an approach which emphasizes variety, resourcefulness, and an energetic and risk-oriented seeking out of new talent, as opposed to a reliance on the tried and trusted. In recent years the company has enjoyed a growing international reputation with invitations to perform at the Covent Garden Festival, the Opéra Comique in Paris, the Brooklyn Academy of Music in New York, Expo 1998 in Lisbon, Oporto, and the Melbourne Festival at the end of 1997. While OTC generally enjoys a very positive press in Ireland, it has also elicited an excellent response from British critics for productions presented in the U.K.

Though repertoire has been a fraught area for the company from the beginning, given the combination of resourcing and audience considerations faced by OTC on a continuing basis, it has undertaken twenty-eight productions[1] in the eleven years of its existence to the time of this study, and so may be said to have identified a body of work, however eclectic, which fits its ambitions and resources. So far, the company has concentrated on baroque and modern operas, itself a challenging record, given the preference of the company's audience for the nineteenth-century repertoire.

TABLE 4.1
Opera Theater Company Productions, 1986-1997

17th century	18th century	19th century	20th century
2	10	5	11

Source: Company records.

Since its founding the company has commissioned several new operas from Irish and British composers and writers. OTC has also introduced a number of Irish theater directors to opera, in accordance with the aim "to stimulate the creation of music theater forms in people who don't normally think of themselves as composers and writers." All the work has been performed in English as a bid to win new audiences to what has always been a minority art form in Ireland. Similarly, OTC has engaged with writers who had never before written librettos and uses visual artists as designers. The Director of the company, James Conway, has himself written, adapted, and translated four librettos.

In addition to the above indicators, an innovative approach is apparent in many other aspects of the company's work: the choice of unusual venues—Dublin's Kilmainham Gaol for "Tamberlane" in 1992, or the presentation of "Katya Kabanova" on the Aran Island of Inis Oirr in 1996; the acknowledged challenge to a composer by proposing an electroacoustic version of a seventeenth century work; or the grouping of a newly commissioned twentieth century piece with a nineteenth century Leoncavallo opera. In these and other ways, it is characteristic of the company that it crosses boundaries without fear of embarrassment and is constantly willing to do whatever is necessary to present high-quality and fresh interpretations believing, in the words of its Director, that "mistakes are much better than inertia."[2] The above factors render it a suitable case for investigation as an exemplary innovative organization in Ireland.

History of OTC

Although the smallest of the Irish opera companies in terms of budget (Table 4.2), OTC provided almost half of the opera nights in Ireland in 1995, and has staged three productions per annum since 1991.

The aim of the company is "to tour orchestrally accompanied and theatrically committed opera productions to all parts of the country."[3] Since its launch in 1986, OTC has toured to thirty-five towns and cities throughout the country, North and South. A company limited by guarantee (registered since 1986) and with charitable status, it is governed by a Board of twelve directors (all of whom are co-opted by other members), which (now) meets quarterly. The Board of OTC has remained rather compact over the years and has shown a healthy turnover in membership.[4]

The company's main source of income is its grant from the Arts Council, which shows a steady upward trend. Box office income and sponsorship supplement this. Table 4.2 shows income trends from all sources, from 1991 to 1995. These figures reflect a healthy growth in box office income, though a decline in sponsorship in recent years. In 1995,

TABLE 4.2
Income of Opera Theater Company, 1991–1995 (in percent)

Income	1991	1992	1993	1994	1995	1995
Arts Council	64	64	60	53	64	50
Box office	15.5	20	23.5	33	25	40
Sponsorship / other	20.5	16	16.5	14	11	10

Source: Submission by OTC to Opera Development Group, The Arts Council, 1996.

18.5 percent of the expenditure of the company addressed administration costs and the remaining 81.5 percent went to cover production
(artists' fees, other production costs, marketing, publicity, and touring).

The company at the time of this investigation employed four full-time
staff members—Director, Administrator, Marketing/Education Officer,
and Publicist/Administrative Assistant, and a part-time Technical Director. The Administrative Assistant is employed through a Department
of Labor employment scheme. OTC operates a Friends/Patrons scheme
(fifty-four in 1996) and estimates that it achieved an overall seat occu-
pancy of 80 percent in 1996.

Beginnings of Company. The beginnings of OTC are fairly atypical in
terms of the history of performing arts organizations—either opera or
theater—in Ireland. This is evident from a glance at its funding history.
The company was formed in 1986, a year of severe cutbacks in the arts,
with the aid of a substantial grant from the Arts Council.[5] This grant,
in the first year of the company, exceeded that of the two long-estab-
lished opera companies (much to their outrage, as evidenced by press
reports at the time). If one looks at the company in the context of theater
rather than opera, its initial funding is even more unusual, given that
most theater companies in Ireland over the past twenty years have
started with funding of under £10,000 and usually take many years to
build up to even a modest level of annual funding (see table in Notes,[6]
p. 123). Thus it can be said that the company benefited considerably
from its placing within the opera budget.

Furthermore, the general funding context of the arts in Ireland in 1986
was not conducive to support for new ventures. Describing it as a "very
difficult year" the Arts Council with a total budget for 1986 of £5.8
million "with very great regret but with very limited options ... de-
cided that it would have to suspend grant-in-aid to a number of festivals and in the area of theater touring."[7] The grant to Wexford Opera
Festival was thus reduced from £77,700 in 1985 to the 1986 level of
£30,300 to allow the organization to fund its permanent staff and over-
head costs through that crisis year. The Dublin Grand Opera Society

TABLE 4.3
Arts Council Grant-in-Aid to the Three Main Opera Companies in the Irish Republic, 1986–1997 (in £000s)

Year	DGOS/Opera Ireland	Wexford	OTC
1986	61.2	30.3	80
1987	142.5	100	80
1988	141.5	100.4	85.5
1989	200	101	91.3
1990	250	130	110
1991	259.8	143	158.5
1992	267.5	145.5	158.5
1993	295.5	180	151
1994	297	234	182
1995	350	300	230
1996	350	300	230
1997	370	330	279

Source: The Annual Reports of the Arts Council (1986–1995) and Art Matters (Issues No. 22 and 25).

(DGOS/Opera Ireland) also had its funding cut from £84,700 in 1985 to the 1986 level of £61,000. The question as expressed in the *Irish Times* was whether "an untried group [should] be given funds that could have been used to support an established major festival."[8]

The birth of OTC followed on the controversial decision, issuing from a review of Arts Council opera policy, to discontinue funding the Irish National Opera Company (INO) in 1985. INO had brought scaled-down productions of grand opera with piano accompaniment to small regional venues in all parts of the country and its demise was much lamented by the devoted following it had built up over the years. A further concern for the Arts Council at the time was the dearth of opportunities for Irish singers, the tradition at the Dublin Grand Opera Society and Wexford being to use mainly foreign artists. There was also widespread dissatisfaction with the standards that currently applied to opera in Ireland and the Arts Council was endeavoring to professionalize the Dublin Grand Opera Society in an effort to develop the practice of the art form.[9]

All of these factors were live issues on the occasion of the press reception to launch OTC on 29 October 1986. The aim of the company was "to tour theaters throughout the island of Ireland, presenting opera to as wide as possible an audience with equal weight given to the musical and theatrical values."[10] Its first application to the Arts Council offered a read on the current situation and demonstrated a neat combination of ambition and pragmatism, articulating the intention of the company to present "clear, thoughtful productions in venues people are used to, at prices they can afford and in a language they can understand" and a wish "to get away from the conception of opera as a circus animal performing against a lavish, glittery, expensive looking background." The application placed notable emphasis on marketing: "The publicity and marketing strategy will be shot through with this intention to popularize and demystify and the company see the appointment of a Public Relations (PR)/Marketing person who identifies with these aspirations and has the ability to orchestrate publicity to those ends as the very next step in its operation." The company made a strong pitch for total funding, even suggesting that the Arts Council should look outside its relatively poor opera coffers: "We feel that an imaginative, across the board approach to our submission would have due regard for our desires to cut across existing boundaries in music and theater."[11]

Not only did the new company receive significant funding in a year of cutbacks, but also, to their own shock, they received £5,000 more than they had requested from the Arts Council. The first company Manager describes his reaction: "I have to say I was terrified. Because one always expects to get less from the Arts Council than you ask . . . then you can say if you'd only given us what we'd asked for, it would have been perfect. When you're actually given more than you asked, you're in deep trouble!"[12]

It is clear from the account given by a founding member of the beginnings of the company that the Music and Opera Officer of the Arts Council was closely involved with the establishment of the company, putting some of the founding members in touch with each other. While the impulse to establish a new company was triggered by the bad experience of the founding members with existing opera provision and practice on the ground, the fulsome response of the Arts Council to the OTC funding application may be accounted for by the fact that, in the context of suspending funding to INO, the Council was sensitive to the continuing imperative to provide access to opera throughout the country. Thus it would seem that OTC came into being as a result of a confluence of interests, personal and political/strategic, and by comparison with most arts organizations in Ireland, had an unusually easy birth.[13]

Founding Members and Agenda. The team that made the initial proposal for a touring opera company to the Arts Council comprised a Theater Director with some experience of having directed opera, Ben Barnes; a Conductor with an interest in theater, Proinnsias O Duinn; the Manager of the Irish Chamber Orchestra, Randall Shannon; and Maureen Loughran, an Arts Administrator. Ben Barnes and Proinnsias O Duinn had already worked together on some opera projects—Young Irish Artists—and Randall Shannon's involvement was suggested to him by the Arts Council.[14] While the professional and personal interests of the artists (Director and Conductor) in establishing a new company might be obvious,[15] Randall Shannon too had a strategic interest in furthering work opportunities for the full-time orchestra which he was managing, seeing OTC as "one of the building blocks."[16]

Phase One: Opening Production. The company's initial plans after an opening production of Britten's "The Turn of the Screw" were to present a new production in 1987 followed by two annual tours to twelve regular venues from 1988 on.[17] The "Turn of the Screw" was chosen "for the modernity of its music, the theatricality of its dramatic conception, the modest size of its cast and orchestra, its literary antecedent, its imaginative design possibilities, and its English language libretto."[18] The initial approach described by the Manager of the company in the *Irish Times* was notable for its pragmatism: "The work fits exactly into the size with which we can operate, the number of artists we can find, and also the size of venues that we can play in."[19] There was also a commitment from the beginning to education, as to high standards.

The "Turn of the Screw" opened in Limerick's Belltable Arts Center on 6 November 1986, thus signaling OTC's commitment to serving the country outside of Dublin, and went on to play three other venues—Dublin, Sligo, and Belfast—giving a total of thirteen performances. Directed by Ben Barnes and conducted by Proinnsias O Duinn it proved to be a popular (though not a box office) success, confounding those who regarded the piece as too avant-garde for an Irish audience. At this stage a company was formed and a Board of Directors was put together. It is worth noting that the Arts Council did not insist on having nominees despite their substantial first grant to the company. The Board comprised an impressive mix of artists and arts administrators with one (nonartist) regional representative (chosen by virtue of his position as a County Manager[20]). Randall Shannon was Manager and Company Secretary of OTC and Ben Barnes and Proinnsias O Duinn shared its Artistic Directorate as Director of Productions and Music Director, respectively. Having come in to carry out the marketing function in 1987, James Conway (the current Director of OTC) was appointed Administrator in 1988. Various accounts convey the contagious excitement and "spirit of adventure"[21] of the early days of the company.

Phase Two: Stormy Waters. As shown, the beginnings of OTC were unusually smooth. Problems arose when it came to discussing a second production: either the operas available did not lend themselves very well to scaled-down versions, or they were such that they would not win an audience for OTC:

> The repertoire that's open to a company like OTC is either adaptations of standard repertoire like what we did to Mozart[22] or post-1945, like "Turn of the Screw." And post-1945 isn't that acceptable to the public. There is a huge repertoire out there but because we were aware that the audience we were taking out stuff to were people who had never seen opera before or very little of it, and we wanted to introduce them to opera, not just give them an evening out, so our planning or thinking was much more along the lines of adapting nineteenth century . . . but it was very unthought-out.[23]

Though no minutes of Board meetings exist before 3 February 1988, it is clear from reports to the Board, as well as from interviews, that the second production—"Cosi fan Tutte"—was proving controversial. Divisions were becoming apparent between the two Artistic Directors. Problems related to funding, to programming, in attitude differences to Dublin performances—their primacy or not, whether or not to play at the Gate Theater, to the divisions between theatrical as opposed to musical values, and casting. Personality differences between the two Artistic Directors as well as a clash of approaches and interests gave rise to heated exchanges and a shower of vitriolic reports to the Board. There were tensions too between the artistic direction and the small executive, attributable in part to an overlap or lack of clarity between executive and Board functions. Despite attention being drawn by the Manager and the Administrator[24] to the necessity for an artistically integrated (theater and music) rather than a solely theatrical product, to the need for planning, the importance of self-definition with reference to the other companies on the island, of greater clarity in role definition internally, divisions degenerated into acrimonious exchanges and the two Artistic Directors adopted polarized positions. The veil of aesthetic difference failed to disguise the major personality clash between them. Reports and proclamations proliferated during 1988 until at a Board meeting it was suggested that they be "thanked"[25] and a new (single) Artistic Director sought. In January 1989, the actor and former Arts Council member (until December 1988), Barry McGovern, was appointed to this role. However, planning difficulties and personality differences persisted: the Administrator and the new Artistic Director did not see eye to eye in relation to key aspects of the functioning of the company. Indeed, the former, now the Director of the company, recalls this whole period from 1989 as one when the interests that had established OTC were being replaced by a different approach. "I think I was probably asserting myself in terms of administration. Administration in a way asserted itself. Listening to audiences."[26] He perceived this period as one of breaking away from the interests of the Artistic Directors and loosening the metropolitan hold on OTC, which was bound up with those interests.

> The company was attempting to do interesting treatments in mainstream repertoire that would advance the career of the two performing artists who were the Artistic Directors. . . . And moving—also in the same period—I think, out of the sphere of influence of a number of Dublin theatrical organizations. The company was very much in the sphere of influence of the Gate[27] for the first few years. And then the only avenue of growth was perceived as being the Dublin Theater Festival and I was impatient with both of those. . . . So [the alternative was] to move out of those associations and really strike out much more on our own.[28]

By December 1989 a board meeting minute recorded the suggestion "that the relation between the Artistic Director and the Board required discussion"[29] and his contract was terminated in July 1990. Legal discussions ensued and the matter was eventually resolved. At around the same time a small grouping from the company made informal soundings to the Arts Council about the possibility of forming another company but these were not encouraged.[30] Once again it seemed as if disintegration was but a hair's breadth away. James Conway was asked by the board to assume artistic responsibility until 1991 and requested to prepare a three-year plan for the company. The post of Director was advertized in November 1990. It would seem to have become apparent at this stage that the current Administrator was the obvious candidate, and in January 1991 he was appointed by the board, now chaired by Gemma Hussey, former Irish Minister of Education, who had been invited by the Administrator to join the board on her resignation from politics in 1990. "And that was the beginning of stability."[31]

That the company survived this very turbulent phase is worthy of some comment. After all, two of the founding triumvirate had fallen out and the next move lurched OTC into a further crisis, which might have easily precipitated its demise. The Arts Council had a continuing interest in the company but at this point was standing back somewhat from the company. That one of the founding members who had a close working relationship with the Music Officer acted *in loco parentis* during this phase would seem to account in no small way for its survival. He is explicit about this: " I really felt like a parent."[32] Also the presence of an experienced Chairperson was crucial in steering the company towards more tranquil water:

I had the advantage of having no connections with anybody in this place, coming new to it and having, I suppose—because I had been so recently Minister—a certain aura of authority.... A lot of organizations have stormy beginnings and also a lot of organizations—and I'd say this probably applies in a lot of arts organizations—to get from being the brain-child and baby of some people who feel very strongly about something, they have to move into the mainstream and have to get proper structures and proper boards and proper accounting because they're moving into an era of accountability.[33]

The use of the family metaphor here is indicative both of the young age of the company and the corresponding need for care and a degree of tolerance. In the words of a former board member, "Gemma became Chair and was fabulous. She and the Director worked very well together."[34]

Stability/Planning. During the early years of the company, Board meetings were held on a monthly basis. Table 4.4 shows the trend, which reflects the turbulence of the beginning, relaxing afterwards, into a more desultory pattern.

Minutes of Board meetings from 1991 onwards turn to discussions of repertoire, programming, and sponsorship, but it is clear by mid-1992 that from the planning problems which bedeviled the company in its early stages, OTC had by now moved into a smoother phase with discussion on forthcoming productions taking place a year or so in advance. From 1991 the company undertook three productions per annum, counting revivals; initiated a developmental dimension to the work—a training program for artists comprising workshops and masterclasses as well as an education program of school workshops in tandem with productions; began to engage in co-productions; and to present its work overseas.

The Director, who may at first have been less surefooted than he is now, enjoyed the full support of his Chairperson. Although Arts Coun-

TABLE 4.4
Frequency of Board Meetings at Opera Theater Company, 1988–1996.*

Year	1988	1989	1990	1991	1992	1993	1994	1995	1996
No. of board meetings	10	10	11	7	6	5	5	3	5
Arts Council presence	7	2	3	3	1	–	–	–	–

* Minutes of meetings that took place from 1986 to 1988 have disappeared.
Source: Minutes of Board Meetings, OTC.

cil attendance at OTC board meetings had been intermittent (Table 4.4), the Arts Council Opera Officer supported the approach taken by the new Director, who, from 1994, moved into a more public creative role by directing productions for the first time.

Life Cycle. Though not an old organization, OTC by the standards of the arts sector is quite well established. One informant identified four stages in the life of OTC to date (Table 4.5).[35] Although it has enjoyed a reputation for innovation throughout all stages, the fact that the organization survived Stage 2 has been worthy of mention. While the current Director was not a founding member of the organization, he has been present almost from the very beginning and may be said to have grown up artistically with the company. Furthermore, as shall be apparent later, he has shaped the company as it is today, not only in terms of its artistic program but its entire character—Board membership, strategic thrust, staffing, financial, marketing, and other policies. OTC may be said to have moved through the full life cycle of a performing arts company (Gainer 1997) rather quickly and to be recycling now in Stage Three. It is thus on the cusp of what B. Gainer has termed the hardest transition phase, when the question of the artistic vision of the organization is linked to succession issues.

In a number of respects the company is clearly in transition: with a turnover of almost half a million pounds and facing its first deficit, the mechanisms for managing its finances now require reshaping; similarly the volume of overseas work is putting a strain on its Irish operation. It may be that some recent initiatives will satisfactorily address these issues at least in the short term, but if the company is to survive what Gainer terms the "danger phase" and continue as a highly innovative organization, more challenges lie ahead.

Summary. The remarkable easy birth of OTC is in certain contrast to the habitual uphill trudge of arts organizations in their quest for fund-

TABLE 4.5
Stages in the Life Cycle of Opera Theater Company

Stage 1	Set up	1 year 1986
Stage 2	Turbulence	3 years 1987–90
Stage 3	Initial stability and growth	4 years 1990–4
Stage 4	Period of Director's role in stage directing	3 years 1994–7

ing and legitimacy—generally a long haul, which is so common as to seem almost a necessary condition!

While there was some history of two of the founding triumvirate working together, there is little sense of a group which had toiled in the wilderness for many years eventually making a breakthrough. The beginnings of OTC seem much more strategic, based on accurate gap analysis and the proactive approach taken by the funding agency in shaping a proposal. This differs from the mythology which often surrounds the formation of arts organizations—the notion that their formation and growth has to be organic and that somehow a strategic intervention will be less effective, being in some way artificial or insufficiently rooted. The subsequent success of the company—though this could not have been guaranteed—endorses the direct and proactive intervention of the funding agency to establish an organization to meet a specific objective, provided that the environmental scanning undertaken by the funding body is accurate and based on a sound understanding of the sector.

Furthermore the granting of adequate financial assistance at the outset, also highly unusual, runs somewhat counter to the belief that arts organizations are better left to struggle. This myth feeds on the reality that arts organizations do survive for a time and may even thrive on an inadequate funding base. The OTC case shows that the opposite is at least equally true.

The fact that OTC survived the conflict and turbulence that all but sunk the company in its early years is demonstrative of the value of a sound structural base. The continuity provided by a well-chosen Board comprised of people with experience in organizations, and especially the presence of a committed and experienced manager, were both crucial to its survival, a lesson which is of interest to arts organizations in a state of transition.

The medium to long-term approach adopted by the funding agency and the generally expansive attitude taken vis-à-vis the artistic policies being put in place by the new Director from 1991 were rewarded by the success of the company. While it had been necessary during its more turbulent phase for the Chairperson of OTC to reassure in writing the Chairperson of the Arts Council, the latter was generally noninterventionist and allowed the company to follow its own artistic course. This is due in no small measure to the financial viability of the company which, in stark contrast to most arts organizations, has managed for most of its existence to break even.

Finally, one may characterize the history of the company in terms of a weaving of relationships—between artists and Board members, and with the Arts Council—which have proved durable and effective. This will be apparent from the discussion that follows.

APPLICATION OF RESEARCH FRAMEWORK

Management of Transactions: Structure

The core structure of OTC is simple (Mintzberg 1983) and resembles that of a small entrepreneurial organization, which, like most performing arts organizations in Ireland, expands in size with each production, giving rise to issues of interface between the core administration and the artistic sides of the company. A company limited by guarantee, OTC comprises a Board of Directors and a small executive group which is largely informal in terms of how people behave, dress, address each other, communicate, and so forth. This contributes to the flexibility that seems central to its operation, allowing it to tack and jib as necessary, embracing the variety that the Director sees as central to its project and the different imperatives that shape each artistic endeavor. "The projects [are] completely various. There's almost no pattern depending on the artists involved and also the degree of my involvement. . . . What I would stress is that each project has its own imperatives and the thing is it may appear that there is no pattern but, in fact, the imperatives are clear somehow in each situation. They are different but they are clear."[36] At the same time, the company works within a definite set of constraints and to a number of planning deadlines that are essential to its smooth operation. The above features—flat structure, low formality, high variety, and flexibility—are sufficient to classify the company as organic (Burns and Stalker 1961), Whether this is the full story remains to be seen.

The Board of OTC comprises twelve members with considerable social cachet in the Irish context and a fairly high age profile. Notably urban and metropolitan, it does not include artists: "We don't need a dose of playwrights on the board and they're lovely people and I love them but we need administrators, business people, vision people."[37] Criteria for membership includes a willingness to lend respectability, to be "a public face," as well as having a "strong interest [in music] and a feeling of wanting to bring music to people."[38] In addition, their ability and willingness to use personal influence to win sponsors and patrons for the company is important. The Board is conscious of its general social perception and more specifically how the Arts Council sees it: "people looking at that from the outside, the funding body, potential sponsors, all that kind of . . . look at the list of names and say 'Oh, they're good, they're solid citizens' or whatever."[39] At this stage in the life of the organization, meetings tend to run smoothly and are generally quite informal. Commitment among Board members is high, as evidenced by their attendance not only at performances but also at education workshops and master-classes. The Board contributes to the company at other levels too: putting up visiting artists and holding social 'dos' for sponsors, patrons, cast, and staff members in their houses. It has an understanding of its functions.

> To oversee general policy, in other words, to make sure that the company is fulfilling the mandate for which it gets State funding . . . It sets general . . . policy with the Director. It looks after all staff matters, I mean in terms of setting salary levels and all that kind of stuff. But its very important role is as a backup and support in terms of getting sponsorship funding, lobbying, all of those kind of things for the company. But its primary and most important role would be to make sure that everything is being done right in terms of getting money and spending it and fulfilling its mandate.[40]

As a means of evaluating the ongoing work of the company, the Board receives a report from the Director at its Annual General Meeting and it is admitted frankly that "these sessions are usually self-congratulatory!"[41] The input of board members on the artistic front seems at most tentative: "the style of the board always has been to give James . . . [his head]. We really have rarely . . . we wouldn't dream of telling him, 'Oh don't do that!' But we might; we would discuss general policy with him and we might say, 'Oh, listen here James, this is all terribly ascetic stuff. Maybe we should think about next year going a little more mainstream.' That kind of general remark."[42] In terms of the more innovative work of the company, their attitude is generally supportive: "We're doing shortly a new commissioned opera . . . which will probably be all frightfully difficult and esoteric but that has to be. That's important. . . . We scrabble around for money for that. That's not our mainstream work but we feel we have to do that."[43] While the company is enjoying its current success and continued solvency, there is no reason to expect a change in this. As DiMaggio (1987) points out, "conflict often remains latent until a financial crisis requires trade-offs between artistic and fiscal imperatives" (1987, 213).

Similarly the Board's attitude toward audiences is bathed in the glow of such incidents as the account of the company's presentation of the Janacek opera, "Katya Kabanova" in Inis Oirr (Aran Islands), or the Board members' personal experiences of rapt audiences in humble regional venues. The almost mythic power of the Inis Oirr visit, complete with stormy Atlantic boat trip, to capture the imagination is such that it can have a dual effect. Like all symbolically powerful accounts, it motivates organizational members. However, it may also cloud or seem to render grudging any rigorous questioning or exploration of the intrinsic as opposed to the PR value of the experience. The Board would seem generally to attribute poor audience response to the inadequacy of venue managements around the country: "We do evaluate in that we're always worrying about some of the venues where attendances are poor, and worrying about the fact that some of the venues, the local people, the local organizers do a hopeless PR job or a hopeless selling job. . . . They [the Board] worry about all that kind of stuff."[44] Board attitudes to staff are colored by the perception that arts people are somehow different, a viewpoint which entails the necessity for some form of special treatment.

> In the artistic world, it's a different kettle of fish [from] employing staff in a bank. It requires an extra amount of understanding and care. I think creative people . . . by their very nature, don't follow the normal tram-tracks that the vast majority of us unfortunately do, and I think you really . . . you have to try and understand them. . . . Also, I mean I enjoy the company of creative people. I'm very conscious of the fact of staff development and not taking them for granted and making sure that as far as we can, they're paid decently, although the arts community generally is not paid very well. But since all the Board puts in a lot of the work voluntarily, at least they see that; at least they know they have that back up.[45]

The low level of staff pay is partly explained in terms of this attitude and partly something in which arts administrators themselves conspire, as evidenced by the Director's own ambivalence towards pay. Prompted by the many recent changes in personnel, the board has established a management subcommittee to deal with staff matters—"to look at staff structure and how much they'll be paid and where we get them from and all that,"[46] but opinions differ as to how active this committee has been.

On the whole, the Board, much like an effective voluntary committee overseeing the work of a small young organization, is active, in regular interaction with the staff of the company and very much part of the machine that is OTC. The good working relationship between the Board and the staff means at a minimum and in contrast with many other arts organizations (see Ouellette and Lapierre 1997), that time and energy are not wasted in acrimony arising from the political dimension of the organization and that the focus of the Board is clear and distinct. However, assumptions about the "particular" nature of both artists and arts work are pervasive and conspire to the maintenance of a status quo which may in time inhibit aspects of organizational development. Furthermore, it seems clear that the Director sets the dominant agenda at the Board level and that self-questioning would rarely venture beyond the parameters set by him. The importance and the nature of the environment interface of the company are inscribed in the composition and activities of OTC's current Board. This is illustrative of the company's careful and sophisticated manipulation of the levers of power, usually in informal ways. The solidity of the Board is demonstrable in having enabled the company to survive two succession crises, while its ability to attract funds, both public and private, has been considerable. The inclusion of the great, the good, and the well-heeled of Irish metropolitan society (and the absence of artists or members from outside the urban centers—which might well be expected in a company set up and funded to tour) is an indicator of how OTC has chosen to manage its environment interface. This has served it well in terms of legitimacy and resources and places it appropriately in a niche it is able to exploit.[47] Furthermore it has acted as an effective buffer in relation to those areas where its operation is showing signs of weakness (the response of regional audiences), whether by its processes of sense making—to itself and to others—or by the social weight which in itself enables OTC to override setbacks.

Management of Transactions: Staffing and Systems

Since his appointment in 1991, the Director of OTC worked with a small closely knit team, which was relatively stable until 1997. In February 1996, he was able to say: "We have a great team here, committed people who love their jobs, and I've got a real good board—they're hard-working people, they like me, and they trust me."[48] Others corroborate this: "They were a very very close team; essentially four people who seemed to know all each others' bumps and corners and all the rest and seemed to be able to work in that way. I mean it was like some sort of organic unit nearly."[49]

At this point the Administrator left, triggering a period of turbulence in terms of staffing.[50]

Recruitment at OTC is typically on the basis of some sort of contact with the company and specifically with the Director. Almost everyone, including the Director, started on a trial basis, carrying out a short-term project on contract, often under a Department of Labour scheme. Induction is rapid: staff members describe having hit the ground running. Because of the output of the organization, staff almost inevitably join in mid-project and have to learn to swim by immersion. While the company operated as a closely knit unit, information circulated easily with a high reliance on verbal exchange and mutual adjustment.

In 1996, with the partial break-up of the team, downsides became apparent. There is some suggestion that the early departure of a new Administrator after just six months may have been in some part due to a difficulty in adapting to a certain modus operandi which had been in operation for some time; a degree of groupthink perhaps: "There's a certain amount of conflict because people are used to working in a well-worn groove. If you jar, then, in that groove, it can create a certain amount of tension."[51] As new staff has joined, the smooth transfer of information seems more problematic and ways of working have seemed at times "idiosyncratic."[52] Jobs in the past had a fluidity that accorded with the organicism and flexibility needs of the company: "My brief has expanded as the work has expanded and as needs arise really . . . I guess the job descriptions are shifting slightly as one needs to assess all the time."[53] Low formality is still a feature of the organization—contracts, for instance, have not seemed to be very important, at least in the past. "I think now James probably intends being perhaps a bit more clear on that just for the sake of the company's operation and that everybody knows exactly what they're doing. I think OTC is different in that there sometimes can be quite an overlap in what people do. . . . But you know, I suppose I know clearly what I'm doing but you interact with other people a lot as well."[54]

The sense that the organization is in transition is borne out by a recent shift both in the type of staff employed (no longer music specialists) and the closer delineation of functional roles—marketing, touring, and so on. The Director would seem to give serious thought to the best deployment of staff for the good of the organization and for their own satisfaction or stimulation. However, the change has gone only so far: a more formal approach to communication mechanisms like staff meetings,[55] for instance, has yet to be established: "They do happen, yes. But with the best of intentions . . . other things take over because we're kind of too busy. I think they're good. In terms of planning and looking at where we're at and what we need to do and things to be aware of. But I think certainly when you've got new people on board, it's important just to keep everybody abreast of what's happening and to keep everybody informed."[56] The Director attributes the recent instability in the staffing of the organization to a sectoral shift. Recognizing that the future may of necessity involve staff staying for shorter periods because of what he sees as greater mobility in the arts generally, he muses about the next phase of the organization which, as a consequence of what he terms the increased "openness" in the office, will have staff operating more as his equals and holding responsibility for discrete areas of their own. He is keen to encourage autonomy and teamworking: "I work hard to make people feel that they are a team and they have their own responsibilities. My authority is consultative. . . . Basically if I give somebody charge of something, I would want them to spread their wings and not to think I am looking over their shoulder every second."[57] In support of this, all of the staff claim to enjoy autonomy in their work: "I think it's an environment where . . . in one sense you're quite autonomous and you get on with it yourself. Of course you interact with others and you can consult, but at the end of the day you're doing the job and you're largely responsible for yourself and it's up to you how you do it."[58]

However, the notion of autonomy within OTC needs to be interrogated a little, as does the informality that would seem to be the tenor of relationships within the company. While there is no crudely imposed hierarchy of authority within the organization, this is not to suggest that all is free and easy. First, there is a palpable sense of people hard at work and a strong air of discipline within the organization. In addition the Director shapes office relationships with care and is highly vigilant about all aspects of the company's operation. The configuration of office space (three small adjoining and interlinking offices taking up the top of a city center commercial premises) demonstrates the two sides of an open door policy: little can happen that everybody in the office is not aware of. One former staff member felt herself totally free in relation to her brief: "James gave me a complete free hand. I would employ whoever it was for the duration of the project. Always. That was one thing that was great at OTC. If you had an idea you were let run with it. You weren't held back."[59] Yet, the situation has its own in-built controls: "To a certain extent you were let run with your brief, whatever it may be, but everybody knew what everybody else was doing because, as I said we worked so closely together. . . . We would all get together and have meetings . . . it wasn't that everything you were doing was being overseen by somebody else. You were given responsibility and you were let off."[60] So the closeness of staff was in itself a form of control. It is worth noting too that the freedom or autonomy to which younger staff members refer does not extend to having a budget. The aforementioned staff member may have had a free hand with her projects but had to raise the money for anything she wanted to promote. Being young, inexperienced, and highly motivated, she did not even perceive this as a constraint. Furthermore a high degree of seriousness and a reflexive attitude to one's performance is encouraged:

> If you want to focus on press, it's looking at the coverage and seeing well, where did you actually get the coverage. Not just how much you got, but where you got it, who did you get it with, what was the tone of it and . . . relating it to other organizations and seeing what they get and . . . how consistent it was . . . and did you get the message through regularly and consistently and did you place it properly and that sort of thing.[61]

The habitual high standards of the Director and his distaste for self-congratulation or complacency means that few bouquets are offered or expected. Rewards are "the satisfaction of a job well done," the challenge and the excitement of the work, as well as esteem: "In terms of how you work professionally, I suppose you realize that you're working with a good reputation and actually you are held in quite high esteem."[62]

Although there is no obvious evidence of the application of conventional control systems, and while the literature emphasizes the organic, participative side of creative organizations, such a picture gives an incomplete impression of OTC. The control system of the company first kicks into operation in relation to staff selection. The professional approach of the staff arising from their backgrounds in music as well as their sense of the value of the work acts as a type of auto-control. In addition the organization quite literally revolves almost completely around the Director who is aware of and takes an interest in the detail of everybody's work. No task is completed until he is "across" it and though cloaked in informality, there is in fact a highly vigilant approach coupled with an exceptional work ethic. This is not to suggest an oppressive or unfriendly atmosphere, rather a palpable seriousness. Conflict levels are low because of the frequency of verbal interaction and the perception of autonomy.

The increased autonomy of staff to which the Director aspires is not reflected at present in any notable way in increased responsibilities or authority being given to the Administrator (in OTC for four years). Even fairly routine tasks go back and forth between her and the Director. There is some suggestion that the departure of the previous long-term Administrator may have had something to do with a clash of wills: "I was never exactly sure why she left but she swore to me privately that we've no problems: she left because she had a child and she needed time out. But also . . . there might have been a hint of a problem between herself and James in that she is a very strong character, and in fact, if this was a bigger country, she should be heading up some bigger organization administratively."[63] Although the Director sees the organization moving toward greater autonomy, the salary levels of the staff are not commensurate with extensive responsibility and the company shows no sign of moving toward the dual (artistic/managerial) directorship which the Director sees as a possible next phase (after his departure). It would seem to follow that the role of the present Administrator should now be strengthened in preparation for this but no move is being made currently in this direction, despite the fact that the Director refers easily to his departure as something which might happen in the near future.

The structure of OTC expands and contracts as productions commence or finish, thus adding to the complexity of staffing in the organization and making the relationship between the core administration and the artistic side of the operation central to its creative output. Discussing the desirability of a permanent base for OTC, the Director takes an active role in managing the company/artist interface and bemoans the problems that regularly arise.

> I do think [a base] would enable us to experiment. To have a base for rehearsals would make for a more satisfactory relationship between administration and indeed artistic administration and artistic teams. It's a constant strain and a boring repetitive antagonism that develops between office and rehearsal and . . . it's partly to do with disposition, but it just also [is about] whether the phone works, and how far it is and how much it rains, that sets up an antagonism between—on occasions at least 30 percent of the time or maybe more—an antagonism between the office and the rehearsal room.[64]

The effort to communicate well with artists seemed to be a particular aspiration of the company in the past and is regarded as a key factor in the early success of OTC. This is not to suggest that artists were treated with any particular reverence, but rather that their handling was part of the team-building effort so vital to the operation of the company. The capacity of OTC to attract artists of quality depends on the sense they have of being valued: "We pay respectably and it's a professional engagement obviously but I think freelance artists, if they are in a position to choose their work, are careful to look for situations where they think they are valued. . . . It is something that I think we have shaped and are very conscious of in the office and, [we are] I hope increasingly conscious of showing people we value their work, which means trying to make them comfortable."[65]

Friendship gives an extra dimension to the management of transactions within OTC and relationships based on this constitute a subset of the relationships the company develops with artists. The nature of the artistic work undertaken by the company would seem to benefit from a degree of intimacy and requires a compatibility that either arises from or may become friendship. Therefore strands of friendship are discernible in some of the associations the company has developed with artists. The Director readily acknowledges that this is likely to affect the way work is produced and tends to underline the professionalism of any such transactions, converting them into "on-paper, very cool, legalistic, transactions."[66]

However, the use of friends seems to be linked with the propensity of OTC to make unconventional choices in terms of artistic personnel for artistically interesting reasons. It has already been pointed out that a striking innovative feature of the work of OTC is its use of people who are new to opera or new to the particular task being asked of them; for example, the use of an architect as a set designer or of a textiles specialist to do costumes. The Director explains the advantages and consequences of this for staff and for the work itself.

> It is risky. It is certainly more labour intensive from an office point of view because there is time spent in nurturing and explaining the task. There is more time from the Production Manager, apart from me, in processing the work that they do but I know that the Production Manager that we have finds it more fulfilling . . . his satisfaction is not purely technical. It's artistic as well. And that is why he is suited to the organization. He has more artistic satisfaction in working with artists. . . . Yes and he'll put in the time. It costs money but he'll put in the time and I think that somehow we end up getting something—well, occasionally, I think we end up getting something more special. That isn't to say we don't work with professional designers. Of course we do, lots of times. But if there is a pressing reason to work with someone different, I think it is reflected in the product—in the art at the end of the day, very directly. And it does give a lot of satisfaction to [the production manager], I know. I think it enables him to think about his own work when he does it. To think about standards. To think about making good work rather than to process someone else's design. You wouldn't want to do it for every show in the year but you might want to do it once a year. And then it can have its terrible frustrations and really, really backfire.[67]

This is a very complete statement of the attitudes that prevail in the company: conveying the merits of deroutinizing as well as the risks, frustrations, and satisfactions of a more challenging approach; the essential reasons for adopting it; and the reasons why it works. It shows why flexibility is of the essence in producing work that has something special or extra and points to the importance of motivation in bringing this about.

Finally it should be noted that although the temporary system which incorporates the main artist interface with OTC is somewhat apart and sheltered from the direct pressures of the core organization, and although the stage directors working with the company would seem to concur in their feelings of the autonomy granted them in their work, there are nevertheless at base key control mechanisms and power levers which operate between the core and the temporary system, well-articulated linkages which go a long way towards ensuring the effective functioning of the temporary system from OTC's perspective; that is, the selection prerogative of the core company, their control of budgets, and timetabling.

Management of Transactions: Strategy

We have already noted the strategic origins of OTC. By comparison with Druid and Macnas, there is evidence of a more planned approach to the output and programming of the opera company. The Director describes this as falling into a three-year cycle.

> I am really conscious of trying over a three-year period to have a balanced program of something that offers some mainstream repertoire, some twentieth-century repertoire, some baroque or early classical work that we can do very well, enough work with new composers to ensure that the art form goes ahead—but at the same time not more than we would hope to sell or develop reasonably—and also some work which is deliberately focused on enlarging the audience or catering to a section of the potential audience that isn't normally addressed, so that within three years we will do a kid's opera and maybe tour. It is mostly a question of balance.[68]

The annual programming of the company more or less bears this out: in contrast with the other two case studies there is a clear effort to win audiences by the traditional means of mixing the popular with the more experimental, thus catering for the usual opera audience while trying to win new aficionados.

This effort is underpinned by an impressive level of functional delivery, as evidenced by the comments of those who engage with the company in a professional capacity, in relation to all aspects of OTC's operation—negotiations, touring, and marketing.

> The thing I like about Opera Theater Company is they don't take [the audience] for granted. An awful lot of companies will come and . . . they will take the easiest answer. You will say to them "Well, actually Daniel O'Donnell[69] was playing up in the Concert Hall so that obviously affected your audience," and they'll say, "Grand, so." OTC will want to know what went wrong . . . you're on your toes with these [OTC] because you know they are on their toes. Sharp![70]

> I have always thought that they were the most serious company I have ever dealt with. When there was an OTC show coming on, you thought, "Oh, pull your socks up now!" You have to have everything done, every 't' crossed and every 'i' dotted because . . . they will be on the phone going—"What interviews are happening? What is the coverage? What papers have you talked to? Can I get a list of the papers and the journalists for our files?" Oh yes. On the ball! And the schools, they would remember the schools that were in and they would actually come back and say something like—"But have you not got school bookings?"[71]

Functional effectiveness combined with a high degree of flexibility makes of OTC a well-tuned instrument to pursue the variety that the Director regards as central to the innovation of the organization: "We must make our work as absolutely various as possible if we are bringing in so many different kinds of people. I'm against having a company identity. Would fight against it because the company has to be a channel through which, in which artists are able to express themselves in the best way they can."[72]

The above discussion of structures and staffing in OTC highlights the former organicism of the company and the fact that it is now in a somewhat reluctant or enforced transition to a more professional bureaucracy-type configuration. We have observed a certain lag in structures and systems in response to this change. Noting in particular the high level of functional achievement of OTC, we have pointed both to the informality of the company and the sense of autonomy among the staff and have looked behind these to paint a somewhat different picture which throws light on the expert and adroit manipulation of a range of controls to explain more adequately the levels of achievement of OTC. We note too that a number of factors—the small size of the organization, the expertise of the Director, the necessity for almost continual adjustment and retooling, and the governing attitudes within the board and staff—contribute to the heightening of the managerial or leadership function within the company, an issue which is the focus of the next section.

Management of Context: Leadership

As in the other two organizations studied here, the small size of OTC almost inevitably focuses attention on the leadership of the company, which, just as in any entrepreneurial type organization, emerges as one of its most striking features.

Following the considerable focus in the literature on leadership on leader traits, it is certainly possible to trace the continuation of personal characteristics of the Director throughout the organization and to acknowledge the pervasiveness of his influence in virtually all aspects of the company. His approach to work, personal confidence and daring, lack of complacency, attitudes to risk and control, cosmopolitanism and even—by his own account—his "meanness" are all readily manifest at the organizational level.

> The understood rule is that you work hard. . . . Work [matters]. I think it comes from James first of all . . . you would have observed him yourself and you would get a *suss* of what sort of person he is. . . . James has a total puritan work ethic.[73]

> If James hadn't had the neck, for want of a better word, to actually say, "well look, we can go . . . why can't we go to the Covent Garden Festival," then we would never have gone. And if he hadn't had the confidence to contact New York and to invite . . . it's a measure of his

confidence you know, in himself and in the company. And, when Melbourne was first mentioned, it was a joke.[74]

The Director has an enormous gift for absorbing opinions. He will lift the phone to anybody in the world and ask their opinion about something, regardless of how eminent or experienced or whatever they are. I think that's a great gift he has. He's not afraid to say "I don't know" about this or that.[75]

I am quite keen on—I am sort of addicted—to self-criticism but also that reflects then in the fact that I get very impatient with people who are uncritical—people who work for the company who are uncritical of the company. If we get chuffed and pat ourselves on the back. These [staff] meetings are kind of very very irritating.[76]

He admits to being a perfectionist and a control freak.[77]

It's exciting to think that we don't have to serve custom in this art form in this country. We can turn weaknesses (no opera house in a city which can support one, no opera orchestra, and little financial support compared even to a modest German provincial city) to a lively search for assets (many fine singers, interesting if unpretentious middle scale venues, a national broadcasting corporation with two good orchestras, and a collaborative spirit) and an approach to the art form unencumbered by tradition.[78]

I am terribly mean and you know we do break even. Not through any sophisticated financial management.[79]

Similarly the values of the Director constitute the lodestone of the company, informing its mission, objectives, and standards to which it aspires. The importance he attaches to variety has already been shown—his belief in the value of "shuffling the pack more regularly"[80]—as a means of triggering attention as well as a determined expression of the need to continually plough new furrows.

There's almost no pattern. . . . I think variety in these things is probably good and also shuffling the pack more regularly. . . . There's a sense of course: can they sing the role? Can they act the role? But will this be the right dynamic? Will it be a fruitful collaboration? And that's the great gift that my job is. I think I'm lucky. I had to exert pressure there that I might not exert on someone else . . . to say that . . . "well look, I really think that this is the partnership that I want and if you don't want it then I will ask someone else."[81]

The energy evident from these attitudes derives from the conviction that the Director brings to the enterprise his "passion for art," as well as his belief that "making good art is the most important thing."[82] The charisma of the Director combined with their own background and fueled with pride engendered by the continuing success of the company ensures that the staff shares these attitudes.

> It's a passion from a different side because it's a belief in the importance of the work, and the reason for doing it and using young singers and using good singers, exciting singers. . . . I'm very motivated by the work that we're doing. I'm motivated by the music and I think I would probably find it hard to survive without that. [I believe in] the value of what we're doing and doing it properly and challenging and moving forward and saying something in what we're doing, and I think, crossing the boundaries, all the time.[83]

Equally his persuasiveness wins the day with the more conservative elements of the Board. Speaking of innovation,

> I don't think it would be necessarily a shared value in my Board. It never has been. But that said, there have always been people on the Board who have felt that way. And then others who have come around. You know, I can think of one Board member who . . . would have been quite conservative in her expectations of the company to begin with and I think there was a certain amount of being swayed by a charismatic approach from me.[84]

Just as in Druid, there is a certain identification of the Director with OTC. One can cast the relationship in at least two ways. One account would point to his having shaped every aspect of the organization—the Board, staffing, programming—as a platform for his undisputed talents. An alternative account would show how the Director grew with the company, developing in experience and being afforded the chance to test and display his talents, while enabling both the survival of the company at a crucial transition point and its success in defining and realizing its own potential. In any case, the closeness which he develops with each project undertaken by OTC, whether by virtue of his knowledge of and enthusiasm for it, his attention to detail, his focus on shaping it in a particular way, or his artistic involvement (through having translated or written the libretto, for instance, or because he is directing) seems an important part of the innovative dimension of many of the productions.

In terms of style, it is clear that the Director of OTC exerts a strong measure of control but with sensitivity to the preferences and particularly to the experience of both core and artistic staff. He displays an awareness of the appropriate distance to take from a project or an individual, some situations demanding close interventionist behavior while others require him to be more or less "invisible." The degree of experience of the Director, conductor, or other artists involved in a production is the decisive factor in judging this: "If it's an experienced theater designer, you're a facilitator. If it's a visual artist with no experience of the theater, you know that you are going to do a lot more counseling and provide for much more time."[85] As his own experience has grown, he has developed a surer touch in this regard by learning lessons and developing new rules for himself: "I wasn't assertive enough. . . . I wouldn't work with a conductor I don't know again."[86] He would seem to have a wide repertoire in terms of leadership style, developed through experience and is adept at cycling them from "invisible" to "interventionist" as required.[87]

The personal consequences of the high investment placed by the Director in the company are also worthy of comment. He points out that the fact that he does not have family obligations has benefits for OTC: "I think it could well be a function of my character curiously that I don't live in the country where my family live and that I am unmarried and have no children. . . . It's lamentable in ways but it's a way that I can see that the company as benefited from my *disponibilité*!"[88] It is reasonable to assume that this also entails a degree of isolation, loneliness, and personal sacrifice which others might regard as a high price to pay for the innovation which characterizes OTC.

The leadership of OTC recalls the entrepreneurial mode. The company, built substantially around the Director and both driven and informal, has been infused with a culture of pride; its leadership has forged institutional norms for flexibility, high achievement and hard work and, through a combination of direct and vigilant supervision and a degree of autonomy of staff members, has shaped a core organizational framework which is highly effective in managing the successive temporary systems which are central to its operation. Even though each project undertaken by OTC is different to the last and may have special requirements, the high functional achievement of the company assured by a well-tuned and flexible structure and maintained by a blend of hard work and commitment, constantly monitored by the Director, ensures the effective articulation of the core permanent and temporary systems within the company.

Management of Context: Culture

Features of the culture of OTC that are also common within the sector include a strong commitment to the development of the art form, a willingness to work for low salaries in order to achieve this, a belief in the worth of the work, a drive towards the new or the avant-garde: "I think it's one of the better things; it's one of the things that makes the lower salaries in the arts worthwhile, where you can actually be part of a collaborative process to do some interesting things."[89] As already noted there is within the company a specific commitment to discipline and hard work as evidenced not only by the long hours put in by the staff, but also the feeling of application apparent from the office: "It was a very productive place to be. There was always something happening, always something going on and you were always working towards it—it was very productive and the amount of work, even during the period I was there, was phenomenal.[90] The work ethic of the organization is reflected in the office décor, which is notably free of personal decoration of any sort.[91] Furthermore any notion that the long hours and low pay are compensated for by the fact that work in the company is fun is vehemently resisted: "Forget that! It's a business!"[92]

The Director uses the term "family" loosely to describe the company as in the expression, "part of the family," and frequently refers to "nurturing" or "enticing." His understanding of the family embraces a wider circle than the company itself and his introduction of the idea of an "artificial family" underlines the manufactured or constructed dimension of his use of the term.

> I think there is a sort of artificial one which we nurture so that people will feel associated with OTC, will come back to the shows, will feel that their responses to the shows are taken account of, and that they may become donors. There is certainly that and that's generated very deliberately and we think about the frequency of communication with people like that. . . . And then at a more intense level of involvement, there are people on the Board and some more than others are what I would call part of the family.[93]

However, this is changing. The Director no longer regards the core staff so much as a family: "When A, B, and C were here it certainly was and I think it had been in a way in the past, although it was just so small. There were periods when it was and then times when it wasn't, and I think it has changed over the last six months and it's become a little looser."[94] A former staff member corroborates this: "I will say one thing about Opera Theater Company. It was a very tightly knit staff. . . . All of us worked very closely and some people might think that it was quite too intense at times because we were all passionate about what we were doing and we were all passionate about music because we all had music backgrounds."[95] The Director develops the image of a bell jar and regards the change that has come about as sectoral rather than attributing it to organizational factors:

> It is becoming much more of a career and people are treating it like a career and shifting and shunting around I think a lot more. A lot of people leaving jobs and thinking about looking ahead, whereas we had—we seemed to

have—for a period of a few years [it] was almost as if one of these glass cylinders had been put on top of us, like to keep the cake fresh, and we were four people who were really devoted to advancing the company. . . . It was an extraordinary grouping; in the meantime the sector had changed.[96]

Suffocation, which is the flip side of the bell-jar image, is borne out by indicators of the stress engendered by such intensity: "[It goes] back to the same thing I suppose that fueled you and kept you going. There was so much going on. Sometimes you would get very exhausted and you would be literally worn out."[97] As an extension of the family image, the question of a "home" arose, leading the Director to muse on the desirability of having a physical base which he feels "would be the next important step that a company like this could take."[98] The role of friendship in the company has been discussed above. The Director sees his work and personal/social life as being intertwined, something he is less than happy about: "Resentful some of the time. I think that because I am such a work-dominated person, I don't see the people I used to see who were friends in other connections. I am grateful for people that I have met, but I don't like the fact that I am called at home a lot. I never encourage people to call me at home but they do."[99] This is less true, to varying degrees, of the other staff members. One has the impression that a certain distance has been held, possibly as a means of self-protection: "X is very careful about her personal life and very wisely so."[100]

In conclusion, while culture may be said to affect aspects of the way it works and while it impacts on the control system which operates in the company, it is not so distinctive or special as to account in any significant way for the success of OTC, at least no more than in the case of any other arts organization. While staff members share a strong company allegiance and take satisfaction in the triumphs of the organization, the self-critical approach, already referred to, prevents this taking on any cultish characteristics.

Management of Context: The External Environment

Its audiences represent a crucial dimension of the external environment for OTC. Touring performing arts companies in Ireland face the dilemma in the Irish context of trying to reconcile the need to address regional audiences which have been underexposed to artistic experiences of an avant garde nature. Therefore a gap has to be bridged. OTC would seem to have achieved a redefinition of opera in Ireland.

Opera was, in our culture, a compensation. It was, as they say in the United States, counterfactual. And as compensation it had to be as far from reality as small budgets and tacky sets could possibly make it. We didn't really have opera companies—we had opera festivals: opera as a holiday, an escape. And you don't go on holidays to see more of what you've left behind. What is so different, and so important, about James Conway's work with OTC is that it isn't compensating for anything any more. Conway shows no interest in the escapist side of opera. . . . That we can afford, even in opera, to stick with life as we know it must be a sign that life itself is becoming bearable.[101]

While OTC would seem to have grasped the nettle of relating opera to Irish life at least on an aesthetic or intellectual level, there would still seem to be a gap to be bridged in terms of audiences.

On the one hand, there is evidence of OTC's interest in audience opinion—the company has undertaken three basic audience surveys in the past decade, and the Director's claim to take audience preferences on board is borne out by the inclusion of one more popular choice in each annual program. The company is also aware of the need to address different audience segments, especially the Arts Council, their primary source of income. Both from their own accounts and in that of outside venue managements (as already described), there is a feeling that the company will leave no stone unturned in the search for an audience, and are without complacency in this matter.

This does not, however, extend to any level of substantive discussion with venues in relation to repertoire and programming. Options such as a policy of concentrating on developing audiences in particular venues do not seem to have received serious consideration within the company, despite recent nudges from the Arts Council in this direction. The dwindling audiences of OTC in some venues are indicative at least in part of a repertoire problem. However the solution pursued by OTC is to increase their own efforts at functional effectiveness and to pressurize their partner organizations to a higher level of delivery.

And there has been antagonism too because I have not thought that marketing really was as good as it should be. I have real knockdown drag-out fights with people because I would say, "our shows cost more per night." . . . It's a financial reality that when a show is costing £5,000 for one night and if there are not 300 people on the seats, there has got to be a really good reason. So I think I am kind of a bit rebarbative about that and would be hard on publicity people in venues if I didn't think we were getting special attention.[102]

In a highly visible sector like the arts where information is asymmetrical and where there is such an acknowledged dependence on the chattering classes, the manipulation of reputation is of vital importance in attracting audiences but also in influencing the level of grant aid received by the company. OTC has clearly opted for a low-cost, maximum effect policy in this regard, exploiting its ability to put a spin on a story or provide an eye-catching image. There is little question but that the company excels in its use of the traditional mechanisms by which one reaches an audience, repeatedly receiving excellent and exceptional media coverage. Their success in this is attributable in part to clever marketing flair, as illustrated by the following program note: "Opera Theater Company presents all kinds of opera all around Ireland. That may mean putting on modern Czech music theater with piano accompaniment in a Leitrim village or a hall on Inis Oirr; it may mean mounting a baroque tragedy in a cathedral, a prison or an opera house; it may mean trying a new opera by an Irish composer in regional theaters and festivals."[103] In addition, assiduous and sustained organizational energy are expended in this domain. Image and reputation is regarded as a vital strategic asset and care is taken to represent it in the most positive way. Observers comment on the capacity of the company to "talk up" its successes.

> He [the Director] is extremely good at making the company look well and what the company does is always presented in the right way. Who doesn't know where they have toured to internationally? [We all know] the exciting things they have done even in England. I think they did something in the Wigmore or something like that. You will always get to know about [it] without seeking it out. You will always get to know about it—they are working on that.[104]

However, this approach may be criticized as an inadequate response, in that it takes insufficient account of the reality of opera in the Irish context. Alternatives such as some sort of rapprochement between the company and the audience, perhaps through the agency of venues, are not an option that seems to have been explored. Similarly it would seem reasonable to assume that the company's education policy might impact on this problem, but one venue finds this is not the case: "When they tour I have never seen the benefit of their education policy. It seems to be completely separate from their touring policy—I am not sure how it complements the touring policy."[105] However up to now, the OTC approach has proved sufficient to provide an acceptable level of box office income and to date the company shows no sign of taking the audience issue on board in any more profound way.

Therefore, the management of reputation, mostly through its relations with the press and its marketing, characterized both by sophistication and assiduousness, is a factor of the efficiency of the core organization and a major lever in the manipulation of OTC's environment. The extent of the coverage it receives in the press, the reporting back of overseas successes, and a house style which reinforces a positive image at a word-of-mouth level—always significant in the Irish arts scene—are such that they manage to override the effects of a fairly constant negative tone from the premier Irish music critic and to neutralize the effect of any artistic output which is less than successful. Both in its artistic and marketing policies, OTC plays on the preferences and strengths of its Irish audience—theatrical and visual rather than musical—an indication of its approach to the handling of its environment.

In contrast with most other Irish performing arts companies, OTC has also become practiced in networking and developing partnerships with overseas agencies, an aspect in which the Director invested considerable effort in the past and which has considerably enhanced the reputation of the company, while placing a degree of strain in recent times on the small staff. The likelihood of long incubation periods for significant partnership projects, the need to compromise, the marrying of different objectives and approaches, and the handling of inequalities in terms of the balance of power are all aspects of the management of partnerships at which the Director has become adroit. Partnerships at the local level figure less significantly for the company, notably the failure to develop any ongoing relationship with an Irish orchestra. However it is likely that this is currently outside the scope of influence of OTC and would depend on the action of bigger players.

Within Ireland, the Arts Council looms large in actual and potential terms in relation to the external environment of OTC, and the Director is acutely aware of views, developments, and incentives in that quarter. In general, the Arts Council has played a key role in relation to OTC and that its intervention and nonintervention at particular times have been crucial to the operation and even the continuation of the company. Furthermore, the signals it gives about its priorities and the incentives it offers have an important influence on how the company functions.

CONCLUSION—"MANAGERIAL" INNOVATION

Our examination of the structure, staffing, and communication systems of Opera Theater Company show the company to be a well configured, tightly integrated unit, with its compass set firmly on the core enterprise and its structure and systems decisively skewed towards attention management as a means of achieving its aims in a varied and imaginative way. The examination here of the "management of context" of the organization (leadership, culture, and relations with outside groupings and agencies) presents OTC as outward looking, alert, and opportunistic in its relation to the external environment. If this is linked with the earlier description of the internal dynamics of the organization, a picture emerges of a highly flexible body which is capable of both actively scanning for and absorbing external information and translating it effectively and repeatedly into output which is high quality, in terms of production values and innovation level alike.

The type of innovation management to be found in OTC resonates with J. Kay's (1993) concept of organizational architecture. As he sees it, "Some firms have established an architecture that stimulates a continuous process of innovations. Other firms have created an architecture that enables them to implement innovation particularly effectively." (1993, 101) OTC probably best fits the second of these models. The company has built up the organizational knowledge, skills, and flexibility necessary to deliver output which is consistently strong and can handle the challenge of quite various projects, all assembled virtually from scratch.

Though it seems a contradiction in terms, OTC represents almost a formulaic approach to innovation. Process-wise, the company is a well-oiled machine, by now capable of operating almost on automatic pilot. Innovation is well bolstered structurally: the Board is a solid edifice, which confers legitimacy and oversees the relationship with key stakeholders in the external environment (particularly resourcing bodies, public and private) in an effective manner. Internally, the company achieves high delivery on all essential functions: production, finance, press, marketing, and touring areas are all, to continue the metaphor, analogous to pistons in their smoothness, efficiency, economy of operation, and coordination. Thus the company has the character of a well-designed and well-managed entity which in many of its dimensions constitutes virtually a formula for innovative success.

In relation to its artistic output, the company adopts a measured approach to risk taking. By and large it operates well within the conventions of the international opera genre. Its program is a mix of the more popular operas which guarantee a certain level of box-office income, and new work. Where it has pushed out the boundaries (as it habitually does), there are in-built safety measures and usually what risks being a failure on one axis has potential for being exploited as a success on another. The risk in using a director, composer, or designer who is new to opera for instance can be offset against the reputation in another field which he or she brings to the role, or alternatively is minimized by a training or induction process engendered by the company. The use of an unconventional venue—a prison or an island—while it may have integral artistic value, may also be chosen for its potential as novelty-chic and/or can be harnessed as a major press coup. The company has not undertaken any radical interactions with audiences or gone in for community opera experiments, preferring to keep its radicalism for notable reinterpretations of particular operas, and has been credited for achieving no less than a redefinition of the genre in the Irish context.

We have termed the innovation achieved by OTC "managerial" because by developing mechanisms for handling major aspects of its role and its environment, primarily through effective structures and policies and a high level of functional delivery, it satisfies the main stakeholders of the company while at the same time allowing space for innovative work. In fact the company is substantially bolstered by its political, social, and even economic environment, and adroit at manipulating the correct power levers—often informally—to ensure that this continues to be the case. Thus OTC takes an active role in managing its environment in a somewhat selective and altogether sophisticated way. Rather than grappling with the considerable challenges, uncertainties and unknowables inherent in the response of a regional Irish audience to opera, it tends to edit these out and instead pursues an eclectic policy that wins the support necessary to its operation. In this way, the company demonstrates a managed economy of effort and a tolerable level of organizational stress.

NOTES

1. A list of Opera Theater Company productions and coproductions is given in Appendix 4.

2. James Conway, interview by author, tape recording, Dublin, 17/12/96.

3. Statement by founder-Board member at inaugural press reception, 29/10/86.

4. The first Chairperson was replaced in 1990 by a former Irish Minister for Education who retired after four years of service in 1994 and who now remains on the Board as Deputy Chair. None of the original Directors are currently on the Board. The longest serving member and a founder of the company remained on the Board for ten years, resigning in 1996.

5. The amount allocated to OTC was the highest grant to any music organization in that year.

6. The funding history of Rough Magic, a theater company which is comparable in a number of respects, established just the year before OTC, illustrates this clearly:

Arts Council Funding of Rough Magic Theater Company: 1985–1987 (in £000s)

Income	1991	1992	1993	1994	1995	1995
Arts Council	64	64	60	53	64	50
Box office	15.5	20	23.5	33	25	40

7. Arts Council, Annual Report, 1986.

8. Music critic, *Irish Times,* April, 1986.

9. Arts Council, Annual Reports, 1985, 6.

10. Arts Council Annual Report, 1986.

11. Opera Theater Company: Application to Arts Council for grant aid for 1986.

12. Founding member and first manager, OTC, interview by author, tape recording, Dublin 31/7/97.

13. Certain informants refer to OTC as a "baby" of the Arts Council.

14. Founding member and first manager, OTC, interview by author, tape recording, Dublin, 31/7/97.

15. Risible levels of professionalism in the sector and the need to create opportunities for Irish artists.

16. Founding member and first manager, OTC, interview by author, tape recording, Dublin, 31/7/97.

17. Press statement to launch OTC, 29/10/86.

18. OTC application to Arts Council for grant aid, 1986–1987.

19. Randall Shannon quoted in *Irish Times,* April, 1986.

20. Director of a local authority.

21. Former Board member, interview by author, tape recording, Dublin, 5/9/97.

22. The company had presented a critically disastrous version of Mozart's "Cosi Fan Tutte" in 1987 as their second production.

23. Founding member and first Manager, interview by author, tape recording, Dublin, 31/7/97.

24. Paper by Manager to Board, OTC, 2/7/88 and Administrator's report, 8/9/88.

25. Former Board member, OTC, interview by author, tape recording, Dublin, 31/7/97.

26. James Conway, interview by author, tape recording, Dublin, 17/9/97.

27. There would have been an interest among certain members of the company in fostering relations with the Gate Theater as a major and prestigious Dublin venue, in spite of the fact that playing at the Gate was very costly for the company, a cost which, in the context of OTC's main brief for regional opera provision, was difficult to justify in the eyes of some company members.

28. James Conway, interview by author, tape recording, Dublin, 17/9/97.

29. Minutes of OTC Board meeting, 14/12/89.

30. Former Board member, OTC, interview by author, tape recording, Dublin, 5/9/97.

31. Founding member and first manager, OTC, interview by author, tape recording, Dublin, 31/7/97.

32. Former Board member, OTC, interview by author, tape recording, Dublin, 31/7/97.

33. Former Board member, OTC, interview by author, tape recording, Dublin, 27/8/97.

34. Founding member and first Manager, OTC, interview by author, tape recording, Dublin, 1/7/97.

35. Founding member and first Manager, OTC, interview by author, tape recording, Dublin, 31/7/97.

36. James Conway, interview by author, tape recording, Dublin, 17/12/97.

37. Former Board member, OTC, interview by author, tape recording, Dublin, 27/8/97.

38. Board member, OTC, interview by author, tape recording, Dublin, 27/8/97.

39. Board member, OTC, interview by author, tape recording, Dublin, 27/8/97.

40. Board member, OTC, interview by author, tape recording, Dublin, 27/8/97.

41. Board member, OTC, interview by author, tape recording, Dublin, 27/8/97.

42. Board member, OTC, interview by author, tape recording, Dublin, 27/8/97.

43. Board member, OTC, interview by author, tape recording, Dublin, 27/8/97.

44. Board member, OTC, interview by author, tape recording, Dublin, 27/8/97.

45. Board member, OTC, interview by author, tape recording, Dublin, 27/8/97.

46. Board member, OTC, interview by author, tape recording, Dublin, 27/8/97.

47. This is true in a number of ways. First, the social environment for opera in Ireland and particularly in Dublin is conducive to the maintenance of a small company with an eclectic repertoire: while the opera audience is decidedly middle-class and conventional/conservative, it is also large enough and sufficiently well-endowed to associate itself quite happily with an innovative venture as something self-gratifying and worthy. In this context failures are reframed at the very least as attempts at innovation and one can always have recourse to the Emperor's new clothes syndrome—so the company cannot lose! Second, it should be mentioned that set up as it virtually was by the Arts Council to answer a number of imperatives, there is a sense in which the Council needs OTC as much as it needs their funding.

48. James Conway, interview by author, tape recording, Dublin, 17/9/97.

49. Staff member, OTC, interview by author, tape recording, Dublin, 27/8/97.

50. In all three people left without having other jobs but with intentions of freelancing.

51. Staff member, OTC, interview by author, tape recording, Dublin, 27/8/97.

52. Staff member, OTC, interview by author, tape recording, Dublin, 27/8/97.

53. Staff member, OTC, interview by author, tape recording, Dublin, 26/8/97.

54. Staff member, OTC, interview by author, tape recording, Dublin, 26/8/97.

55. Although the Director refers in passing to "our weekly staff meetings," it would seem that these are at best irregular. There is no fixed day or time for them. No minutes are taken and nobody could say when the last such meeting was held. It would be reasonable to assume that the Administrator might be in a position to convene such meetings but this does not seem to occur to her as being within her remit.

56. Staff member, OTC, interview by author, tape recording, Dublin, 26/8/97.

57. James Conway, interview by author, tape recording, Dublin, 17/9/97.

58. Staff member, OTC, interview by author, tape recording, Dublin, 26/8/97.

59. Former staff member, OTC, interview by author, tape recording, Dublin, 4/9/97.

60. Former staff member, OTC, interview by author, tape recording, Dublin, 4/9/97.

61. Staff member, OTC, interview by author, tape recording, Dublin, 26/8/97.

62. Staff member, OTC, interview by author, tape recording, Dublin, 26/8/97.

63. Board member, OTC, interview by author, tape recording, Dublin, 27/8/97.

64. James Conway, interview by author, tape recording, Dublin, 17/9/97.

65. James Conway, interview by author, tape recording, Dublin, 17/9/97.

66. James Conway, interview by author, tape recording, Dublin, 17/9/97.

67. James Conway, interview by author, tape recording, Dublin, 17/9/97.

68. James Conway, interview by author, tape recording, Dublin, 17/9/97.

69. Popular Irish country singer.

70. Staff member, regional venue, interview by author, tape recording, 4/9/97.

71. Staff member, regional venue, interview by author, tape recording, 4/9/97.

72. James Conway, interview by author, tape recording, Dublin, 17/9/97.

73. Staff member, OTC, interview by author, tape recording, Dublin, 26/8/97.

74. Staff member, OTC, interview by author, tape recording, Dublin, 26/8/97.

75. Former Board member, OTC, interview by author, tape recording, Dublin, 5/9/97.

76. James Conway, interview by author, tape recording, Dublin, 17/9/97.

77. Staff member, OTC, interview by author, tape recording, Dublin, 26/8/97.

78. James Conway, interview by author, tape recording, Dublin, 17/9/97.

79. James Conway, interview by author, tape recording, Dublin, 17/9/97.

80. James Conway, interview by author, tape recording, Dublin, 17/9/97.

81. James Conway, interview by author, tape recording, Dublin, 17/9/97.

82. James Conway, interview by author, tape recording, Dublin, 17/9/97.

83. Staff member, OTC, interview by author, tape recording, Dublin, 26/8/97.

84. James Conway, interview by author, tape recording, Dublin, 17/9/97.

85. James Conway, interview by author, tape recording, Dublin, 17/9/97.

86. James Conway, interview by author, tape recording, Dublin, 17/9/97.

87. This notion of a range of styles accords with Glassman (1986) who identified four types of leadership style, from directive through participative and catalytic to nondirective, and suggested that these should be cycled according to the predominant behavior of subordinates—their ability, willingness, performance level, confidence, and developmental levels. Manz, Bastien et al (1989) too identify three leadership styles—visionary, transactional, and participative which are combined and cycled over time.

88. James Conway, interview by author, tape recording, Dublin, 17/9/97.

89. Staff member, OTC, interview by author, tape recording, Dublin, 27/8/97.

90. Former staff member interview, 4/9/97.

91. The walls, notice boards, etc. only hold work-related notices—maps, reminders, contact lists, calendars, and planners. The 1991 AIB Better Ireland reward, an image of the company's success, is framed and on display as are two images from company productions. Telephone calls, though friendly, are noticeably short and businesslike. Personal calls are not encouraged and by and large do not happen.

92. Staff member, OTC, interview by author, tape recording, Dublin, 26/8/97.

93. James Conway, interview by author, tape recording, Dublin, 17/9/97.

94. James Conway, interview by author, tape recording, Dublin, 17/9/97.

95. Former staff member, OTC, interview by author, tape recording, Dublin, 4/9/97.

96. James Conway, interview by author, tape recording, Dublin, 17/9/97.

97. Former staff member, OTC, interview by author, tape recording, Dublin, 4/9/97.

98. James Conway, interview by author, tape recording, Dublin, 17/9/97.

99. James Conway, interview by author, tape recording, Dublin, 17/9/97.

100. James Conway, interview by author, tape recording, Dublin, 17/9/97.

101. Fintan O'Toole, *Irish Times,* 1/10/96.

102. James Conway, interview by author, tape recording, Dublin,, 17/9/97.

103. Foreword in program for "The Magic Flute" by OTC, 1997.

104. Staff member, regional venue, interview by author, tape recording, 4/9/97.

105. Staff member, regional venue, interview by author, tape recording, 4/9/97.

5

"Opportunistic" Innovation: Macnas

That Macnas is synonymous with the anarchic in Ireland, whether in terms of its performance output or its management systems, has certainly been true for most of the life of the company. How then has this been converted into the effective delivery of award-winning spectacles and theater? Does the widespread impression of the company as a highly collaborative unit reflect accurately the process that results in this output? Given that the company has worked primarily with people untrained in arts skills—as opposed to artists—is Macnas an exemplar of the belief, fundamental to the philosophy of community arts, that creativity is a universal wellspring which may be tapped providing an appropriate environment, respectful of the innate creativity of everyone, is furnished? At th outset, this chapter, after a brief run-through of the innovative achievement of Macnas, outlines the main dimensions of the history of the company. We then go on to describe the features of Macnas as per the categories of the Van de Ven (1986) framework. Because of the dramatic change that took place in the company in 1996, we treat the period since then separately before arriving at some conclusions on the shape that innovation took in Macnas.

MACNAS—INNOVATIVE ACHIEVEMENT AND HISTORY

Innovation

There's a reason why the forty theatrical artists who call themselves Macnas have toured the globe, performed with U2, created the opening ceremonies for the MTV European Music Awards, and won armloads of awards themselves: they are fabulously good at what they do.

This is live drama at its electric, engrossing best.

The Seattle Times, 1997.

Physical theatre is almost too polite a term to use for the troupe's style. Pagan ritual is more like it.

San Francisco Chronicle, 1995.

Macnas blends spirits of ancient and modern Ireland into a heady, stunningly theatrical brew. This is the kind of theatre that makes magic feel like an everyday commodity and turns the commonplace mythical.

San Francisco Examiner, 1995.

Ireland should support this troupe as a national resource. We in America should get them back here as soon as possible.

Boston Phoenix, 1995.

Macnas has created a unique and magnificent and telling form of theatre which is as Irish as it comes and yet is totally international.

The Belfast Newsletter, 1994.

Three main factors may be evinced to justify Macnas' designation as a highly innovative organization in the live performing arts. First, the company boldly grasped a tradition of outdoor spectacle which was new to Ireland and, by virtue of its scale and nonverbal nature, quite outside the indigenous theatrical tradition, and reminiscent rather of Chinese- or Rio de Janeiro-type events as much as of mainland Europe. At the height of their operation, Macnas gave this tradition a unique Irish flavor by fusing it with the rich fount of heroic Celtic mythology (as in the "Táin"[1] trilogy) or themes from Irish literature like "Gulliver." Traditionally, Irish theater is regarded as being tethered to the written word and beholden to the Irish writer; Macnas gaily bypassed this, making their own of an exuberant and wholly foreign mode of performance. The company's innovation was of the ebullient—sometimes even volcanic variety, joyful, and anarchic—with wide popular appeal.

Second, the company, also uniquely in the Irish context of the time, devised all their own work as well as commissioning original music. Among the prizes and awards earned by Macnas in recognition of their achievement were the Allied Irish Banks (AIB) Better Ireland Award 1991, the UNESCO award at the Seville Expo in 1992 for their production of the "Táin," and the Best New Irish Production awards at the Dublin Theater Festivals (1992 and 1994) for the "Táin" and "Buile Shuibhne."

Third, the influence of Macnas, spawning as it did a number of imitators in the area of public outdoor events and virtually inventing street theater for Ireland, is indicative of the innovative levels it attained. Arts organizations and artists in other towns and cities sought to emulate the community involvement, visual impact, and color of the street spectacles devised by Macnas, first in a spontaneous way and later through the Macalla network established specifically by Macnas as a more conscious form of propagation.

In addition to the above, commentators who nominated Macnas as highly innovative mentioned such factors as the prodigious energy and the particular extravagance of imagination which they brought to their endeavors, exploding on the Irish arts scene with considerable fanfare and on a scale which outstripped all previous theatrical creations. It can be said that Macnas by cottoning on to the now-current notion of theater-as-event before any of its contemporaries—in effect redefining theater in an Irish context—went on to exploit it in a spectacular way. Their "community arts" approach and their use primarily of untrained people gave the company a freshness and even a daring, widening their appeal by contrast with the more staid "professional" theater. In addition there is a perception that the management and organization structure of the company evolved creatively in tandem with their artistic output, thus evidencing an organicism which is associated both with the participatory dynamic of community arts and friendlier, popular notions of creativity. Finally the company is regarded as having sustained its creativity over a longer period than most arts organizations, showing the ability to reinvent itself and to capture the public imagination repeatedly over the past twelve years.

History of Company

Beginnings. Macnas (a word meaning "joyful abandonment") was founded in Galway in 1985 by four people—Páraic Breathnach (Production Manager), Pete Sammon (Performance Director), Tom Conroy (Costume and Design Director), and Ollie Jennings (Administrator/Secretary). Inspired largely by such traditions of European spectacle street theater as are exemplified by the British gypsy-type troupe, Footsbarn, and the Catalan, Els Comediants, both of which had made memorable visits to the Galway Arts Festival (with which Jennings and Breathnach were closely associated) in the preceding years, the company placed an emphasis from the start on strong visual impact, street processions, and community involvement.

Arts, Community, Education (A.C.E.). The initial impulse of the founding members to come together was prompted by the ACE project, a "community arts" initiative, established in 1985, which was jointly formulated and sponsored by the Arts Council and the Calouste Gulbenkian Foundation, an international foundation which had already been involved in significant initiatives in the arts in Ireland. ACE was essentially an exploratory project, the aim of which was to introduce greater coherence to the new (at least in Irish terms) area of community arts and, through practice, to develop and further inform models of funding in this domain. It thus presented an opportunity for the funding of innovative projects that straddled the worlds of arts and community, an opportunity that was seized by the Macnas team.

The application by Macnas to ACE outlined the thrust of the company: "We interpret the word community in the broad popular sense. We are interested in the pastimes, games, and rituals of our community in the West. We wish to create dramatic, visual spectacles using and exploring these popular forms of communal entertainments. Our spectacles will be created in the community, in large, outdoor, familiar spaces. We hope to make fun and have fun on a grand scale and amongst ourselves." Discussions with ACE expanded on the initial Macnas application which outlined the idea to present "The Game," an enactment of a "satirical spoof football match"[2] to be staged during the interval of the Connacht Football Final in Castlebar in 1986. These discussions resulted in the addition of an education component to the project as well as a year-long program of lead-up events, to be funded by a grant of £40,000 from ACE over two years. The realization of these projects necessitated the employment by Macnas, through a social employment scheme (SES) worth £116,500, under the aegis of the Department of Labour, of some twenty-five trainees.

Placed in context, the significance of the ACE grant to Macnas becomes evident. In 1986, the total Arts Council budget for community arts was just £102,430. In that year too, due to its own inadequate funding (£5.8 million), the Arts Council suspended funding to festivals and to theater touring. Thus the advent of a new fund like ACE, particularly in the field of community arts, which had hitherto been granted such low priority, proved a genuine stimulus to innovative projects in this area.

From the beginning Macnas was run on a collective basis with the same personnel acting as technicians, performers, and musicians. Their commitment was to a nonverbal style of theater, incorporating live, original music and the visual arts. Their ambition was no less than to forge a "new style of Irish theater . . . heavily influenced by Mediterranean and European carnival and masquerade tradition." They prided themselves on "a democratic, collective approach to the nurturing and harnessing of creativity without the barriers, constraints, and conventions of established art forms."[3] The inaugural performance of Macnas was at the opening parade of the Galway Arts Festival in 1986 when the company brought a 16-person dragon to the streets. Participation in local County Galway events at the Ballinasloe Horse Fair, a Wren Boys' Outing, and a New Year's Eve lantern parade followed this.

Funding. The financial pattern established at the outset was to be the basis for Macnas' operation for most of the decade:[4] the company survived primarily by responding to various opportunities or being contracted by different organizations (Dublin Millennium, Glasgow Cultural Capital, National Garden Festival, Ireland Fund); it operated on successive SES, Teamwork, or other Department of Labour schemes which supplied the manpower of the organization, and its funding was uncertain and irregular. Arts Council funding at the outset (Table 5.1) was small and project-based, issuing from various occasional funds within a number of budget headings (community arts, music, dance, and the like).

In 1988 the company exploded on the national arts scene with their recreation of "Gulliver," a twenty-meter model of Swift's character, which attracted unprecedented media attention in Ireland.

In 1990, the company applied for Arts Council core funding, submitting a three-year plan which aimed to address: the low pay of company members; their reliance on employment schemes which obliged them to continuously undertake training from scratch and to battle with motivation problems on the part of some participants; and

TABLE 5.1
Arts Council Funding of Macnas, 1986–1997 (£ under different budget heads)

Year	Community Arts	Theater	Touring	Other	Training	Total
1986	15,600					15,600
1987	18,500					18,500
1988	6,028					6,028
1989	6,000			2,250		8,250
1990	10,000			1,150		11,500
1991	25,000					25,000
1992	41,000					41,000
1993	50,000		30,000	5,000	15,000	100,000
1994	75,000	20,000	30,000	7,100	15,000	147,100
1995	98,000	60,000				158,000
1996	100,000	60,000	30,000		20,000	210,000
1997	107,000	65,000	30,000		25,000	227,000

Source: Figures supplied by Macnas.

the difficulty they experienced in establishing any real degree of continuity. Their arguments for some level of core funding began to bear fruit to a degree in 1991, also the year when they were awarded an AIB Better Ireland Award of £25,000. At this point an effort had been made to restructure the company, notably by establishing a new Board structure with Páraic Breathnach as General Manager and Rod Goodall, formerly of Footsbarn Theater Company in England as full-time Artistic Director.

Touring and Expansion. In the following years Macnas began to tour within Ireland and to perform overseas. A major point in the Macnas year centered on the annual Galway Arts Festival. The company had also begun to work elsewhere in the country with communities and groups who were keen to reproduce the Macnas experience as part of their festivals and parades.

1992, their busiest year, Macnas launched their prizewinning trilogy, drawn from Celtic mythology—the "Táin"—which was presented at Expo in Seville. At this point the Arts Council commented on the "pathbreaking achievements of the company in setting high standards in Irish community arts practice and in charting new directions in Irish drama."[5] From 1992 on, Macnas was the Council's anchor client in the community arts area. In 1993, the company performed as part of the U2 Zooropa tour (forty-three shows in sixteen countries), an experience which still has emblematic importance for the company, as evidenced by the framed note from Bono[6] in their central office/reception area, other office iconography, and the fact that some company members still (five years later) wear gear carrying the U2/Zooropa logo.

At this stage too, the company began to formalize the various aspects of its operation, spawning a number of offshoot companies—MacEnts, to take on special commissions such as the U2 tour; Mac Eolas, a community arts training program funded in the main by various European Union schemes which were then on offer; and MacTeo, a commercial wing for the creation of "unique and unusual" projects, which were able to avail initially some development funds from Forbairt (the Irish Development Agency). However the company was still struggling with inadequate core funding and submitted its second three-year plan to the Arts Council in 1994. This was accompanied by a frank postscript: "We are not getting any younger. Most of us now have children and partners. Commitment, enthusiasm, and friendship have kept us together so far, but without decent wages, a vital force in the Irish arts scene may be lost. If Macnas with its color, spirit, and high media profile fails, what will happen to all those groups for whom Macnas is an inspiration and a role model?"[7]

This plan made provision for the establishment by Macnas of a "National Community Arts Initiative" comprising plans for a "National Community Arts Studio." In 1995, two further offshoots were added to the company: Macalla network comprising nine arts groups from other towns and communities; and Mac Léinn, an education development project. Meanwhile the company continued touring (France and the United States).

Restructuring. At the end of 1995, Páraic Breathnach, its founder General Manager left the company. The vacuum created by this precipitated a thorough self-evaluation and change management process throughout every part of the organization. Funding from the EU Adapt program allowed this to be undertaken in a deliberate and comprehensive fashion, moderated by international consultants over a twelve-month period. The process recognized that "the structure of the company did not lend itself easily to fulfilling the essentials of being an arts-led organization with a very clear sense of direction."[8] To correct this, Macnas appointed a new board, a step which required the resignation of all members of the old Board (30 August 1996); and established a new management structure, requiring the mass resignation of all the staff (1 April 1997) and occasioning some painful redundancies, including those of the two Artistic Directors. Thus to all intents and purposes, Macnas as it was self-destructed. It was reformed as a Macnas Limited, a company limited by guarantee with no share capital; Ace Macnas Limited, which acts as a holding company with charitable status; and three other companies—MacTeo, MacEolas, and MacEnts—which are private companies limited by shares. In January 1997, Declan Gibbons was appointed General Manager of a reconstituted Macnas, which now defined itself as a project-based organization.

Phases. One can identify three discrete phases in the development of Macnas: first, the founding of the company associated with the ACE football match production and up to the departure of Ollie Jennings (1986–1990), the first administrator; second, the subsequent development of Macnas under Páraic Breathnach, which saw the company move from street spectacle to their own particular brand of theater and which included its evolution in management terms to a company with subsidiaries (1991–1994); and third the departure of Páraic Breathnach from his role as General Manager and the restructuring of the company (1995–1998). With a current turnover of about £350,000, it is worth noting that Arts Council funding constitutes a growing percentage of Macnas funding since 1990.[9]

APPLICATION OF RESEARCH FRAMEWORK

Management of Transactions: Structure

For its first decade, Macnas, insofar as it can be said to have a structure, was configured loosely as a project organization. It was decidedly entrepreneurial in thrust in that it followed funding opportunities. A notable idealism is discernible in the impulse that established the organization—a genuinely emotional effort at empowerment with a strong socialist twist, as described by its first General Manager.

> So I was deeply politically motivated at the start of Macnas. Deeply politically motivated. I felt this was not alone a socialist movement, not alone a creative movement, but it was a movement of gathering alternative economic power to get us the respect we needed because everybody was laughing at us. It was very angry and [there were] very deeply politically motivated reasons for the energy in Macnas. It was motivated by anger and by the fact that in the West everybody was always put down by everybody in Dublin. We were always seen as second-class citizens.[10]

As he saw it, the arts were just one of the agendas or instruments for empowerment and one part of an overall mission with high aims.

> My intention was to renew the Macnas' economic power, to empower us all. . . . We saw ourselves as exemplary role models and that it was our duty and our personal wish to empower other groups around the country. And I think we did that very effectively. . . . It's to do with power for us. It's to do with me and my people. The motivation from us was for us, us for us. *Muide na daoine.*[11] We the people. The idea was that we were together as a group of people. We cared and respected and loved each other. Very much so![12]

That the members of Macnas were disinclined towards any formal hierarchies and any but the loosest form of structure would therefore follow philosophically on this.

> There was a democracy in the sense that they were trying to be democratic. They were trying to be very social-minded. There was a great sort of social awareness. . . . A brotherhood, if you like. People took care of each other and if somebody didn't have a few bob then the few bob would be found for them or whatever. If there was a problem, you know, people would help. It was very much—very kind of familyish—it was like belonging to a club.[13]

Issues of governance in any conventional sense did not arise. Macnas had no Board; the Board was everybody "because Páraic had it we were all a cooperative. We were all on the Board."[14] "There was a Board of Directors which was effectively the management team plus a few others, and the reason for that was it was fairly strongly felt that the people who ran the company, and who earned their livelihood from the company, should have a say in where the company was going."[15] "From after 'Gulliver' till after the 'Táin' which was from 1987 to 1993, there wasn't effectively a Board meeting. They only ever met to sign the accounts every year, you know, and they met in a public house and signed the accounts for the Arts Council and that was with the effect of a few pints!"[16]

The closest definition of the company is as a loose project-based organization with drifts of people coming and going. As might be expected this meant periods of frenetic activity followed by periods of slack. Furthermore integration was problematic. As the company developed, a number of distinct strands—community, training, and theater—became apparent. However these interrelated only insofar as they were answerable to and directed by Páraic as General Manager. "You had theater going one way and community going the other. And decisions were made . . . independently of any reference to the other, to anybody else really."[17] "But, yes, it was like three separate companies going in three separate directions without any consideration or appreciation of each other. There was no respect for theater from community, [between] theater and commercial work, and commercial and community. It was like three separate companies. It was an incredible strain particularly on the people who had to work in all of the areas."[18] In fact, despite the democratic aspirations of the company, attitudes within Macnas militated against integration, notably the haughtiness of the theater people vis-à-vis the community arts side of the company: "[With theater] you'd go to more exciting places. Instead of going to Ballinasloe and working with some remedial people, you could end up going to Spain and doing a show out in—you know. I don't mean to sound snotty about it. . . . I worked a lot in community arts but I am not a community artist."[19] Thus the structure of Macnas for the duration of its first decade was fluid and sprawling with minimal or sporadic attempts at governance. Its output clustered around a succession of opportunities with coordination being the exclusive domain of the General Manager.

Management of Transactions: Staffing and Systems

Given the philosophy of Macnas and the circumstances of its founding (the ACE program), the staffing of the company was informed by the social mission which animates the community arts movement, the notion of empowerment through the arts. By virtue of this, the company, in the view of one informant, attracted people who were socially marginalized in one way or another, and by placing government employment schemes at the center of its operation, addressed people who were economically marginalized.

> You've got to realize that Macnas always attracted an element of society that was slightly outside of the norm. . . . So, consequently, you would always have people whose social attitudes were slightly different. It was a kind of a link to something that wasn't quite . . . it's not like a halfway house. I don't mean it in that way. But it was a bridge to many people who couldn't actually fit or work in a group at all, and yet ended up there, and through that process—through the process of being part of a collective . . . the collective process of working in the arts . . . and I can think of loads of people, because hundreds of people have been through Macnas . . . some of them complete head-cases . . . a lot of them have become very well adjusted people. . . . They were very confused individuals. But it has allowed confidence in them mostly.[20]

Recruitment was always by the General Manager on a personalized basis and in a very ad hoc and instinctive manner. Each of the staff members related directly to him and this became more problematic as the staff numbers increased. The company took on the character of a squat or a loosely structured commune rather than any formal type of organization.

> There were hundreds of people wanting jobs. There was a load of people there we had to keep working and it became very hard to get new talent into the company because we had to keep paying the old guys! So that was the problem . . . the input end was very good. It attracted people to the company. In the 1988/1993 phase . . . there was no problem at all attracting people to the company. We had a problem paying them and . . . a lot of people just stuck. Just stayed too long and that became a problem subsequently. . . . I don't think there was ever a formal job advertized in Macnas.[21]

Roles were always ill-defined, sometimes to a positive effect in terms of scope and flexibility and sometimes to a negative effect because the result was wasteful and inefficient: "I can make of my job whatever I want it to be as long as it's still a positive thing for the company. . . . There were sort of grey areas where people didn't know what they should be doing or other people should be doing. . . . It was wasteful ultimately, and there were also things that weren't being done."[22] Nevertheless, accounts of idea generation in Macnas point to a degree of collectivism: at least some of the company members had the impression that they could make a contribution to ideas by engaging in the creative tumble. This was facilitated by the fluidity of roles, which enabled the Production Manager, for instance, as much as the Artistic Director, to put forward an idea: "The basic structure of the show came from Páraic. But then other people contributed a huge amount. . . . So when a show was finally happening it was very much a combination of different creativities, which I think, is what Macnas does best. . . . What was good about it was that sort of combined creative energy."[23] "In the canteen, first thing in the morning, during discussion, somebody will come and somebody will mention something and you can have a whole development of an idea that's gone another stage further, just while you're having a conversation."[24]

The tale of the organization is animated by accounts of close relationships—whether between the General Manager and the first Administrator (Phase One) or the General Manager and the Artistic Director (some of Phase Two)—which first went well and then underwent serious deterioration: "Páraic and I worked very closely together. We were inseparable. Yeah. For a long time. We'd drink together. We'd have lunch together. We'd stay in the office till eleven o'clock at night. Hours weren't an important thing there, you know. And then we'd probably go out for a pint after that."[25] While the explanation offered for breakdown points to different understandings of what collaboration means, it comes down ultimately to a struggle for power and control. "These separations were hugely traumatic. . . . And certainly X's departure from the company was hugely traumatic. . . . It wasn't until X left the company that I was allowed to initiate these movements. He was completely opposed to Macnas having a life of its own."[26]

The staffing of the company also exhibited other divisions and dysfunctional aspects. Despite its democratic and egalitarian aspirations, the company was not without its élitism—or its sexism: "I mean, if I even suggested an idea it was, like, 'but you type!' "[27] "In the old structure there was a lot to do with being female here, in that you were a good typist or good on the phone or you looked good."[28] This extended to the artistic dimension of the company's work: "And very much in our shows as well, all the leading parts went to men. All the strong characters went to men and all the credible characters were men."[29] After the U2 tour, "social" divisions arose between various groups in the company: "Well, say, the twelve that went off [with U2] would have lost a lot of their humility with regard to . . . cleaning out the toilets and doing the jobs that everybody else had to do. . . . The acting troupe then began to act up, as they say, towards the administrators: 'Oh, my hotel room isn't up to scratch.' "[30] As noted above, the cachet associated with the theater work in the company also occasioned divisions: "When there were, say, twenty people on a scheme and ten of them would be involved in a theater show, the other ten would have to do all the dross—this sets people against each other."[31] Somewhat ironically in a company so committed to empowerment, information flows were carefully controlled: "Before, it was very closed. All decisions . . . would have been kept to a very tight group and not a lot was leaked out. And it was almost—in some ways, it was almost probably paranoid—the levels to which people wanted to control the information."[32] "Information used to be very much on a need-to-know basis."[33]

The reliance on mutual adjustment that might be expected of an organization this size and type is not in evidence in Macnas. Most accounts point to the shortcomings of communication within the company: "Communication was bad. . . . We used to have these meetings with people and we'd say 'Well now we're going to do this show this year and we'll have a meeting with everybody on Thursday and we'll tell you what to do.' It would happen all right but, I mean, with that number of people, you know, they'd be able to not be here and you wouldn't even miss them."[34] "Communication was dreadful. . . . So, we had a large but limited resource pool of equipment, people, and resources basically and the lack of communication would mean that at times people were being asked to do two or three different things at the same time."[35] Communication and co-ordination happened via the then General Manager: "Like, for example, nobody knew how much anybody else was getting paid . . . things were controlled very tightly from the top and there was an illusion of participation."[36]

Control systems reverted regularly to the hierarchic model. Macnas could not rely on the motivation levels that applied generally in the arts sector. The difficulties of managing trainees on employment schemes were intensely felt, possibly because of a certain ambivalence about control and discipline, as well as a deficit in managerial experience:

> The people we took on a scheme weren't on the scheme because they wanted to be on the scheme. They were on the scheme because they were interested in achieving something. And they [were] imbued with personal ambition and talent. [Question: But was that not a plus?] It is when they all go in the one direction. But they all go off and diversify and you've agreed with a client to do a job in this way, well then you've got a problem.[37]

When applied, controls were simple and direct: appeals were to team spirit and sometimes even more basic! "Peer pressure. That was the main thing. We were together. Letting the side down. Letting the team down. Letting the town down. Letting the company down. . . . You know 'Your mother asked me to give you this job. Do you want me to go back and tell her you're useless?' Do you know what I mean?"[38] By and large this approach worked, at least for a period; one company member recalls: "You wouldn't let the team down ever. . . . The spirit from 1988 to, say 1990, was unbelievable . . . I've worked a 70- to 80-hour week for nothing. And maybe pay my babysitters to mind my children and do that. Now when I think of it I say, 'Oh Jesus!' But everybody did it."[39]

All in all neither the structure nor the systems in Macnas were sufficient to carry an organization with any degree of ease or efficiency. Little wonder then that the first General Manager described each phase of the company as chaotic and personally traumatic:

> The first four years were complete and utter chaos. . . . At that time it was chaos. Trying to keep things on the rails every week. . . . The "Táin," 1992. That was great. Except it was a pain . . . as well. Again, similar problems. . . . I wrote the show. I was playing the King of Ulster. I was Production Manager. I was Company Manager. I was in charge of the tour and I did all the negotiations. That phase—from 1987 to 1993—was without a doubt, Macnas' most difficult and most traumatic . . . those six years were serious trauma. A lot of people left the company. A lot of rows. A lot of bitterness.[40]

Although records are deficient in this respect, it seems fair to assume that while the company achieved all its successes during this period, there were missed opportunities and failures as well. Furthermore, one must inquire into what actually kept Macnas afloat and a going concern, not to mention how it achieved the level of innovation outlined above.

Management of Transactions: Strategy

The strategy of Macnas was that of a classic entrepreneurial company. Founded on the basis of an opportunity presented by the ACE fund, it continued for a decade to lurch from one funding opportunity to another. Its success in this may be attributed to its high public profile as well as the persuasiveness of its General Manager. The mission of the company was so all-encompassing that it could easily allow it to adapt to widely diverse events, whether civic celebrations or rock music tours. Despite the preparation of some three-year plans to win core Arts Council commitment, planning was rudimentary. Its divisionalization into subcompanies was also funding-driven and quickly became meaningless as funds dried up.

Ultimately the vision of the company was too broad to act as a guide through the funding maze. Furthermore, Macnas' strategy for most of its existence seems to have been substantially deficient in terms of any reflective capacity, beyond learning some basic lessons in technical efficiency.

Management of Context: Leadership

The centrality of its first General Manager to Macnas is undisputed: "It all emanated from him very much."[41] It is clear that his ideas, instincts, and ways of working were what formed Macnas, first in collaboration with Ollie Jennings and then later with Rod Goodall. Everything seemed to depend on him:

> The structure worked well while he was there because of . . . the way he managed things. He managed things with him very much at the center. Which meant he would have a meeting with Peter about community. He'd have a meeting with Rod about theater. He'd have a meeting with me about money. . . . That was fine but if he wasn't there—when you took away that—then people were completely headless chickens. We didn't know what to do when he wasn't there because he influenced every single decision.[42]

"He called all the shots for everything. . . . Páraic used to go off and make decisions and come back and tell us who he hired or who he fired or what we were all going to do for the next six months or what way it was going to be."[43] This sits uneasily with the democratic, participative organization that Macnas purported to be. All accounts render Macnas as a heavily hierarchic organization: "It was a dictatorship!"[44] "We had what was described as a benign dictatorship and [there were], you know, references to fascism and that maybe Stalin had the right way of doing things!"[45] "Páraic was the dictator to a large extent!"[46]

Moreover, there is some suggestion of dysfunctionality in the leader-follower relationship, deriving to some degree from the marginalization of organization participants:

> Because of Páraic's personality it had attracted a very big team who liked to be led. . . . The people that worked in Macnas were very critical of themselves. . . . There was this dictatorship. . . . Really, when it came to their self-worth, they didn't really think that much of their work or themselves. Do you know what I mean? And it was easier for other people not to comment on each other's work because then, "if you don't say anything about my bad community arts projects, I won't say anything about your bad theater." Which is very immature.[47]

The central power of the General Manager is attributed by some to his exceptionally colorful personality:

> He was the big man . . . he walks into a pub and you can't ignore him. So he's a huge personality. He's a huge personality in Galway, y'know. He's Irish. He speaks Irish. He's well known in Ireland now. He has made a

reputation for himself from Macnas and he was able to leave and walk away from Macnas on his own terms and is a fairly big kind of personality. Like he might be invited to do "What the Papers Say" or be on a chat show or something![48]

Or simply there was the "amusement factor"[49] of dealing with him. Company members refer to the "insatiable" nature of the drive he brought to Macnas, his "persuasive and dominant" personality, and the extent of his dedication to the company:

> One, because he was extremely intelligent, and, second because his whole life was Macnas. I at least attempt, when I go home, to switch off, and have a family [life]. Whereas he would—you'd especially notice it on a Monday—have spent the whole weekend thinking about something and . . . you'd take a couple of days to catch up. He'd be ahead of—very much ahead of—most people, which he often found a bit frustrating because he felt . . . that he was waiting for people to catch up, as it were.[50]

That he had the charismatic power to motivate people was indisputable:

> Breathnach would have been at the helm of that stage very much and he had this skill of motivating people that I have never seen since. . . . That to me was his genius. He was fantastic to work for and you worked twenty-four hours a day for him quite happily. . . . I mean, I have seen him get five hundred people into a hall and get them motivated to go down the street and do the right thing and to come back and clean up afterwards and not ask for a pint.[51]

He himself was motivated by his aspiration to empower people, mainly financially: "his heart used to be—'Give the people, give the people the money!' "[52] However, poignantly, the sheer effort of carrying and driving the company took its toll.

> Terrible. Terrible. It nearly destroyed my life. And two years to get over it. But you are in there and you have no option. . . . The first four years were complete and utter chaos in that you were always behind, always fighting to keep people on board. . . . Just the time and money and effort . . . I was the chief designer and construction manager on "Gulliver." I was running the company at the same time. . . . And there were huge technical problems with "Gulliver" and it proved to be very, very, very traumatic. A very, very traumatic event. . . . The last twelve, fourteen years hurt too much . . . Painful . . . I lost my house, my wife, had a nervous breakdown in the middle of Macnas and I wasn't the only one. My health is permanently impaired from Macnas: I've hurt my back.[53]

The picture that emerges is of an organization, which, insofar as it had a structure, was oriented to project work. It was driven by a philosophy which not only did not distinguish between social objectives and the need to function as a going concern, but was emotionally confused and torn between these aims. The company was carried along primarily by the sheer effort of one person at a huge personal cost to him.

Management of Context: Culture

While the loosely structured nature of Macnas did not allow for the development of a uniform culture, the company nevertheless exhibited some traits that seemed to underlie its modus operandi and to set it apart from others. On the one hand the company always offered a level of excitement. A number of informants refer to the variety of work in the organization and the fun of working there. "It was different. Every week was different. Every second month was different. . . . So there was great camaraderie. . . . There were very flamboyant characters here as well . . . there was Páraic Breathnach and Rod and Pete . . . it was fun to come to work."[54] This carried over into their public spectacles:

> I thought it was a fantastic thing to watch, to do . . . to be part of, and also to say to other people, "Come on! Everybody be part of it!" and people to feel they had an ownership in Macnas. They were the special years, I thought, when the ordinary man in Galway would [feel] "I'm part of Macnas" or the kids would go "I'm going to do the Macnas" . . . it gave a load of people a big lift.[55]

When things were good, the central relationships between key Macnas personnel, though often stormy, could be characterized as a "healthy discourse," but when they were bad, they made for an extremely turbulent organizational atmosphere. The conflict took on all the character of a clash of the Titans. "They were very, very creative minds, which sometimes was brilliant and sometimes was horrendous because one person's idea would be fought against the other's."[56]

There was an unmistakable aura of "maleness" and an obsession with scale within the company. From such projects as "Gulliver" or the "Táin" Trilogy or many of their street spectacles, Macnas emerges as the Samurai of the Irish arts world, a (mostly) male band of arts warriors, well heralded fore and aft by their reputation, energetic, exuberant, and decidedly of-the-West, sweeping down in search of adventure, travel, excitement, fun, piloting their own brand of chaos, and specializing in the physical business of "making."[57] As with Robin Hood and his Merry Men, a less agreeable characterization of them as brash adventurers, animated by collective self-aggrandizement, concerned to propagate their own vision and mode of performance, attracted by the grand scale at the expense of the subtle or the meaningful, and tolerated primarily by virtue of the embarrassment or even *Schadenfreude* of urban sophisticates, might also be offered. These opposing images collide frequently in our effort to arrive at the elements that characterize innovation in Macnas.

While reputation and visibility always have an importance in the arts world, the unique importance of scale in the work of Macnas makes this subject worthy of special note. The initial mission statement of the company—one still used today—makes specific reference to "fun on a grand scale." Whether in terms of ambition, artistic output, or impact, the company always aimed for the large scale and spectacular: "Gulliver's" enormous size, the mythological grandeur of the characters in the Trilogy. While this might be a necessary element in the street parades where size was important for impact, one staff member hints at a pathological dimension—"I think it was just mainly the egos, you know? People had enormous egos."[58] This logic of scale explains Macnas' participation in the U2 tour: while an attempt was made to introduce an artistic theme to the roadshow,[59] it is clear that for the company members who participated in the tour, a large part of the attraction was the glamour of the association with U2: "For the twelve people that went on it . . . all of a sudden they had work for, whatever it was, seventeen weeks. They were better paid than they have ever been since. The money was very good. It was an incredible adventure touring all over Europe. With the biggest rock-and-roll circus ever."[60]

This engendered some internal conflict in Macnas, running counter, as it did, to the community arts dimension of the company, which, until 1993, was the primary rationale for its Arts Council funding. However, as already noted, the company's early success in theater and the opportunities this offered for display quickly seemed more attractive than the low-profile work to be done in community arts.

> Maybe this is my personal vision but I think that as Macnas began to develop the theater dominated everything. We were quite successful at doing theater. . . . Community arts basically aren't sexy, you know, compared to theater. You are not going to get to Australia or you're not going to get reviews in *The Irish Times* for doing parades in Ballinafoyle. Whereas you will if you do . . . Maybe I'm being kind of jaundiced here but I think that sort of colored what was going on; that the community art would happen anyway, whereas attention had to be paid to theater.[61]

Some company members recall small-scale projects in the early days of Macnas:

> In the beginning it was lovely because we were doing very small projects. We went to Belmullet. . . . The Arts Festival parade would have been our

biggest thing and then the first year I worked here was the first time we
brought the parade to somewhere else. We brought it to Belmullet and we
brought it to Waterford—you know, we had small things here and there
and in retrospect it was very laid back.[62]

I remember we took thirty students to Inisboffin, he [Páraic] and I,
and we did a little parade there and he'll tell you now that it was one
of the nicest times he ever, ever, ever spent when he was working at
Macnas. Do you know what I mean? . . . the little things that change
somebody's way of looking at things. You know that kind of thing? . . .
[Now] we have to bring a hundred million thousand people on the road
or else it's no good.[63]

However, most of the company fell for their own media hype: scale
alone seemed to give them the attention they craved. The belief that
they were "the greatest arts organization since Gengis Khan"[64] and the
need to sustain that self-image would seem by virtue of its inherent
delusion and its implicit rejection of any form of questioning or
challenge to risk leading the company ultimately to a dead end.

Another frequent source of conflict within Macnas and one that
relates to its innovative approach centered on its refusal of convention.
Though in the nonprofit arts world credits are usually determined or
fixed by convention, the notion of idea copyright became a fraught
issue. This is doubtless attributable to the fact that Macnas was
inventing itself from scratch, as well as the refusal of the General
Manager to accept any existential basis for such conventions. Ownership of ideas became controversial and acrimonious. This was both
a finance and an ego issue, deriving from the general fluidity of roles
within Macnas (reflected in their stage programs)—"you could change
from being a Stage Manager on one show to be an actor on the next
to be a musician on the next"[65]—as well as the proliferation of forceful
egos:

> The ownership of the ideas, who owned them and where they came from,
> who started it . . . who was going to get the bread of royalties for it, wasn't
> an issue in the early days. . . . The biggest row that Macnas had—we had
> a lot of rows all the time—but the biggest row . . . was the program credits
> for Seville. . . . Well, we were getting older and the company started getting
> more successful. The company started making an income. People wanted
> to make an income. We were poorly paid. . . . Also, people—some artists—
> perceived that others were getting [more] kudos. . . . The ego thing became
> a huge problem.[66]

Thus the culture of the company became conflictual and seemed unable
to find ways of resolving issues in such a way as to make for a viable
organizational environment.

Management of Context: External Environment

To what extent did its external relationships and networking capacity contribute to Macnas' achievement and reputation? The key relationships were with its funding bodies, primarily the Arts Council and the Department of Labour.

As already discussed, during its first decade Macnas was unashamedly funding-led and always alive to opportunities (commissions, special schemes, one-off events, EU training programs) which might enhance its income. Although Arts Council funding in the early days might be considered small in absolute terms, since 1992 the company became the major client in the portfolio of community arts organizations and remains in this position today. Relations with the Arts Council through its gatekeeper, Lar Cassidy, the Community Arts Officer, were extremely good and handled by the Officer to the maximum advantage of Macnas.

> Lar[67] was very much our hero and he was very good to us.[68]

> Lar was our great godfather. He helped us out in all things. . . . He was a fantastic man. A man of vision. . . . He gave us great confidence. . . . Well, we were good for him too, you see. We were probably the best area he had in that, you know, we were getting a lot of press. We were getting a lot of all sorts of things and that looked good for the Arts Council.[69]

The relationship was informal and oiled by personal friendship: the officer did not attend Board meetings which, in any case, were few and far between, and he availed of every opportunity to promote a positive reputation of the company. In addition to community arts funding, the company managed to access theater funding and saw this as a triumph in terms of breaking down barriers or preconceptions about the nature of their work.

> And then we got a foot in the door with a touring grant. Getting that was a big thing! This was like the real thing! . . . Macnas did itself very proud by doing that. . . . We'd actually been funded to do theater! So we could beat the Arts Council over the head with that and say "Right. Fund us to do a show!" and they did! . . . There was a lot of battles with the Arts Council as to whether or not we should be funded as theater, because I think there was a certain élitism about theater. . . . We had to break down those barriers and say "Well listen, this is as much theater as anything else!"[70]

While one of the ways in which Macnas sought to justify its Arts Council funding was in the propagation of its mission, the uncritical acclaim that their work received from that source as well as the seeming ease with which they accessed funding gave rise to a degree of resentment among other arts organizations: "I think in some ways that it went too fast and . . . there was a lot of resentment towards Macnas in that they felt it was pushing and dominating the agenda. . . . There was a lot of paranoia about the organization. . . . There was a jealousy towards Macnas. Other groups were jealous of us. . . . We were referred to as the Macnas monster. You know, don't mention the "M" word!"[71] (In 1994, Páraic Breathnach was appointed to the Arts Council.)

Relationships with the Department of Labour as the other major funder were good. This State agency also demonstrated a degree of flexibility, bending the rules to enable Macnas to hold on to trainees for more than one training period so as to enable the company to build up an ensemble: "We kept turning over the same people year in and year out. We didn't abide by the rules of the scheme."[72] This ability of the company to bypass rules must be attributed to the charisma and persuasiveness of Páraic Breathnach, endorsed by the media profile of Macnas.

In terms of other relationships—with audiences for instance— Macnas had no discernible policies other than a high consciousness of the need for a media profile. The frank inwardness of their mission, "have fun on a grand scale and amongst ourselves," seemed to be contagious. The tremendous success of first, their parades and street spectacles, and second, their theater productions, assured them of a public. Press relations were handled by the General Manager whose physical presence and personal color fairly ensured high visibility and extensive coverage. On occasion a professional publicist would be hired to deal with touring in Ireland, but in this as in almost every other functional area, Macnas lacked a system or any form of considered policy.

Macnas Now

Since the innovative reputation of Macnas attaches to its pre-1996 existence, here is given a summary account of the trajectory of the company since then to the time of this study. In 1996, following the departure of its first General Manager, Macnas, enabled by yet another EU fund, undertook what purported to be a root and branch examination of itself, its structures, and operation. This arose at what was undoubtedly a crisis point for the company. The process, aimed at reorienting and focusing Macnas, was long drawn out, taking place over a year, and drew extensively on the skills and advice of external consultants. It resulted in the constitution of a formal Board and a flat staffing structure which has a team of seven managers (all long-term members of the Macnas staff) reporting to a new General Manager. For the first time people were given job titles and a clear sense of their brief. It was also intended to make Macnas more democratic in its operation, allowing for greater input into ideas at all levels in the company. The Board comprises individuals (including Páraic Breathnach) with long associations with Macnas as well as some new people (a number of whom are Dublin-based), chosen for their expertise in relation to such areas as community arts, management, finance, and so forth. The change has engendered a work environment that is virtually a textbook effort to foster the creative capacities of all the company members with frequent meetings, working groups, and discussion sessions. The organization now keeps fairly conventional working hours. Reporting systems have been clarified and regular staff meetings ensure better communication and teamwork, largely due to the efforts of the new General Manager: "Each team has a leader or somebody who oversees their work. . . . If people have grievances they know where to go now. There's proper channels set up. . . . Everybody's got their job and everyone can see at any time where somebody's supposed to be. Those systems are brilliant. They stop people double jobbing. The chain of— not really authority—but responsibility is a lot clearer now."[73] Authority is not heavily enforced as before, but there is greater discipline: "because there's no boss as such, everyone knows that there's no point in being late every day."[74] Company members have a feeling of greater engagement at the level of ideas: "People are more aware of what's happening in community [arts] now and there's much more discussion about things like, for example, the new theater project or directions for the theater. . . . There's a lot more people involved in that."[75] This engagement has spread to the trainee level: "They wouldn't have a lot of say in what they did before, whereas now even the people on the Community Employment (CE) scheme have a say in how they make something [as] 'I think this is a better way because I'm a mask maker and, you know, we're making masks.' "[76] The leadership style is open and facilitative. "I think you have to have somebody in here that would bounce ideas off people. Declan's very good at that and listening to everybody and giving people exercises, as it were. You know—'Think about this and come back to me.' And if you have a terrible idea or if you have a good idea, he always takes them on board. So there's a good sounding board now."[77] Overall there is a greater sense of order: "What we try to do now is to give people more autonomy and give them more long-term strategic planning—of what they should be doing and where they are going . . . so . . . it's much easier to plan your personal life and your working life. And your funding applications always have to be planned. And so the relatively slack times can be used."[78]

Within Macnas this new structure has engendered considerable optimism about the future, tempered with a realization that the company now has to prove itself capable again of successful artistic innovation and achievement. There is a certain feeling both within and without Macnas that, by ridding itself of its artistic staff,[79] the company may lack the brio that previously gave it its innovative edge. Furthermore, in spite of the scope of the restructuring, the question arises as to whether it has been sufficiently radical. Similarly certain issues that would seem crucial to the identity of the company and to its artistic mission remain unresolved, as for instance the relationship between the different strands of the company—theater and community arts: "That relationship hasn't been really worked out yet and it probably won't be worked out until we actually start doing theater and then on the hoof. . . . I think we need to do a bit more work on mission."[80] In general it remains to be seen whether the company has achieved the integration necessary to its overall effectiveness and whether its activity can still be termed innovative. In the view of one commentator "Macnas has repeated itself now for a long time."[81] Nor has the old yearning for scale been excised: "People want to take theater from here to Australia and want to take Macnas to Australia. . . . It's still there... for example, when the Board were talking about things . . . that's what a lot of them want to see. They want to see Macnas travelling. They want to see big shows."[82] While people are happier, there is a feeling abroad that the company may lack internal challenge: "Now it's purely a facility house and it's not a vibrant artistic organization any more."[83] Fundamentally, however, as to the future of Macnas and its likely innovative success, the jury is out.

CONCLUSION—"OPPORTUNISTIC" INNOVATION

To conclude, three questions are addressed: first, what type of organization is Macnas; second, how did it survive for the past twelve years, sustaining a reputation for innovation for much of that time; and third, to what extent does it correspond with the description of innovative organizations offered in the research literature.

The question of Macnas' identity is even today, after over a year of organizational soul-searching, still unresolved. Is it a community arts organization or a theater company, a commercial body or a cooperative? While company members may answer by simply saying it is all of these, this is not as unproblematic as it may seem. These various disciplines are founded on different philosophies and impulses that led to conflict in the past. The identity of Macnas has been serial: its initial direction was a celebratory form of community arts activity. This was substantially displaced by theater work. Commercial work developed an importance along the way. The organization has been entrepreneurial in character, funding-led, and driven by opportunity, tending to shift direction as opportunities arose. Its expansionism in terms of mission, structure, and staffing, its spawning of subsidiaries, and its intent, whether through training programs or through the agency of its network organization, Macalla, to develop mini-Macnas organizations around the country, recalls the behavior of a multinational—without the financial capacity or success. This is at least mildly surprising given the socialist impulses that formed the company. Reference has also been made to the pathological dimensions of the company—its obsession with scale and display, its power/dependency relationships manifest in the willingness of company members to bend to the will of dominant personalities, its sexist attitudes, and, most seriously, its absence of challenge which led to a chronic strain of groupthink.

How, given the continuous turbulence that characterized its operation, did Macnas survive for as long as it did? Furthermore, how did it develop and maintain its reputation for innovation? The company lurched from crisis to crisis in an unreflective manner. Structure and systems failed to evolve effectively over its first decade: the same problems and issues recurred from one project to the next. This lack of reflectiveness was evident in relation to the aims, objectives, policies, and strategies employed by the company: new directions were adopted as opportunity arose, all being subsumed in the greater quest for money and reputation. The survival of Macnas may be attributed to three factors: first the unquestionable influence and energy of its founding General Manager who, at considerable personal cost and by sheer force of personality and commitment, simultaneously drove and dragged the organization along; second, the cushion of public funding provided in the main by the Arts Council and enabled primarily by the unreserved support of its officer; and third, the highly successful media management of the company, which from "Gulliver" on, attracted national coverage for their activities almost as a matter of course. The lack of a coherent artistic vision was compensated for by its chameleon-type adaptation whereby the company shaped itself according to the environment: for want of a sense of itself, the company became whatever was required. (The deontas[84] mentality of the west of Ireland, accustomed and practised as it has become to surviving on state aids, may well have influenced this approach.)

Macnas does not correspond with the accepted image of innovative organizations as organic as opposed to hierarchical. Its history, during its first decade at least, runs counter to the notion that such organizations are consciously built around a respect for the ideas of company members and that they actively seek to create conditions that allow for the flowering of the process. On the contrary it was heavily hierarchical; integration was made possible only through the central conduit of the

General Manager and the relatively small size of the organization; and motivation was firmly focused on extrinsic as opposed to intrinsic rewards. The company has now reorganized itself along the more organic model with increased attention to lateral communication and the spread of information, as well as scheduled opportunities for idea development and exchange. The artistic results of this process remain to be seen.

NOTES

1. Heroic cycle in early Irish literature.
2. Arts Council, Annual Report, 1987.
3. Macnas briefing document, 16/2/94.
4. For a list of productions with dates, see Appendix 5.
5. Letter from Community arts officer of the Arts Council to Páraic Breathnach, 14/2/92.
6. Lead singer with Irish pop group U2.
7. Macnas grant application to the Arts Council for 1994.
8. Macnas grant application to the Arts Council for 1997.
9. From a low of 2 percent in 1990, Arts Council funding in 1997 represents 65 percent of the total turnover of the company.
10. Páraic Breathnach, interview by author, tape recording, Dublin, 28/1/98.
11. "We the people" (Irish)—a sort of socialist battle cry.
12. Páraic Breathnach, interview by author, tape recording, Dublin, 28/1/98.
13. Former company member, Macnas, interview by author, tape recording, Galway, 26/1/98.
14. Former company member, Macnas, interview by author, tape recording, Galway, 27/1/98.
15. General Manager, interview by author, tape recording, Galway, 26/1/98.
16. Páraic Breathnach, interview by author, tape recording, Dublin, 28/1/98.
17. Staff member, Macnas, interview by author, tape recording, Galway, 27/1/98.
18. Staff member, Macnas, interview by author, tape recording, Galway, 27/1/98.
19. Former company member, Macnas, interview by author, tape recording, Galway, 26/1/98.
20. Former staff member, Macnas, interview by author, tape recording, Galway, 26/1/98.
21. Páraic Breathnach, interview by author, tape recording, Dublin, 28/1/98.
22. Staff member, Macnas, interview by author, tape recording, Galway, 27/1/98.
23. General Manager, interview by author, tape recording, Galway, 26/1/98.
24. Staff member, Macnas, interview by author, tape recording, Galway, 27/1/98.
25. Senior staff member, Macnas, interview by author, tape recording, Galway, 26/1/98.
26. Páraic Breathnach, interview by author, tape recording, Dublin, 28/1/98.

27. Staff member (female), interview by author, tape recording, Galway, 27/1/98.

28. Staff member (female), interview by author, tape recording, Galway, 27/1/98.

29. Staff member, Macnas, interview by author, tape recording, Galway, 27/1/98.

30. Former staff member, Macnas, interview by author, tape recording, Galway, 27/1/98.

31. Staff member, Macnas, interview by author, tape recording, Galway, 27/1/98.

32. Staff member, Macnas, interview by author, tape recording, Galway, 27/1/98.

33. Staff member, Macnas, interview by author, tape recording, Galway, 27/1/98.

34. Staff member, Macnas, interview by author, tape recording, Galway, 27/1/98.

35. Staff member, Macnas, interview by author, tape recording, Galway, 27/1/98.

36. General Manager, interview by author, tape recording, Galway, 26/1/98.

37. Páraic Breathnach, interview by author, tape recording, Dublin, 28/1/98.

38. Páraic Breathnach, interview by author, tape recording, Dublin, 28/1/98.

39. Former staff member, Macnas, interview by author, tape recording, Galway, 27/1/98.

40. Páraic Breathnach, interview by author, tape recording, Dublin, 28/1/98.

41. General Manager, interview by author, tape recording, Galway, 26/1/98.

42. General Manager, interview by author, tape recording, Galway, 26/1/98.

43. Staff member, Macnas, interview by author, tape recording, Galway, 27/1/98.

44. Former staff member, Macnas, interview by author, tape recording, Galway, 27/1/98.

45. Staff member, Macnas, interview by author, tape recording, Galway, 27/1/98.

46. Former staff member, Macnas, interview by author, tape recording, Galway, 26/1/98.

47. Former staff member, Macnas, interview by author, tape recording, Galway, 27/1/98.

48. Former staff member, Macnas, interview by author, tape recording, Galway, 26/1/98.

49. Staff member, Macnas, interview by author, tape recording, Galway, 27/1/98.

50. General Manager, interview by author, tape recording, Galway, 26/1/98.

51. Former staff member, Macnas, interview by author, tape recording, Galway, 27/1/98.

52. Staff member, Macnas, interview by author, tape recording, Galway, 27/1/98.

53. Páraic Breathnach, interview by author, tape recording, Dublin, 28/1/98.

54. Staff member, Macnas, interview by author, tape recording, Galway, 27/1/98.

55. Former staff member, Macnas, interview by author, tape recording, Galway, 27/1/98.

56. Staff member, Macnas, interview by author, tape recording, Galway, 27/1/98.

57. This gerund is used intransitively by company members to indicate what it is they do. Thus they will discuss "making," hold workshops in "making," describe a colleague as a very good "maker."

58. Staff member, Macnas, interview by author, tape recording, Galway, 27/1/98.

59. A vacuum cleaner was used to evoke the notion of ethnic cleansing, a message, it could be argued, that was totally lost in the in-your-face technology of the Zooropa event.

60. General Manager, interview by author, tape recording, Galway, 26/1/98.

61. Staff member, Macnas, interview by author, tape recording, Galway, 27/1/98.

62. Staff member, Macnas, interview by author, tape recording, Galway, 27/1/98.

63. Former staff member, Macnas, interview by author, tape recording, Galway, 27/1/98.

64. Former staff member, Macnas, interview by author, tape recording, Galway, 27/1/98.

65. Páraic Breathnach, interview by author, tape recording, Dublin, 28/1/98.

66. Páraic Breathnach, interview by author, tape recording, Dublin, 28/1/98.

67. Lar Cassidy, Community Arts Officer of the Arts Council.

68. Staff member, Macnas, interview by author, tape recording, Galway, 27/1/98.

69. Former staff member, Macnas, interview by author, tape recording, Galway, 26/1/98.

70. General Manager, interview by author, tape recording, Galway, 26/1/98.

71. Staff member, Macnas, interview by author, tape recording, Galway, 27/1/98.

72. Páraic Breathnach, interview by author, tape recording, Dublin, 28/1/98.

73. Staff member, Macnas, interview by author, tape recording, Galway, 27/1/98.

74. Staff member, Macnas, interview by author, tape recording, Galway, 27/1/98.

75. Staff member, Macnas, interview by author, tape recording, Galway, 27/1/98.

76. Staff member, Macnas, interview by author, tape recording, Galway, 27/1/98.

77. Staff member, Macnas, interview by author, tape recording, Galway, 27/1/98.

78. General Manager, interview by author, tape recording, Galway, 26/1/98.

79. All staff members resigned as part of the restructuring process. Then all were reappointed with the exception of the Artistic Director and the Director of Community Arts.

80. Staff member, Macnas, interview by author, tape recording, Galway, 27/1/98.

81. Former staff member, Macnas, interview by author, tape recording, Galway, 27/1/98.

82. Staff member, Macnas, interview by author, tape recording, Galway, 27/1/98.

83. Former staff member, Macnas, interview by author, tape recording, Galway, 26/1/98.

84. Irish for "grant." The willingness of individuals and organizations to do almost anything for a government grant has been frequently caricaturized as a feature of Irish life, particularly in the West. This is habitually referred to as "deontas."

6

Innovation in Arts Organizations: An Adjusted Focus

Having considered what is already known about innovation management both in the business and the arts sectors (Chapter 2), and having
examined the operation of three highly innovative arts companies via
an adaptation of A. H. Van de Ven's (1986) framework (Chapters 3–5),
we can now marshall the evidence and refocus the picture in a way
which allows another take on managing innovation in the arts.

We first offer a consideration of certain key concepts that emerge from
the empirical investigation of the three art companies. This discussion
allows us to revisit in a more informed way the three models derived
from Van de Ven (Table 2.5). We then draw together the evidence in the
light of the three case studies and to opt for the accented model as the
one that provides the best account of the management of innovation in
arts organizations. In the final part of the chapter we consider the extent
to which, given the research strategy undertaken for this study, our
findings have relevance to the arts sector as a whole. The book concludes with a statement of its contribution to thinking and theory on
the management of innovation in arts organizations.

FOUR KEY CONCEPTS

Institutional Processes

Throughout the examination of the three cases, the relevance of
"institutional processes" to the management of attention, transactions,
and context has been pointed out as well as the overall resonance of
these concepts and the mechanisms with which they are enacted (Figure

2.2) with the process of innovation. The main import of the discussion in this chapter is vested in assessing the fit between the empirical findings and theory. However, in addition the exploration of innovation-in-practice, through the rich empirical material furnished by the three cases, has highlighted four aspects of the management of innovation and the operation of institutional processes that in themselves contribute to a more highly differentiated appreciation and understanding of the process.

By operationalizing the concepts inherent in institutional processes, the case examination has uncovered certain aspects of the reality of their operation. It has highlighted dimensions that either have been underemphasized in the literature on innovation to date, or else that diverge in some fairly significant way from the dominant interpretation in the theoretical literature.

In the discussion that follows therefore, four vital aspects of the implications of the preeminence of institutional processes in innovative organizations are taken up: the organicism implied by such processes; the consequences of preserving environmental uncertainty as a means of managing attention; the management of reputation, which has emerged as inextricably entwined with the management of innovation; and the nature of leadership, which is pivotal to the operation of institutional processes.

These themes are not only important in relation to the conceptual framework but also emerged as significant in common across the three cases examined here. They are singled out for one or more of the following reasons: because their current treatment in the literature either has suffered from a degree of elision and thus may give an erroneous or distorted impression of the innovation process; they have not been explored or elaborated to the extent that the consequences attendant on their presence have received full consideration; or they have been treated in a somewhat uni-dimensional way which is at odds with the empirical evidence.

Thus there is a need to reconceptualize these core dimensions of innovation management and to rebalance them, as it were, within the innovation equation. The other aspects of innovation management have been more adequately represented or can be dealt with more summarily in the course of the discussion. The modified understanding that emerges from this more detailed consideration of these concepts will be subsumed into the reprise of the cases presented later.

Organicism. Attention has already been drawn to the affinity of Van de Ven's model for innovation with the features of organic organizations as described by T. Burns and G. M. Stalker (1961). Indeed the overall consensus in the theoretical literature is that organic structures are most conducive to innovation.

An organic organization is characterized by mutual adjustment, flat structures, a shifting locus of control, "realistic" job design, and intensive communication. Essentially such organizations are low on formality and hierarchy and depend instead for their purpose and cohesion on shared values and commitment. The suggestion is that innovation is fostered more readily by drawing on the ideas of all organizational members—more at least than would be the case in a hierarchic type organization—and that the realization of those ideas is also more likely given the high degree of participation and thus of ownership in their genesis. However, Burns and Stalker do not talk in absolutes: rather they see the hierarchic/organic axis as a continuum along which different organizations—or even the same organization at different times—may locate themselves, or itself.

To what extent do the three cases examined here meet the description of an organic organization? Each company shows clear evidence of a degree of organicism at all stages in their life cycle to date. The organic origins of both Druid Theater Company and Macnas have been noted and also, despite its more strategic beginnings, the operation of Opera Theater Company (OTC) for much of its existence has been very much that of an organic unit. However, it would seem too that there are varying degrees or levels of participation at different stages in the realization of each project (Figure 6.1). Idea generation at the very first stage is seen as the task and prerogative of the Director. As the idea begins to take shape, other staff members become involved, contributing their advice and ideas. Finally in the actual realization of the production, a number of other players come into

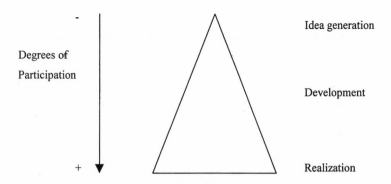

Figure 6.1 Participation Trends in Innovative Arts Organizations

greater focus and have a chance to contribute—the Stage Director, Conductor, technical personnel, and artists. While Figure 6.1 does not reflect the iteration that is typical of any real-life artistic project, it does describe an overall top-down thrust. However this does not take from the fact that ideas introduced at any level may affect the overall assessment of the level of innovation achieved by the company. The degree of mutual interaction and adjustment therefore confirms an overall tendency towards organicism.

However, in two important respects, the structural configuration apparent in the three cases does not accord with the classic organic model. First, while it is clear that the successful realization of their project supposes a genuine level of interaction between the parties to the enterprise and a real contribution on their part, the exercise of authority and control in these companies is not as Burns and Stalker or, indeed, as what little arts management literature as exists on the subject, would seem to suggest.

While there is variation in style between the three companies, the location of authority and control does not shift nor for the most part are matters "settled by consensus" (Burns and Stalker 1961, 122). Control remains firmly with the Director. In the case of OTC, authority derives from a number of factors: a range of in-built mechanisms; the symbolic power of the Director as an expert whose reputation has been sanctioned by the relevant cultural indicators; his close attention to detail and tight supervision of the operation of the company; and the inculcation within the staff of a way of doing things which is particular to OTC. Even in that part of the organization that seems most fluid and where control would seem to shift—the rehearsal period—the strategic elements of control still rest within the core company and more precisely, in the person of the Director, through such mechanisms as selection of program and personnel, budgetary allocation, and determination of deadlines. This control would seem for the most part to be lightly handled by the Director and, as such, to engender compliance rather than resistance. Hierarchy is not obvious or heavy-handed although the relatively high turnover of staff in recent years would suggest that personnel could either accommodate themselves to a certain modus operandi or not.

A more basic type of organicism is evident in Druid insofar as the organization is highly project-oriented and with less developed functional specialisms than OTC—though, at least in aspiration, moving in the same direction administratively as the opera company. The more classic organic mode (in terms of control) may have applied to the operation of the company from 1991 to 1994—during Maeliosa Stafford's period as Artistic Director. However, hierarchical control is much more evident in this case, with what minimal structures as exist

sent from an organization where staff members are buffered by structure or policy from the awkwardnesses—ambiguities, inconsistencies,
dissonance—of the outside world. The idea is to trigger the "action
threshold" (Van de Ven 1986, 596) of workers. Double-loop learning,
being more radical than single-loop, supposes a willingness to question
the operating norms of the organization and is thus by definition
unsettling. Again, the mechanisms for effective management of transactions by underlining the virtues of autonomy (and thus responsibility) also increase strain, while the preservation of uncertainty is by
definition painful except perhaps for those rare individuals with a high
tolerance for ambiguity. Thus all the strategies described by this author
are, almost of necessity, stress-inducing.

There is considerable evidence from the case studies of organizational
stress. First, the overall uncertainty of the arts environment poses
difficulties. According to the six dimensions of environments described
by H. E. Aldrich (1979), the arts environment is lean (in terms of
resources available); heterogeneous (insofar as the sector incorporates
a wide variety of organizational types and forms); unstable (in that
there is a high mortality rate for organizations); tends toward concentration (in resource distribution); is more characterized by domain
dissensus than consensus (in that the sector is still in the course of
professionalization and legitimacy building and in the case of many arts
organizations, there is little to prevent another company setting up and
staking a claim on territory which was formerly that of another); and
turbulent (the arts environment is growing in size and diversity with
concomitant increases in interlinkages and connections which are not
readily understandable by individual organizations). This puts the arts
environment into a category of unstable, concentrated, and turbulent
organizations, exhibiting a high degree of uncertainty "because the
rules governing environmental changes are themselves changing" (Aldrich 1979, 73). Funding is from year to year. Organizational legitimacy
is insecure. The outcome of an artistic project is uncertain. Audiences
are fickle. Competition for these audiences is within a wide entertainment sector and as such difficult to read. Barriers to attendance are
complex and being education and background dependent are not easily
overcome. While it is probably possible to guarantee a degree of success
in financial terms, for example by choosing a well-known play with
well-known actors presented in a comfortable venue, such options are
not usually open to an innovative company. The quotient of unknowns
is necessarily higher in work that is exploratory or experimental: it is
the essence of experimentation that there are few or no givens, even the
conventions of the genre being open to question. In addition, despite
the safety net of public funding, the situation is fraught with quanda-
ries: Will resources be adequate to realize the artistic ideals of the project

and the experimentation, which is the core of innovation? Will the project work with audiences? How will they react to the unfamiliarity or the interrogation/subversion of the familiar? In a situation of annualized funding, how can planning be properly managed? Will the affective mix so necessary to the live performing arts prove effective? And how will the core/temporary system dynamic operate? These imponderables are a factor in project after project.

Second, the efforts to combat organizational inertia and the stasis induced by institutionalization while preserving the value orientation, commitment, and organizational loyalty necessary to peak performance require considerable directed effort on the part of the organization and its leader. The personal exposure and high visibility of artistic work is also likely to increase the pressure on organizational members, and the high dependence on intuition as a guide, albeit informed or experienced intuition, envelops every decision in an atmosphere of risk. In addition, a number of writers have pointed to the legitimacy of conflict in innovative organizations (Cummings 1965; Thompson 1965; Zaltman, Duncan, and Holbeck 1973)—a consequence of the diversity regarded as conducive to innovation. This risk, uncertainty, and (often personal) exposure constitute a heady cocktail that almost inevitably places a strain on organizational management and relations.

How does this stress manifest itself? It is evident in high staff turnover (endemic in the sector, Clancy 1994) with many accounts of personal rifts and enmity, accusations of self-interested behavior, tales of personal pain, betrayal and disillusionment, and the demise of long-term friendships.

In addition, the insight provided by the case studies into the personal lives of the Directors of these companies is suggestive of considerable self-sacrifice and in general terms, a high price being paid for the innovative success of their organizations. It is worth noting, for instance, that to the extent that one can judge,[2] the dedication necessary to this task means that a personal family life may have been forfeited. Allusion has already been made to the necessity for a high-ambiguity threshold on the part of leaders of creative organizations. Though typically regarded as being endowed with a crystalline artistic vision and a readily accessible "sure touch," closeness to the organizations allows observation of the agonies of decision making, attributable to the uncertainty described above, especially in a situation where there is such high exposure and finely tuned awareness of the consequences and ramifications of decisions.

The absence of pattern on the artistic side at OTC heightens both attention and anxiety. And the effort to preserve organizational flexibility at Druid, its refusal of institutionalization, even a modicum of structure, and its tenacious hold on organizational autonomy all make the organization a prime exemplar of stress. The fact that there are no sacred cows at Druid and that everything is continually up for discussion and questioning means that staff members are constantly on unsteady ground, while at the same time much is demanded of them. This tension emanates from—and perhaps at the same time is most keenly experienced by—the Director because of her central and driving role in the organization. The same is true at Macnas (pre-1996) where the absence or outright rejection of convention made almost every aspect of organizational behavior a subject of contention. The sheer effort of leading such organizations, the personal sacrifice in terms of the time to nurture relationships or for a private life, and the resulting loneliness (expressed by two of the Directors interviewed) seem almost unavoidable and constitute a dark side of the innovation process which is curiously absent from many accounts of entrepreneurship.

Thus there is considerable evidence from the empirical work of the burnout associated with managing innovation, deriving both from the notable instability of the environment and the actual mechanisms necessary to the process. The highly driven nature of the organizations and the considerable demands on all organizational participants are in stark contrast to a prevailing view of arts organizations as happy places dedicated to the realization of personal creativity, and revert instead to a more feasible portrayal of the effort and costs associated with high achievement in any sphere. As Mintzberg (1996) puts it in his account of the innovation context: "Combining its ambiguities with its interdependencies, the innovative form can emerge as a rather politicized and ruthless organization—supportive of the fit, as long as they remain fit, but destructive of the weak." (1996, 692)

The Management of Reputation. The management of reputation emerged as a key dimension not only from the empirical aspect of the work undertaken here but also because it was impossible to discount it in terms of such important issues as the selection of companies for examination purposes. Although the topic is worthy of a detailed examination in its own right, the discussion here is confined to its significance as an aspect of institutional processes at the core of innovation. Furthermore, the use of the word "reputation" and related phrases in this section is intended to be value-free and without any suggestion of inauthenticity.

While Van de Ven makes (1986) no mention of the management of reputation as such, it is relatively easy to establish a link between this and his description of institutional processes as being focused on "the creation of an ideology to support the founding ideals; the use of personal networks and value-based criteria for recruitment; socialization and learning by sharing rituals and symbols; charismatic leadership; and the infusion of values as paramount to structure and formalize activities" (1986, 602–3).

Ideology, the preeminence of the personal, values, rituals, symbols, and charisma, might be termed the ingredients of reputation. Their pervasiveness in this study of performing arts organizations is such that it merits ringfencing as an aspect of innovation in such bodies.

The formation of an institution in the sense understood and described by Van de Ven has to do with the infusion of value into an organization or sector; thus institutions are in the first instance institutions of the mind and are based on values built up over time in complex ways. The tracing of these processes and mechanisms, their "structuration," is a whole area of study in itself and is related to reputational effects, including the evolution and development of fads and fashions,[3] as well as to the intrinsic value or worth of an organization or a sector: an interplay of shadow and substance. The exercise of forces that are both deliberate and subliminal—and deliberately subliminal—play a role in this process.[4] Of particular interest here is the part played by image and reputation management in the acquisition of institutional status as an innovative entity, especially in a small country and within a highly visible sector where much is played out at the level of the media.

Reputation had an impact on the selection of cases for this study. First, the opinion survey that constitutes an essential part of the approach to this, by virtue of seeking some form of consensus, recognizes implicitly the role of reputation. Second, the comments of informants— for example, the admission of some that at times they were naming organizations whose work they themselves had not necessarily seen— as well as the currents discernible by the researcher in the responses— the tendency to follow certain trends or fashions and the likely fluctuations in what is deemed innovative even within a relatively short time span—are indicative of the inextricability of the two concepts of innovation and reputation. Such dependence on perception is all the more likely given the absence of clear criteria, the shifting boundaries around the concept, and the endemic nature of controversy in relation to innovation.[5] (The indulgence of our own initial reaction to a substandard work by one of the organizations selected for detailed examination was also revealing in this respect.[6])

Whether construed as identity building, "deep" marketing or branding, or as a profoundly symbolic or semiotic process, whether constructed or intuitive, the management of reputation has consequences for both internal and external organizational operations. It is traceable in the Board selection processes of OTC where the key criterion of the public perception of members as "solid citizens" lends a legitimacy to the company, allowing it to fly its own kite. Each of the case studies is explicit about its significance in relation to the management of key stakeholders like the Arts Council. Its impact on audiences is clearly a determinant of box office response. Its overall effect in terms of internal operations may be characterized as a mirroring of its external impact. The docile nature of OTC's Board—its non-interference in artistic matters, its nonquerying of what might be regarded as disproportionate attention to policies which are peripheral to its main aim—is related to the reputation of the company (though also, as already acknowledged, to its solvency). Allusion has been made to the quasi-mystical "specialness" of Druid for some organizational members—even those with every reason to feel bitterness about their personal experience of the company in recent times. Similarly, the reported dominance of company members in Macnas was tolerated largely because of their perception of the spectacular success enjoyed by the company on the national and international front. In each case the association with a glowing public reputation had an overriding effect. Thus the reputation of a company has a potent impact on the organizational culture as well as on the outside world.

The mythical dimension—with its rich potential as a reputational storehouse—has been alluded to throughout the description of each of the cases. It is interesting that two of these are Galway-based companies, this fact in itself affording them a rich mythology which each of the companies exploited: on the one hand the romanticism of the west of Ireland, directly tapped into by Druid in its association with Synge, and by Macnas in its exploration of Celtic lore and heroic saga; on the other hand the east-west divide in the country as a whole—the traditional exploitation of the (rural) west, its institutional neglect and the concomitant defiance and bravado with overtones (however fictive) of the championing of the underdog, versus the metropolitanism of the (urban) east. The permission—or even license—afforded by such "historical halos" (Denzin 1983, cited by Owen Jones 1996, 11) is worthy of comment: it may be that elements such as the above allowed both companies to safely adopt a "David versus Goliath" stance, with reasonable expectation of ultimate triumph (in a way which might be considerably more difficult for a Dublin-based company, for instance).[7] However, as well as rendering organizations mobilizable, the stasis-inducing dangers of a nostalgic-type reliance on such myths are discernible from the organizational drift experienced by Druid from the early 1990s.

Reputation management may offer a solution to the dilemmas presented to an innovative organization by the necessity for uncertainty reduction. Kimberly's account of an innovative medical department traces its evolution from innovation to success via institutionalization.[8] In his view, as an organization ages certain processes inevitably take shape which reduce or remove its innovative capacity—"the transition from personal to impersonal and from instrumental to collective points of view" (1980, 39). As he defines it, this process of institutionalization has to do with uncertainty reduction—both internally in relation to social control and the structure of work, and externally to the organization in its relations with the environment. In his account, the environment offers certain opportunities at the time a new organization is created—the new body pushes its way into an available space or vacuum. However its longer-term survival means that it must knit itself into the surrounding environment, much as adaptation is necessary to ecological survival. Does reputation in some sense offer a way out of this, an escape route as it were? What if, rather than conforming to the rules, standards, and norms of society, one acquired a reputation which put one in a category of one's own—does this endow an organization with greater freedom, at least for a period? If one sees the environment mainly as a resource provider and thus the necessity to conform to it primarily as a means of ensuring resources, then the problem for an organization not wishing to conform is to find another way to acquire or guarantee those resources. Reputation may afford this window by winning the confidence of resource controllers (Van de Ven and Polley 1992).[9] In the arts world reputation attracts different kinds of resources—artists, money, and audiences—and thus obviates the necessity to conform. So a good reputation means that one can ignore or even break the rules.

Company reputation is managed through the manipulation, both instinctive and deliberate, of personalized networks and societal levers in such a way as to maximize the freedom of the company—its space to innovate. Rather than being a simple uncertainty reduction device, it is a tool to exploit it; a form of leverage that, when handled adroitly by people whose very element is the world of image making, may be used to make meaning, shape the environment to fit the organization and expand its potential to take risks. The ability to weave worlds and to "spin" is of inestimable value in a sector where there are potentially infinite ways of casting organizational action.

Each of the three cases described here achieved this in a notable way, availing of the components of reputation—whether company mythology or public perceptions or media image—to buy themselves the security necessary to their operation as an innovative entity. It is used to attract resources or, by reordering the environment, to carve out a space for innovation. While its application within the arts world may seem obvious, there is also good reason to extend it further: N. Nicholson's (1990) description of the semiotic, hermeneutic, epistemological, and ideological issues surrounding any study of innovation repeatedly points up its susceptibility at these different levels to the process of reputation management, independent of any sectoral specificities. The importance attributed to reputation by Kay (1993), who identifies it with architecture and innovation as one of his three legs of corporate success, is a further case in point.

Leadership/Autonomy. Van de Ven (1986) regards the infusion of charismatic "transformational" and supportive leadership as vital to animate the institutional processes necessary to innovation. N. King (1990) concludes from his review of the literature that there is a consensus that the type of leadership most conducive to innovation is supportive. Such leadership is consonant with the concept of autonomy central to Van de Ven's holographic metaphor and traceable in a number of other features of the framework model—for example, redundant functions, self-organizing units, and so forth. However, it is perhaps in relation to the leadership dimension that there is the greatest variance between the arts innovation literature and the empirical evidence collected in the case studies.

The notion of supportive leadership does not accord with the findings here which, as a regular feature, detail a more or less autocratic style of leadership and at worst, describe considerable breaches of trust between organizational members and leaders. This impression is no doubt reinforced by the emphasis that the small size of the organization inevitably throws back on management and leadership, as well as the explanation advanced by Kanter (1983) and DiMaggio (1992) who highlight the importance of leadership in the "integrative" organization. In the three cases examined here, the interplay of power differentials and the practiced use of these, impacts intimately on the functioning of the organizations. Not only is leadership dominant and tending at times towards the autocratic, but also in each instance, structures are skewed, albeit to varying degrees, to ensure the centralization of power.

How can this contradiction between the literature and the empirical findings be resolved while accounting for the paradox inherent in the actual feelings of autonomy expressed by staff members, despite the clearly discernible exercise of top-down control? The fact that this study enabled the interviewing of staff members at all levels of each organization means that these opposing positions may be refined, qualified, and hopefully reconciled.[10]

Two explanations may be advanced for the feelings of autonomy described by organizational participants. First and most cynically, these feelings may arise more from the youth and inexperience of staff members, faced with managers who undoubtedly possess sophisticated interactional skills and are adept at the manipulation of power levers. Staff members explicitly acknowledge the "persuasiveness" of the three organizational leaders in question, a feature that is undoubtedly reinforced by their stature in the arts world. Second, it would seem that there is a genuine sense in which the individual input of organizational members is necessary to the innovation process and that, for this to be released, a degree of autonomy is vital. Indeed such autonomy is more demanding than a prescriptive approach, as for example, a list of detailed instructions or the rules and regulations one might expect in a bureaucratic organization. The space allowed for individual input, the absence of prescription, the knowledge that expectations and standards are high, and the relative infrequency of approbational comment all challenge staff or other participants to bring a notable degree of attention to their work and trigger innovative strategies and solutions. L. Smircich and G. Morgan (1982) discuss the concept of leadership as the management of meaning, showing how this "can develop in ways that enhance, rather than deny, the ability of individuals for the definition and control of their world" (1982, 271).

The most vivid illustration of the authority/autonomy dilemma is the rehearsal process at Druid, which different actors describe in conflicting terms. While some feel that there is a genuine effort to arrive at a shared meaning and are conscious of the reality and depth of their input into a production, others describe the process as one in which they feel pushed and harried into delivering a rendition which is primarily in the mind of the Director. Thus, while both parties or points of view regard the process as demanding, the reasons given are opposing. This paradox may be resolved by the suggestion (borne out by the performances achieved by the company) that the type of collaboration demanded by the experience involves a detailed self-searching on the part of each participant to arrive at the "truth" of the experience or the character; such efforts are always difficult and may involve pushing the performer beyond the usual limits and her/his more habitual experience of directors in the more workaday world of theater, where, as in all other spheres of existence, outcomes are more frequently banal. So, in summary, the type of interaction and collaboration exercised or exerted by innovative organizations is high voltage and in sharp contrast to the friendly, all-in-this-together image of participative organizations. The conflicting accounts of the process also reflect the different levels of tolerance of the different actors.

Therefore, in these companies the relationship between leader and follower is not determined by role, rules, regulations, or even by any particular form of embedded custom or tradition; it is reinforced primarily by the symbolic power of the Director rather than by the checks and balances of the bureaucratic structure, and even though despotic and at times even seemingly ruthless in style, it is deeply dependent for maximum added value on an actively engaged rather than a passively compliant participation on the part of the other organizational members.

Summary

In this part of the chapter, the operationalization in the empirical work of some aspects of the "institutional processes" basic to Van de Ven's (1986) organizational innovation framework has been summarized: the characteristics of the organicism which is regarded as the most appropriate configurational arrangement; the burnout attendant on the application of primary innovation levers as identified by Van de Ven and others; the inextricability of reputation and innovation; and the paradox inherent in the combination of autocratic leadership with sentiments of autonomy.

Rather than being clearly organic, these companies manifest a hybrid-type structure, which, while they all share a number of clearly organic features, diverges from the classic model in the top-down, hierarchical style of their operation. While this conforms with Mintzberg's simple structure, it is worth pointing out that these organizations do not conform in some important respects to the classic organic structure, most notably in relation to the location of authority. Furthermore, the informality associated with organicism and with arts organizations alike is shown to be somewhat misleading as an indicator of both the tempo and the temperature of these organizations, diverting attention from their highly driven nature and the stress redounding from this. This account begs speculation as to whether in fact the organic/mechanistic distinction is useful in describing the dimensions of these organizations and if, as a means of capturing their essential character, it is itself in need of revision.

The burnout which is more than an occasional feature of such innovative companies, deriving from the fundamental effort to strike an appropriate balance between order and chaos in a highly uncertain context, merits greater attention than it is customarily given in the research literature. It undoubtedly explains in part the high turnover of organizations in the sector and as such is of considerable interest in public policy and resourcing terms.

The association of reputation and innovation emerges as more crucial than the incidental comment it has occasioned in the literature so far, and ranges from identity building, through the direct exercise of marketing, to the subtle and deft manipulation of levers and the interplay of forces which may seem ephemeral. The in-depth exploration of this dimension is beyond the scope of this study but merits further examination.

Finally, the type of leadership required for innovation, as evidenced in this study, is in stark contrast to that prescribed in the literature. However to describe it as simply autocratic is to underplay the interactive dimension of this type of leadership and to fail to account adequately for the degree of autonomy felt by organizational participants and necessary to the innovative project.

It is suggested that the above discussion fills out and enriches some of the vital components of innovation management, crystallizing their operation in the real world of practice. As such this constitutes a useful foreword to the following section, which represents the theoretical core of this exploration of the innovation process.

THE DRIVERS OF INNOVATION

Theoretical Consideration of Three Case Studies

In this section the task is to establish the drivers of innovation as uncovered in the empirical examination. First, a short reprise is offered of the three case studies—one that distills the essence and character of their particular variety or style of innovation. This enables a consideration and weighing of the evidence in order to determine conclusively which theoretical model best captures and most convincingly explains the phenomenon of sustained innovation in these performing arts organizations, against the background of the alternatives developed from the theoretical literature, as discussed in the last section of Chapter 2.

Druid Theater Company: "Primitive" Innovation. Twice the age of OTC and Macnas, Druid has managed to sustain a reputation for innovation for longer than any other Irish theater company. Its designation as an innovative performing arts company does not reside in its introduction of a new art form (Macnas) or in the presentation of a repertoire unknown to Irish audiences (OTC). Operating well within the conventional parameters of theater—the well-made play delivered in a building which is often but not always a theater—its innovative contribution derives primarily from a radical interrogation, even an excavation, of the corpus of Irish theater, past and present, desentimentalizing and revitalizing it and presenting it anew.

The character of the type of innovation that emerges from an examination of Druid, and here dubbed "primitive," inheres in two aspects of its operation: first, a distinctive trait that differentiates the company from the other case studies; second and related to the first, a difference in terms of degree or intensity in its functioning that is sufficient to set it apart from the others. The first salient characteristic of primitive innovation exemplified by Druid is its "degree zero" approach to its work. It is perhaps necessary to the radical interrogation referred to above that nothing is taken for granted in the operation of the company. Even though one could describe the nature of the work as repetitive— the production of one play after another—and even though it is conceivable that the establishment of a more or less smooth and efficient system would be feasible for such a task, the work at Druid has continually the character of a "first-time-ever" endeavor, where all its aspects are repeatedly subject to scrutiny in the relentless search for *the* right way for each project. The lessons of the past have a limited shelf life; experience is as likely to be dulling as it is to be enhancing, and professionalism as a designation or title has to be earned rather than taken for granted. As such, the company breaks all the rules, even those with the character of a natural law.[11]

The resistance to institutionalization which constitutes in analytic terms a prime feature of the company is endemic to this approach: it stands to reason that the norms or habitual ways of operating inherent in institutionalization are rendered suspect in a context where convention is constantly open to question and repeatedly has to prove its worth or usefulness. It is not that such norms are rejected as a matter of course in an iconoclastic fashion; rather they have to be continually subject to test and to demonstrate their value. This is attributable to an unflinching spine of authenticity which, while it may have faltered at times during the history of the company, has nevertheless in the main held its line with notable courage or cussedness (depending on one's perspective) in the face both of blandishments and tribulations.

Much of the pressure towards institutionalization comes from the environment, towards which Druid typically adopts a combative stance. It is as if the main dimensions of the outside world constitute a considerable counterforce, against which the company must wage an incessant battle if it is to achieve its artistic aims. External forces are regarded as at best suspect, at worst hostile, pushing the company towards an institutionalization which it resists: even gifts are potential poisoned chalices. The hostility of the environment is felt at every level: through the lethargy which is a normal human and organizational characteristic; the pressure to move in directions which might make sense in ways other than the strictly artistic; the parsimony of funds available; or even the seduction of success. All are resisted if they run counter to or seem inauthentic in the context of the motives or directions of the company, or obstruct in any way the imaginative realization of its enterprise.

The second distinction that sets Druid apart is the degree to which it exhibits an almost ferocious energy and tenacity protecting its flexibility and autonomy as an organization. Described variously by its Director as a "fight for insecurity" and a need for "constant retooling," this approach has resulted in the company periodically reinventing itself and its enterprise and reshaping the context of its work, while all the time retaining a strong distinctive competence. It also gives the turbulence, which is a feature of the operation of the company, the character of an inevitable side effect—rather than being, for instance, an indicator of incompetent management as such. Thus it can be said that Druid operates at a level of intensity and in a consistently higher gear than the other two case studies examined here.

Having considered the character of primitive innovation at Druid, the discussion now turns to its primary drivers. While leadership is an important driver of innovation in each of the three cases studies, the continuous fine-tuning necessary to maintain the "insecurity" which seems essential to Druid gives this dimension a primary focus in the configuration of innovation that best describes the company. The total commitment of the Artistic Director to the project, the intense and consuming attention she brings to the minutiae of the company's operation (notwithstanding her nominally part-time role), and her considerable personal prestige have carried Druid through projects and crises alike, justifying the frequent and commonplace identification of the two: "Druid is Garry; Garry is Druid." While this accords with the characteristics of most entrepreneurial organizations, it has been deliberately preserved in Druid: what structures and systems that do exist have developed and continue to be oriented so that decision-making power and control are highly centralized and vested in the person of the Artistic Director. Its leadership determines the salient characteristics of the organization—to the extent that these can be readily cast as extensions of the personality of the Artistic Director. Though organizational reorientations, with their attendant turbulence and high stress levels, have been presented persuasively as direct consequences of environmental conditions or change, it is just as likely that intimation of these outside factors and, as a consequence, policies and decisions issue from the intuitions[12] of the Artistic Director. Similarly, the position of the Director vis-à-vis the external environment is analytic and hard-nosed, intolerant of any sign of organizational complacency or drift.

While there is ample evidence of the operation of institutional processes as described by Van de Ven, the preservation of environmental uncertainty is particularly notable at Druid. Instead of the uncertainty reduction techniques, which can be shown to operate to a degree at both OTC and Macnas, environmental uncertainty is irradiated within Druid in a way which seems intimately connected with the level of innovation achieved by the company. Here, more than at the other companies, one has a sense of the "unstructured"[13] nature of the uncertainty with which the company has to contend. The reluctance of Druid to close off options and its willingness to take on board as fully as possible such dilemmas and problems as are associated with reaching an audience, for instance, while assuming considerable artistic (and financial) risks, are indicative of its full embrace of outside uncertainty.

Figure 6.3 (next page) summarizes the salient characteristics of Druid as outlined above according to the dimensions of the conceptual framework.

To what extent does the primitive innovation encountered at Druid correlate with the framework of the investigation. In every respect—founding ideals, recruitment, socialization, leadership, and attitudes to formalization—the institutional processes that are regarded by Van de Ven as pre-eminent in innovative organizations underpin the operation of the company. With the caveats described in the first part of this chapter, such dimensions as ideology, personalized networks, values, rituals, myths, and ideals all have greater explanatory value in interpreting the operation of the organization than the more technical processes of planning, formal policy making, and so on. There is ample evidence of double-loop learning in Druid's capacity to reformulate its mission in the light of changing environmental conditions.[14] However, most striking is the extent to which the company can inhale environmental complexity and uncertainty, coming up with novel solutions to the strategic issues that present themselves as a result. Closure (the most obvious means of uncertainty reduction) is typically resisted by Druid. There is little structure worth speaking of to act as an effective support or buffer. Flexibility is regarded as paramount and sudden reversals are the order of the day. Unlike OTC, Druid's strategy for uncertainty reduction depends not on the establishment through structures of set mechanisms for handling the environment to acceptable levels; rather it depends on the fluidity of the organization itself, its cohesion, and capacity to adapt, while keeping its compass fixed firmly on its overall vision.

Opera Theater Company: "Managerial" Innovation. The character of innovation in OTC is markedly different to the "primitive" innovation approach exemplified by Druid. This is termed "managerial" to convey a certain smoothness of operation, even a formulaic approach (though without negative connotations), which OTC has developed to create or clear a space for innovation as a regular feature of its enterprise. This is not to underplay the impact that all aspects of the behavior of OTC have on innovation in the company: rather it is intended to emphasize how deliberately and precisely this aspect of its operation is managed. Thus, as in the case of Druid's "primitivism," the "managerialism" of OTC refers more to the process or functioning than the actual output of the company. It describes an altogether more rational approach—captured perhaps by Kay's (1993) concept of "architecture," than that of the theater company.

In spite of the variety and the uniqueness emphasized by the Director in relation to each of the opera productions undertaken by OTC, and the range of permutations and combinations that can impact on each project, there is a reasonable level of expectation of innovation by virtue

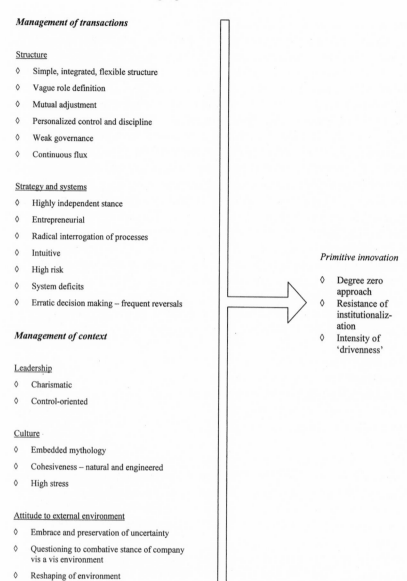

Management of transactions

Structure
◊   Simple, integrated, flexible structure
◊   Vague role definition
◊   Mutual adjustment
◊   Personalized control and discipline
◊   Weak governance
◊   Continuous flux

Strategy and systems
◊   Highly independent stance
◊   Entrepreneurial
◊   Radical interrogation of processes
◊   Intuitive
◊   High risk
◊   System deficits
◊   Erratic decision making – frequent reversals

Management of context

Leadership
◊   Charismatic
◊   Control-oriented

Culture
◊   Embedded mythology
◊   Cohesiveness – natural and engineered
◊   High stress

Attitude to external environment
◊   Embrace and preservation of uncertainty
◊   Questioning to combative stance of company
    vis a vis environment
◊   Reshaping of environment

Primitive innovation

◊   Degree zero approach
◊   Resistance of institutionaliz-ation
◊   Intensity of 'drivenness'

Figure 6.3 Features of "Primitive" Innovation (Druid Theater Company)

of the approach typically adopted by the company. Like a well-oiled machine, OTC delivers its wares in accordance with principles, norms, and standards that seem altogether more measured and predictable than the Druid way. On the whole it is fair to say that risks at OTC are more calculated—the company has not experienced the swings of fortune which are evident from Druid's history—and a generally more strategic orientation underlies its innovative achievement.

What then drives this managerial innovation? The reference above to architecture points to a response that has to do with the configuration of OTC. The structure of the company—comprising as its permanent side, a Board and core Executive (technical and administrative), and as its temporary system, a highly variable selection chosen from a pool of freelance artists—is well-constituted and, in general, particularly by comparison with the other two cases, runs smoothly and effectively. Its operation—touring, marketing, press, and staging—is marked by a significant degree of functional effectiveness, each organizational role reflecting a major strategic concern of OTC and performed, often in a classic manner, to a sophisticated level of delivery. Although like the other two organizations the company exhibits in recent years a fairly notable staff turnover, continuity is maintained (up to now) by the presence of a couple of key staff members, well-embedded norms of performance, and a satisfactory level of forward planning.[15] The existence of some administrative systems (though these are kept to a minimum), and a range of what are usually termed "soft" controls, help to ensure that standards of performance are relatively constant, while a high degree of mutual adjustment means that the company retains impressive organizational flexibility. Stress levels ebb and flow with the intensity of work demands, and while the latter remain fairly constantly at a high level, the output of the company being considerable, the degree of internal conflict or burnout would rarely seem to degenerate to the extremes experienced by the other two cases. Nevertheless, a strong work ethic and a pervasive company ethos are notable features of OTC. High performance is a *sine qua non*, norms for this are internalized, and those who cannot stand the heat leave.

The style of the Director is more managerialist than in the other two cases. As is clear from the financial history of the company—and in sharp contrast with both Druid and Macnas where competing agendas are reviewed only by virtue of necessity—the business side of OTC receives as much attention as the artistic, and at times in the history of the company has superseded the artistic dimension. While the director's vigilance has been noted, the diverse organizational elements (Board and Executive) of OTC have achieved an impressive level of autonomy which require for the most part a "tweaking" by the Director rather than the full-blown leadership which is so necessary to Druid and which has been a prime driver at Macnas.

OTC manifests a degree of sophistication in relation to the management of its environment. This is itself sufficiently well endowed in the resources (money and people, whether as artists, Board members, or even audiences[16]) necessary to sustain the company. To this dimension of its operation, OTC brings a high awareness, a keen understanding of the location and manipulation of power levers, and a capacity both to choose its focus of attention and effort and either to edit out or to manage to an acceptable level those aspects of its operation which interest the company (and its Director) less: again an instance of adept managerialism. The company has developed voices appropriate to different interests or constituencies, and its organizational structures are tailored to cope with major dimensions: the Board takes responsibility for the business of resourcing and the "management" of key stakeholders, particularly in terms of optics, thus allowing OTC to exploit the relative munificence of its small but elite audience, both in terms of funds and social standing; and functional roles in the company address marketing, education, press relations, touring policies, and sound financial management. Thus uncertainty is controlled, adequate levels of satisfaction are maintained on a number of axes, and the requirements of stakeholders are addressed to the extent that they allow the organization to pursue its innovation strategy unhindered.

This capacity is reflected in the company's programming which achieves a mix of the popular and the more avant garde, its exemplary record in financial management, and its strategies vis-à-vis the changing requirements of stakeholders. Its touring policy is a case in point. Funded to tour, the OTC approach to this has not developed in any substantive way over the years, is dependent on effective delivery of traditional approaches, and despite fairly spectacular marketing coups has failed to break the basic mold of audience interaction by reframing its environment in any notable way. Rather, operating almost as a sole trader or a monopoly in an environment with significant entry barriers,[17] what it does is adequate. The fact that the company has not experienced any real pressure from the Arts Council to develop audience relationships and the maintenance of a reasonable level of touring box office income are indicative of it having 'satisficed' in this regard. Perception and reputation are regarded and treated as a vital dimension of the environment. The expertise with which this approach is handled means that the indifference or even hostility of particular stakeholder groups to innovation therefore becomes irrelevant.

Thus the structure of OTC and its way of managing its environment bolster the company. The ingredients of its operation combine a degree of social standing and a high media profile (delivering legitimacy), a level of structural stability (delivering continuity of performance), a standard of satisfaction of key stakeholders (delivering security and a degree of licence), and clever artistic direction (delivering innovation). Indeed it is almost as if the shape of OTC is the result of a thoroughly worked out and finely balanced recipe which determines in detail exactly what is necessary to ensure survival, to meet stakeholder requirements, and to allow the space for innovative work, while at the same time keeping organizational stress to an acceptable level. Its expertise in this respect affords the company the room to take risks and to experiment in a manner that has earned it a high currency in the innovation stakes. In this too the company exhibits a careful approach: a Director new to opera will be coupled with an experienced Music Director; training courses prepare composers for composing for opera and singers for acting; inexperienced artists receive a greater degree of "care." Thus while risks are taken, they are calculated on the basis of the sensitivity which OTC has gained from experience.

Figure 6.4 summarizes the above along the dimensions identified in the framework outlined in Figure 2.3 (page 18).

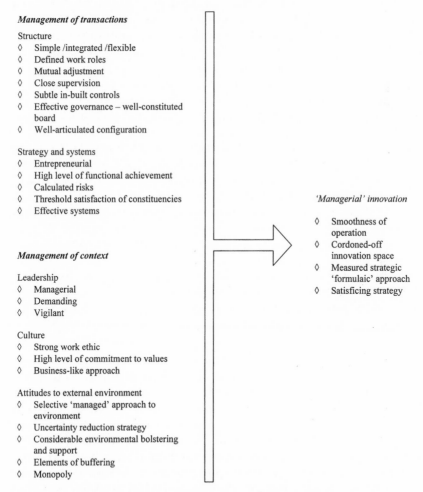

Management of transactions

Structure
◊   Simple /integrated /flexible
◊   Defined work roles
◊   Mutual adjustment
◊   Close supervision
◊   Subtle in-built controls
◊   Effective governance – well-constituted board
◊   Well-articulated configuration

Strategy and systems
◊   Entrepreneurial
◊   High level of functional achievement
◊   Calculated risks
◊   Threshold satisfaction of constituencies
◊   Effective systems

Management of context

Leadership
◊   Managerial
◊   Demanding
◊   Vigilant

Culture
◊   Strong work ethic
◊   High level of commitment to values
◊   Business-like approach

Attitudes to external environment
◊   Selective 'managed' approach to environment
◊   Uncertainty reduction strategy
◊   Considerable environmental bolstering and support
◊   Elements of buffering
◊   Monopoly

'Managerial' innovation

◊   Smoothness of operation
◊   Cordoned-off innovation space
◊   Measured strategic 'formulaic' approach
◊   Satisficing strategy

Figure 6.4 Features of "Managerial" Innovation (Opera Theater Company)

What then is the degree of correspondence between the empirical findings and the framework for innovation adopted in this study? Again, as with Druid, taking account of the provisos, qualifications, and omissions elaborated in the beginning of this chapter (e.g., organicism, leadership, etc.), innovation at OTC would seem to accord in general with and to reflect the main dimensions of the Van de Ven framework. Once again, institutional rather than technical processes are predominant in the management and behavior of the company; although OTC is more managerialist and businesslike than ritualistic in its operation, the balance of evidence is weighted firmly in favor of an ideological, value-driven, and personalized approach. The main techniques identified by Van de Ven for the management of context and transactions and thus of attention are all present to some degree or can be detected at some point in the history of the company—the directional influence of values and standards ("negative feedback"), the evolution of structures and systems implied by double-loop learning,[18] and the importation of some measure of environmental uncertainty.

However it is perhaps in this final dimension that OTC departs most noticeably from the Van de Ven framework in that, as shown in Figure 6.4, the company employs uncertainty reduction techniques to a significant degree, creating a safe space for risk taking within a delimited artistic domain in such a way as to present no real threat to the survival of the organization. In this regard it is less bold or reckless than Druid is. There is a sense in which the "big" question of how to engage an Irish audience, unaccustomed to opera and uneducated in music, with an unusual and difficult repertoire is not addressed in any way that would bear comparison with the relentlessly searching approach of the theater company. Nor has OTC experienced the organizational redefinition or repositioning noted in Druid. This is not to say that OTC is docile or acquiescent in its relationship with elements of the outside world,[19] but rather that it has developed mechanisms that constitute an effective buffer against the inchoate mass of uncertainty, which constitutes the environment of arts organizations.

Macnas: "Opportunistic" Innovation. As in the case of the other two companies examined here, it is as a function of the process which operates in the organization that the type of innovation exemplified by Macnas has been characterized as "opportunistic." While the output of Macnas up to 1996 was exuberant, iconoclastic, and contemptuous of convention, its style of operation was strongly determined by and built around opportunity and funding. In this the company took its lead from the environment, shaping itself to fit the opportunities which arose. While initially Macnas embodied a distinct and forceful identity which burst with considerable impact on the arts scene of the time, confounding neat categorization, ultimately, unlike OTC and Druid, its response to outside forces was not guided by any principled vision or set of values other than the vague and all-encompassing credo of people empowerment and the impulse to have fun "on a grand scale." Having established its core idea, the company became adept at tapping into opportunities and was happy for much of its history—belying its iconoclastic image—to change its shape accordingly, shimmying into whatever the environment-as-resource-provider wanted it to be. Thus the Macnas type of innovation is characterized as much by a lack or absence as the presence of any particular traits or features. This shall be related to Van de Ven's terms in due course.

That Macnas' innovation began as a result of a response to an environmental opportunity is not unusual—many innovative projects may be traced to just such incentives, which by allowing the breaking down of barriers or the fracturing of convention, stimulate high commitment and an unusual or fresh approach from respondents. Such projects are frequently and almost by definition short-term. The main interest of Macnas, as with the other two cases, lies in how it managed to sustain this innovation over a long period. While the chameleon-like adaptation to the environment is a classic survival strategy, a full embrace of the uncertainties associated with the outside world is likely to be too turbulent to allow for the continuity and even the minimal levels of stability necessary to organizational life.

Macnas may be classified as a hybrid of Druid and OTC both in terms of what drives innovation in the company, and over time. Like Druid, the survival of the company and its innovative impact may be attributed to its leadership, which by dint of its sheer energy and force (and clearly at great personal cost) pushed and pulled Macnas through its first decade. Other factors that contributed to its success—reputation and public profile, may be traced directly to the charismatic nature of its leadership. The impact of this was such that, also like Druid, Macnas succeeded in redefining its environment on a number of levels and to an extent that was unprecedented for an arts organization: it introduced a pagan ebullience into Irish society, which makes it meaningful to talk of a "pre- or post-Macnas" period; it redefined the notion of a parade, moving away from its only antecedents in Ireland—the religious procession or the clapped-out queue of tractor-drawn commercial floats which constituted the St. Patrick's Day event (pre-Macnas); and finally within the arts sector it established the notion that theater was not bound by the written word,[20] did not have to happen within a theater building, and by challenging the boundaries of operation in the Arts Council (as evidenced by its extraction of funding from a variety of budget categories and subheads; see Table 5.1, page 131), won a legitimacy for street theater as an art form. Similarly, its resistance to traditional boundaries, rules, and regulations in government training schemes was an indicator of the success of the company in challenging accepted notions of training and employment, again effectively achieving a form of redefinition. As well as a high degree of persuasiveness, this necessitated an instinctive tapping into the psyche of a country poised for change, much as Druid responded to the audience feel for a fresh version of old stories.

However, as time passed Macnas' fount of ideas seemed to run dry. Its strongly hierarchical mode of operation meant that idea generation, while it had a collective dimension, was largely from one source. This was overly focused on scale and limited in perspective to a superannuated notion of male heroism. Since neither of these concepts offer much in terms of scope or depth, the strategy of the company turned to the propagation or harvesting of its idea. To do this Macnas focused on certain aspects of the environment, seeking to ensure its survival by satisfying the requirements attendant on these. The internal changes adopted by the company (divisionalization) were largely inappropriate for an organization of the size and scant resourcing base of Macnas (although consistent with their obsession with scale and the company's preference for centralized control). Having made its initial mark, Macnas' strategy vis-à-vis the environment was therefore more one of uncertainty reduction: spotting opportunities, fitting itself to exploit these, and attempting as far as possible to harvest its then unique brand of packaged chaos. It is almost certain that this strategy lengthened the life span of this phase of the company, with resource providers showing themselves appreciative of the willingness of Macnas to shape itself to their requirements.

The uncertainty reduction strategies of OTC in their "managerial" approach to innovation have already been pointed out. However the resemblance between the two companies is superficial: while OTC retains control, it seems that Macnas lost it, lacking that core confidence, sense of direction, and identity that so clearly brands the opera company. Its mission, clouded by mere opportunism, dissolved into disillusionment and drift. It is almost as if by virtue of shape shifting and becoming whatever the environment required, the company mislaid its own identity. Its chameleon quality coupled with the inability to learn from its experience resulted in the dilution or drying up of its artistic wellspring and a growing sense in recent years of the company rehashing a single idea or an old formula.[21]

Moreover, in spite of a strategy that latterly is broadly similar to that of OTC, there was a difference in style. For most of the period which is under consideration here, Macnas never developed the structures or systems that allowed for some level of organizational security and calm, and that preserved a well-defined space for innovation—in the OTC fashion. This is a further indication of the inadequacy of reflection within the company.

Over the years, it failed to learn even rudimentary lessons as to how it might function, thus continually experiencing the same problems and conflicts by operating out of perpetual turbulence. This state of precariousness was ultimately more a result of the company's inability to convert its experience: a form of incompetence rather than a deliberate consequence of its modus operandi—as seems the case with Druid.

Macnas' dependence on leadership is also like that of Druid in that it produced some of the same effects: considerable organizational turbulence and conflict and a high degree of personal sacrifice and burnout. However since the engagement of the company with the environment lacked the sureness, deliberateness, and uncompromising nature of the mode adopted by and integral to Druid, and without the structures and techniques adopted by OTC, Macnas' survival as an innovative entity after 1996 was uncertain.

Figure 6.5 (next page) depicts the features of the "opportunistic" type innovation that characterizes Macnas.

To summarize, pre-1996 Macnas may be regarded as the manifestation of a hybrid type of innovation, which shares over time and in relation to structure and strategy some of what is to be found in Druid and in OTC. While, like the former, it is driven primarily by the enterprise, energy, and sheer force of its leader, more akin to the latter, it opted in the final analysis for a strategy of uncertainty reduction vis-à-vis its environment. As observed, Macnas, fundamentally rudderless, shifts as need arises or as opportunity presents, unimpeded by the radical authenticity discernible in Druid and unaided by the architecture (structural configuration, systems) of OTC. Where OTC controls the environment, the environment controls Macnas. Its formula was ultimately less flexible than that of the opera company.

Therefore, in Van de Ven's (1996) terms, there are notable deficiencies within the company in relation to a number of key dimensions—the preservation of environmental uncertainty and the necessity for double-loop learning. While some evidence of both is available at an early stage in the company, these rapidly dissolved or became distorted. This is indicative of a failure in what Van de Ven terms "institutional leadership," that is, the functions of "defining the institution's mission, embodying purpose into the organization's structure and systems, defending the institution's integrity, and ordering internal conflict" (1986, 602). This default leads to organizational drift which is accompanied by "loss of the institution's integrity, opportunism, and ultimately, loss of distinctive competence" (Van de Ven 1986, 602), all of which are clearly traceable in Macnas.

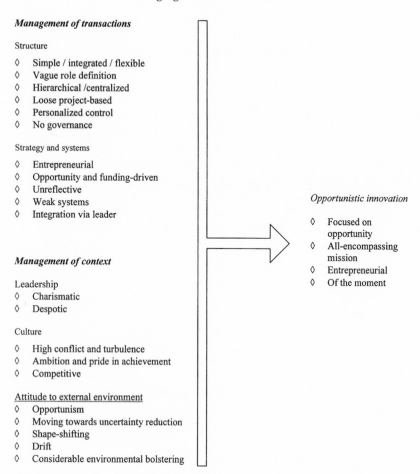

Figure 6.5 Features of "Opportunistic" Innovation (Macnas)

Comparison of Three Case Studies: Distinctive Features

Having shown that innovation differs in character at Druid, OTC, and Macnas, it is appropriate to consider briefly whether certain intrinsic features of the companies might account for this difference. The analysis to date has demonstrated that both OTC and Macnas benefitted from a significant level of environmental support over and above that normally enjoyed by other publicly subsidized theater companies. Also it is likely that their marginal location was of some advantage to Druid and Macnas.[22] The question is whether these factors account for the differences in innovation type.

All three companies operate within the subsidized arts sector, which already provides for a certain level of uncertainty reduction. Audience differences between opera and theater, while they may impact at the microlevel on resourcing, do not do so to the extent that they affect the fundamental financing equation to be solved by each organization. While the nature of opera might be said to necessitate a more planned approach than that of theater or community arts, there is ample evidence of opera organizations that exhibit considerable deficiency in this area. Therefore a planned "managerial" approach cannot be said to be a necessary condition or a logical consequence. Despite the high entry barriers, no arts organization can afford to be complacent about the continuation of Arts Council support—after all, the predecessor of OTC, which enjoyed considerable popular support, was summarily disbanded in the 1980s. While the championing of Macnas may have prolonged the life of the company in its pre-1996 manifestation,[23] it cannot be said to have provoked the innovation characteristic of the company during that period—especially since Macnas seemed to incite the same support in State organizations other than the Arts Council. Finally, though their marginal location may have impacted on the drive and energy of Druid and Macnas, the differences in innovation type between these two companies are more significant than their similarities.

Therefore while acknowledging certain differences and advantages, it is nevertheless unlikely that these are of a scale that would impact on fundamental organizational dynamics and override the drivers which distinguish between the types of innovation exemplified by the case studies.

The Accented Model

Common and Individual Characteristics. It now remains to show how, of the three models proposed in Chapter 2, the accented model represents the most persuasive theoretical account of the innovative process as exemplified by these case studies. First, Van de Ven's contention that "institutional processes" are central to the management of innovation is largely borne out. To illustrate their pervasiveness, Figures 6.3–6.5 have been integrated in Table 6.1 (next page). This shows the traits common to all three organizations as well as the main axes of difference.

The column in Table 6.1 showing common features corresponds by and large with Van de Ven's listing of institutional processes by virtue of its emphasis on personalized and ideological factors. However, there is a range of other organizational characteristics or processes that are as, it were, added to this basic recipe in order to account for innovation at Druid, OTC, and Macnas and which makes for the different character of innovation in each. The table also helps to clarify the similarities in

TABLE 6.1
Integration of Figures 6.2–6.4

Common features		Distinctive features		
		Druid— *'Primitive'*	*OTC—* *'Managerial'*	*Macnas—* *'Opportunistic'*
Structure	Simple, integrated, flexible structure, characterized by mutual adjustment	Poor governance Vague role definition	Well articulated architecture and effective governance Defined work roles	Poor governance Vague role definition
	Personalized control and supervision		Subtle in-built controls	
	Sense of continuous flux			
Strategy and systems	Entrepreneurial, intuitive strategy formation	Highly independent stance	Effective systems Calculated risk	Opportunity and funding driven Unreflective
		Radical interrogation of processes		System deficits
		System deficits		
		High risk		
Leadership	Highly driven personalized and charismatic leadership as a major driver		Managerialist	
Culture	Embedded mythology		Business-like approach	Ambition and pride
	Value driven			
	High stress			
External environment policies	Degree of uncertainty penetration	Embrace and preservation of uncertainty	Selective 'managed' approach	Opportunism and shape-shifting
		Questioning, combative stance	Uncertainty reduction	Uncertainty reduction
		Reshaping of environment	Considerable environmental bolstering	Considerable environmental bolstering
			Monopoly	Drift
				Monopoly

structure between Druid and Macnas and between OTC and Macnas in their attitude to and handling of environment effects, as well as highlighting the features of the more "managerial" innovation as exemplified by OTC.

From the preeminence of institutional processes, it can be assumed that the mechanisms by which these processes operate (negative feedback, double-loop learning, and preservation of uncertainty, as illustrated in Figure 2.2, page 15) are all present to a substantial degree within the three companies, at least for a period of time. The differences in emphasis in respect of these have already been pointed out, the most notable being the low reflective capacity of Macnas and its corresponding deficit in learning.

The three models proposed in the conceptual framework for this study (see Table 2.5, page 39) are located on an axis which moves from full to incomplete support for Van de Ven. While the clear presence of institutional processes in all three companies might point to support for the first of these, or the *integral* model, it does not account for the notable differences in the character of innovation discernible here. Fundamental to the accented model is the presence of certain organizational traits associated with innovation to a degree that is highly pronounced, while others exhibit a moderate or threshold level of influence. This allows for variation in the character or color of innovation and points to a diverse pattern of findings. The correspondence with the findings of this study seem clear.

To demonstrate this, Tables 6.2.–6.4 compare the characteristics of the three companies with the dominant expectations of the research literature, and identify the main and secondary drivers of innovation, thus offering a more detailed exposition of the theory underlying the accented model as it applies to Druid, OTC, and Macnas. A general sympathy with the research literature is noted. The "highly pronounced" column describes the main drivers of innovation at each company, already elaborated in some detail. To note the dominance of certain organizational features is not to underplay the necessity for other dimensions that kick in at a more basic or threshold level of influence, as indicated by the third column of each table.

Alternative Models. In arguing for the accented model of innovation, the claims of the other two models suggested in Chapter 2 must be considered. The integral model, which supposes full support for the Van de Ven (1986) framework, describes an almost ideal organizational configuration in innovation terms. As already suggested, the sustaining of such a level of institutional innovation with all that this implies— negative feedback, double-loop learning, and the preservation of environmental uncertainty—will inevitably entail a high level of

TABLE 6.2
Drivers of Innovation (Druid Theater Company)

Dominant expectation from research literature	Main drivers (highly pronounced influence)	Secondary drivers (moderately pronounced /threshold influence)
in relation to STRUCTURE: Organicism; holographic type; issues surrounding 'innovation dilemma'; some caveats arising from contingency theory.		Basic scaffolding (nominal board); strong concentration of power and authority; low functional definition; task orientation; intensive communication; co-ordination by mutual adjustment.
in relation to STRATEGY AND SYSTEMS: Some tendency to highlight entrepreneurial type strategy though simple formulations discouraged; 'soft'systems as in organic organizations; dynamic and fluid processes.	Notable level of control using both hard and soft mechanisms; High strategic self-awareness	Intuitive or ad hoc approach to governance, planning, reporting, appraisal and evaluation; uncertain efficiency; flexibility mixed.
in relation to LEADERSHIP: charismatic, supportive, pervasive	Charismatic and hierarchical; leader main source of ideas and policy; personalized approach; strong identification with and overriding influence on company	
in relation to CULTURE: dearth of research but importance of as a substitute for hierarchy; shared values, rituals, symbols; informality		Broadly shared value system; embedded general mythology; informal relationships; amenable to change.
in relation to EXTERNAL ENVIRONMENT: mostly speculative but preservation of uncertainty; active approach to scanning; general receptivity of.	High level of uncertainty penetration; tendency of organization to confront environment; high-risk approach; evidence of organization having reshaped environment.	Partial scanning; selective or strategic awareness of stakeholder concerns.

organizational burnout. Therefore a more likely scenario would suggest that such features could be sustained only for a certain period: it is unrealistic to expect a continuously high level of attention. Furthermore, as noted above, the integral model does not account for the variation in color as well as the diverse pattern of findings clearly discernible from these three cases.

TABLE 6.3
Drivers of Innovation (Opera Theater Company)

Dominant expectation from research literature	Main drivers (highly pronounced influence)	Secondary drivers (moderately pronounced /threshold influence)
in relation to STRUCTURE: Organicism; holographic type; issues surrounding 'innovation dilemma'; some caveats arising from contingency theory.	Well articulated structural components (board and executive) with distinct roles and a degree of autonomy; clear lines of authority dispersed across these; well-defined jobs; effective co-ordination and integration; impressive flexibility.	
in relation to STRATEGY AND SYSTEMS: Some tendency to highlight entrepreneurial type strategy though simple formulations discouraged; 'soft' systems as in organic organizations; dynamic and fluid processes.		Intuitive or ad hoc approach to governance, planning, communication, reporting, appraisal and evaluation; adequate control systems; internalized standards of performance.
in relation to LEADERSHIP: charismatic, supportive, pervasive	Leader—main source of ideas and policy; charismatic; managerial, vigilant.	Team emphasis; some diversity of input.
in relation to CULTURE: dearth of research but importance of as a substitute for hierarchy; shared values, rituals, symbols; informality		Company ethos; identifiably distinctive approach; work ethic; amenable to change.
in relation to EXTERNAL ENVIRONMENT: mostly speculative but preservation of uncertainty; active approach to scanning; general receptivity of.		Tendency of organization to accommodate itself to environment – to a degree; partial scanning; calculated approach to risk-taking; selective or strategic awareness of stakeholder concerns; reputation management; perceptible influence of organization on environment within a limited sphere.

The componential model offers another alternative and, on first consideration, might have been posited as an explanation for innovation in Macnas. The substantial presence of some features and a seeming deficiency in others would appear superficially to correspond with the "opportunistic" type of innovation. However, on balance, while

TABLE 6.4
Drivers of Innovation (Macnas)

Dominant expectation from research literature	Main drivers (highly pronounced influence)	Secondary drivers (moderately pronounced /threshold influence)
in relation to STRUCTURE: Organicism; holographic type; issues surrounding 'innovation dilemma'; some caveats arising from contingency theory.		Basic scaffolding; strong centralization of power and authority; low functional definition and sporadic integration and co-ordination.
in relation to STRATEGY AND SYSTEMS: Some tendency to highlight entrepreneurial type strategy though simple formulations discouraged; 'soft' systems as in organic organizations; dynamic and fluid processes.	Entrepreneurship; strong control orientation.	Intuitive or ad hoc approach to governance, planning, communication, reporting, appraisal and evaluation; uneven delivery.
in relation to LEADERSHIP: charismatic, supportive, pervasive	Charismatic and hierarchical; leader main source of ideas and policy; personalized approach; strong identification with and overriding influence on company	
in relation to CULTURE: dearth of research but importance of as a substitute for hierarchy; shared values, rituals, symbols; informality		Broadly shared mission; recognisable company ethos.
in relation to EXTERNAL ENVIRONMENT: mostly speculative but preservation of uncertainty; active approach to scanning; general receptivity of.	High level of uncertainty penetration at times; identifiable reshaping of environment by organization at certain periods.	Tendency of organization to accommodate itself to environment; partial scanning; opportunistic approach.

Macnas did not manage to sustain the different elements as identified by Van de Ven to the same extent as the other cases (a factor which led to its demise, at least temporarily, as an innovative unit), it can be shown to have exhibited these for a certain period of its existence. Were this not the case, it is reasonable to assume that it would not have achieved the innovation level it so clearly did for a time.

Life-cycle Considerations. Certain dimensions of the companies make it feasible to speculate that, within the accented model of innovation, the completeness or otherwise of accounts of the process (King, Anderson, and West 1991; Van de Ven and Rogers 1988). Thus the notion of leadership as supportive may be one which has been promulgated primarily by leaders!

11. Paradoxically the turbulence associated with the transition from founder to second Director (Gainer 1997) did not correspond with that event in Druid; the crisis instead breaking with full force on the return to the company of the original Artistic Director, thus, by a neat trick, bucking the usual life cycle of such organizations.

12. In any case, Druid has not conducted any research to inform such decision making.

13. Gibbons and Lai Hong Chung (1995) after Ackoff (1970) distinguish between structured and unstructured uncertainty. The former occurs when the top management team is aware of "the range of potential conditions [but] is unable to encode probabilities on their likely occurrence" (1995, 21); the latter arises when management "does not know the range of potential states of nature" (1995, 21).

14. As, for example, most recently in its recasting of itself as a project or event-led company with a national and international focus (even if some pieces of the jigsaw are still missing).

15. It is true that the intrinsic demands of the genre require more planning than is the case in theater—the international context of opera requires that artists, especially singers, be engaged considerably more in advance than actors, for instance.

16. Not that opera audiences in Ireland are considerable, but OTC, by virtue of extensive touring, has the potential to reach different audiences often on a fresh or first-time basis.

17. Another national touring opera company is unlikely to receive Arts Council support.

18. It is notable that this is directed more at internal processes in OTC than in Druid—hence its "managerialism."

19. We have seen that the opposite is the case.

20. Notably the prevalent tradition in Ireland.

21. We have already noted that it is too early to comment on whether the company in its current manifestation will manage to transcend this.

22. Concomitant with the neglect of the west of Ireland has been the psychic onus on State agencies to correct this imbalance and despite the disadvantages of peripherality, it can be argued that its Galway location has privileged both companies.

23. The privileged position of Macnas must be placed within the context of the development of community arts in Ireland. Since 1992 Macnas has been the major beneficiary of funding from the Arts Council's community arts budget, due in no small way to the personalized championing of the company by the Arts Council officer who held responsibility for that budget subhead, both because of his belief in and close personal affinity with the company and his political need to boost the status of community arts (which benefited from the national and international reputation of Macnas) within the Council. Thus both by virtue of its uniqueness and influence within the Irish context as well as for the above reasons, Macnas enjoyed something of a monopoly position, akin to that of the dominant player in a field or industry.

24. This corresponds with what Kimberly (1980) found in his examination of the history of an innovative medical school.

Appendix 1

Opinion Survey of Key Informants

An opinion survey of key and active informants in the Irish arts domain was conducted to establish which organizations were regarded as most innovative and to ascertain the dimensions of innovation and the meaning attached to it within the sector (Nicholson, 1990). Respondents were asked to name the five organizations in the live performing arts that they regarded as most innovative and to give a reason for their choice. As might be expected (Nicholson, 1990), many of the reasons given by respondents for their choice of organizations were circular: creative companies were described as new, inventive, imaginative, and so on. Nevertheless a consensus emerged as to what constituted an innovative company in the live performing arts.

First, it is evident that innovation is associated in particular with the capacity of companies to come up with new, bold, and exciting work. One respondent termed this the ability to go beyond the merely incremental; to take as it were an imaginative leap, independent of context. The fact that one would not know what to expect from a company was seen as indicative of its uniqueness and originality. Boldness, assertiveness, bravery, energy, and extravagance is valued, and even the scale of the work of certain companies was mentioned. Whether this imagination manifests itself in the fact that the company devises its own work, operates in unusual contexts, "pushes out the boundaries," demonstrates high variety, or is otherwise radical in approach, it is consistently associated with a willingness to take risks, to suffer big "highs and lows," and to operate with vision and energy. The fact that a company had spawned followers or imitators or had acted as a seedbed for talent was seen as a further indicator of its imaginative energy. The association of imagination with a particular person, usually an Artistic Director, was noted repeatedly.

A set of comments alluded to the intellectual dimension of some artistic work. The innovation level of one organization was said to derive from a scholarly base, which enriched its output. An ability to be selective, to commission intelligently or imaginatively, and to articulate a distinct policy or define a repertoire also sets the organization apart. Subversion of text in theater or of form itself in dance or opera gives an innovative dimension to traditional work and causes the audience to reevaluate their notions of the work or art form.

Second, and related to the above, are allusions to ways of working which people associate with innovation. The more conventional ways of stimulating new work, for example through commissioning, was sufficient to merit a rating. However, it is frequently the handling of material that renders a company innovative: a multimedia approach involving the linkage of art forms; the use of the traditional idiom in a new way; the ability to send up tradition or to give it a new life; the incorporation of more popular forms; the reanimation of the avant-garde; the ability to transform the conventional; fluidity of staging; and unconventional interaction with audiences—all single out certain companies. Respondents alluded frequently to the incorporation of European and world influences and their combination with Irish modes of expression to produce something distinctive. Linkages not only between different art forms but also involving partnerships with different categories of participants, as for instance community groups, young people, or people with disabilities, result in fresh forms of expression. In addition a contemporary orientation which speaks to today's audiences was found to be a feature of innovative work, either by making it relevant or rendering it more accessible—the use of English translation and a modern idiom in opera for example. In general close attention to process would seem to give a unique quality to artistic work.

In spite of an idea that innovation might be associated primarily with the avant-garde and thus by definition likely to be abstruse or esoteric, a number of comments took account of audience response. The fact that a company stimulated "spectacular public access" was seen as an indicator of innovation. In general, far from being regarded as inimical to the avant-garde, popularity was applauded as being indicative of an effort by an organization to relate to an audience. At the same time there was admiration for companies that rigorously pursued their own aesthetic, eschewing certain external pressures, and trusting that such artistic integrity would in itself create an audience without any dilution of the artistic mission.

Respondents referred frequently to qualities associated with commitment: the fact that companies work very hard; their ability to overcome constraints of repertoire and resources and their devotion to the aim of making "good art"; the phoenix-like characteristics indicative of continuous effort and high integrity; discipline and disregard for a seemingly peripheral location—all were referred to as traits associated with innovation. A "David-bias" was discernible in replies insofar as a fairly common theme was the triumph of the small, the poor and, in some cases, the socially committed. Another feature of this is the effort or courage to do the difficult, for example to make opera popular and accessible. Such traits as persistence, determination, discipline, and control were strongly associated with innovative artistic achievement.

Though high-quality work may be differentiated from innovation (DiMaggio 1987), respondents seemed to feel that a consciousness of high standards is a necessary component. The capacity to carry out work which meets the best international standards in terms of production values and ambition was lauded. Also it was felt that some companies, by virtue of these traits, set benchmarks for the sector as a whole. In cases where the innovative level of companies may suffer lapses, respondents still rated them on the basis of their track record and consistency and the fact that their overall body of work is impressive. The ability to reinvent themselves or to alter, to remain intellectually alive and questioning, and to avoid repetitive or formulaic repetition of past successes is part of this.

Even though the questions focused on output rather than management, administrative skills were referred to in a way that suggests their close connection with innovation in the minds of the respondents. The presence of a clever administrator; good planning, business, and marketing skills; appropriate positioning; able programming; the ability to get resources and use them well; a professional approach; technical expertise; the maintenance of a good team spirit; and a creative management structure were all seen as part of the innovative package.

Appendix 2

Data Collection and Information Sources

	OTC	Druid	Macnas
Interviews*	15 interviews: Director Deputy Chairman Founder member 2 current staff 1 composer 1 conductor 2 performers 2 stage directors 2 venue management personnel	11 interviews Director/Founder- director Chairperson General manager 1 former Artistic Director 2 former General Managers 2 former staff members 3 artist associates	7 interviews General Manager Founder-director Former artistic director 3 current staff members 1 Former staff member
Archival material	Records of productions Programs Brochures Minutes of board meetings (from 1988) Arts Council files and submissions Press files	Archive of 1st ten years, University College, Galway Press records, *Irish Times* Minutes of board meetings (from 1989 —with some lacunae —notably 1996) Arts Council files and submissions Press files: *Irish Times* Published material	Programs and brochures Company meetings minutes 1986/7 Board meetings from 1996 Arts Council files and submissions Some minutes of staff meetings Records of fromal change process Press files Video recorded productions and promotional material
Observation	Attendance at production rehearsals Observation in office Informal discussions with staff	Observation not possible because of cramped office conditions (company in transit) Informal discussions with staff	Some observation in offices Attendance at staff meeting Informal discussions with staff

Appendix 3

Druid Theater Company Productions, 1975–1989

Year	Name of Play	Author
1975	Playboy of the Western World	J.M. Synge
	It's a Two Foot Six Inches Above the Ground World	Kevin Laffan
	The Loves of Cass McGuire	Brian Friel
	Orison	Fernando Arrabal
	Act Without Words	Samuel Beckett
	The Glass Menagerie	Tennessee Williams
	An Entertainment on Marriage	David Campion and James Saunders
	Children of the Wolf	John Peacock
1976	It Should Happen to a Dog	Wolf Mankowitz
	Countdown	Alan Ayckbourne
	Who's Afraid of Virginia Woolf	Edward Albee
	Treats	Christopher Hamilton
	The Pongo Plays	Henry Livings
	The Glens of Rathvanna	J.M. Synge
	The Pot of Broth/Purgatory	W. B. Yeats
	Off Obie	Various Authors
	Happy Days	Samuel Beckett
	Mother Adam	Charles Dyer
1977	S. W. A. L. K.	Various Authors
	Tom Paine	Paul Foster
	Birdbath	Leonard Melfi
	There Are Tragedies and Tragedies	George Fitzmaurice
	Playboy of the Western World	J. M. Synge
	The Pursuit of Pleasure	Garry Hynes
	The Promise	Aleksei Arbusov

Year	Name of Play	Author
1977	Aladineen O' Druideen	An Original Production
1978	After Magritte	Tom Stoppard
	Sean, The Fool, the Devil and the Cats	Ted Hughes
	The Proposal	Anton Chekov
	The Enchanted Trousers	Oliver St. John Gogarty
	The Tinker's Wedding	J. M. Synge
	The Colleen Bawn	Dion Boucicault
	Bar & Ger	Geraldine Aron
	Woyzeck	George Buchner
1979	Threepenny Opera	Bertolt Brecht
	Village Wooing	George Bernard Shaw
	An Evening at Coole	Lady Gregory
	Eternal Triangle	Frank O'Connor
	A Galway Girl	Geraldine Aron
	The Importance of Being Earnest	Oscar Wilde
1980	The Real Inspector Hound	Tom Stoppard
	Thirst	Myles na gCopaleen
	Island Protected by a Bridge of Glass	Garry Hynes
	Fascinating Foundling	George Bernard Shaw
	Sundance	Meir Ribalow
	A Doll's House	Henrik Ibsen
1981	I Do Not Like Thee Doctor Fell	Bernard Farrell
	Master of Two Servants	George Mully
	Dial M for Murder	Frederik Knott
	The Nightingale and Not the Lark	Jennifer Johnston
	Geography of a Horse Dreamer	Sam Shepard
	Endgame	Samuel Beckett
	Much Ado About Nothing	William Shakespeare
1982	Private Dick	Maher and Mitchell
	Accidental Death of an Anarchist	Dario Fo
	The Shaughraun	Dion Boucicault
	Shadow of the Glen	J. M. Synge
	Playboy of the Western World	J. M. Synge
1983	Action	Sam Shepard
	Mother Courage	Bertolt Brecht
	The Rivals	R. B. Sheridan
	Rising of the Moon	Lady Gregory
	A Bedtime Story	Sean O'Casey
	Wood of the Whispering	M. J. Molloy
1984	Famine	Tom Murphy
	Same Old Moon	Geraldine Aron
	Beggars Opera	John Gay
	On the Outside	Tom Murphy/ Noel O'Donoghue
	The Glass Menagerie	Tennessee Williams

Year	Name of Play	Author
1985	Playboy of the Western World	J. M. Synge
	Conversations on a Homecoming	Tom Murphy
	'Tis Pity She's a Whore	John Ford
	The Importance of Being Earnest	Oscar Wilde
	Bailegangaire	Tom Murphy
1986	Dracula	A Frank McGuinness adaptation of the Bram Stoker Story
	Loot	Joe Orton
	Same Old Moon	Geraldine Aron
	Conversations on a Homecoming	Tom Murphy
1987	Conversations on a Homecoming	Tom Murphy – Irish Prisons Tour
	Waiting for Godot	Samuel Beckett
	A Touch of the Poet	Eugene O'Neill
	A Whistle in the Dark	Tom Murphy (in association with the Abbey Theatre)
	Oedipus	Sophocles
	The Hostage	Brendan Behan (including Irish Tour)
	Festival Playboy of the Western World	J. M. Synge
1988	The Factory Girls	Frank McGuinness, London/Irish Tour/ Glasgow
	Trumpets and Raspberries	Dario Fo
	Little City	Seamus Byrne
	I Do Not Like Thee Doctor Fell	Bernard Farrell
1989	A Little Like Drowning	Anthony Minghella
	Wild Harvest	Ken Bourke
	Lovers	Brian Friel
	Wild Harvest	Ken Bourke (Dublin & Irish Tour)

Appendix 4

Opera Theater Company Productions, 1986–1997

Year	Name of Production
1986	Turn of the Screw
1987	Cosi Fan Tutte
1988	Carmen and Don José
	Opera Nights
1989	Country Matters
	The Soldier's Tale
1990	The Rape of Lucretia
	Late Night Weill
1991	Falstaff
	New Opera '91
	Hansel and Gretel
1992	The Human Voice/ A Waterbird talk
	Tambourlaine
	Combattimenti
1993	High Fidelity
	(revival) 4 Dublin Operas
	Tenufa
1994	FlavioPagliacci/Frankie's
	From the Diary of Virginia Woolf/12 Poems by Emily Dickinson
1995	That Dublin Mood
	Tambourlaine
	Orfeo
1996	Zaide
	Amadigi
	Katya Kabanova
1997	Life on the Moon
	The Magic Flute

Opera Theater Company Coproductions: 1986–1997

Year	Production	Co-Producer(s)
1988:	Carmen and Don José	Opera Northern Ireland
1991:	Hansel and Gretel	Opera Northern Ireland and Welsh National Opera
1995:	Zaide	Transparent Muziektheater, Antwerp and RTE
1997:	Life on the Moon	Opera Northern Ireland
1997	My Love, My Umbrella	Eastern Touring Agency—Year of Opera and Music Theatre

Appendix 5

Macnas Productions, 1986–1996

The Silver Apples of the Moon (schools' show)
The Game
Gulliver
Tír faoi Thoinn (parade)
Alice in Wonderland (first indoor show)
An Slua Sí (parade)
Treasure Island
EP Moran and the Fir Bolgs
The Serpent and the little Big Game Hunter (children)
Circus Story
Táin
Capal
Noah's Ark
Moses Moran and the Three-and-a-half Wonders
Sweeney/Buile Shuibhne
Moby Dick
Hay Fever
Balor
Rhymes from the Ancient Mariner
Spellbound

Bibliography

MANUSCRIPT AND UNPRINTED SOURCES

Files

File Repository: The Arts Council, 70 Merrion Square, Dublin 2
    Applications for financial assistance, 1997, The Arts Council
    Druid files, The Arts Council
    Macnas files, The Arts Council
    Opera Theater Company files, The Arts Council

File Repository: Druid Theater Company, Druid Lane, Galway
    All company files and records

File Repository: Macnas, Fisheries Field, Galway
    All company files and records

File Repository: National Archives, Bishop St., Dublin 8
    Druid files. The National Archive

File Repository: Opera Theater Company, 18 St. Andrews St., Dublin 2
    All company files and records

File Repository: University College, Galway
    Druid archive

Theses

Chiapello, E. Les modes de contrôle des organisations artistiques. (Unpublished Ph.D. dissertation, Université de Paris IX Dauphine, 1994).
Gyllenpalm, B. How does Ingmar Bergman create peak performance in the theater? (Unpublished Ph.D. dissertation, Ann Arbor, MI 1995).

Lectures

Gainer, B. The life cycles of entrepreneurial nonprofit arts organizations. (Paper presented at the AIMAC conference, San Francisco, 1997).

PRINTED SOURCES

Reports, Newsletters Programs, and Brochures

Annual Reports. 1974–1995. Dublin: The Arts Council.
Art and the Ordinary. The ACE Report. 1989. Dublin: ACE Committee.
Art Matters. 1986–1997. Dublin: The Arts Council.
Arts Plan, The. 1995. Dublin: The Arts Council.
Burke, D. 1985. The first ten years. *Druid—The First Ten Years.* Galway: Druid Theater Company and Galway Arts Festival.
Coopers & Lybrand. 1994. The employment and economic significance of the cultural industries in Ireland. Dublin.
Druid—The First Ten Years. 1985. Galway: Druid Theater Company and Galway Arts Festival.
Edwards, D. O. 1985. Giants on the Fringe. *Druid—The First Ten Years.* Galway: Druid Theater Company and Galway Arts Festival.
Lally, M. 1985. A sisterhood and a brotherhood. *Druid—The First Ten Years.* Galway: Druid Theater Company and Galway Arts Festival.
O'Toole, F. 1985. Starting from scratch. *Druid—The First Ten Years.* Galway: Druid Theater Company and Galway Arts Festival.
O'Toole, F. 1996. A Moveable Feast. *Druid, 21 Years.* Galway: Druid Theater Company.
Richards, J.M. 1976. Provision for the Arts. Dublin: The Arts Council/The Calouste Gulbenkian Foundation.

Programs

All extant programs of Druid Theater Company, Opera Theatre Company and Macnas were examined and used as sources. These were accessed through the companies.

BOOKS AND ARTICLES

Acar, W., A.J. Melcher, and K.E. Aupperle. 1989. The implementation of innovative strategies. *International Journal of Technology Management* 4, no. 6: 495–513.
Ackoff, R.L. 1970. *A Concept of Corporate Strategy.* New York: John Wiley.
Adizes, I. 1975. The cost of being an artist. *California Management Review* XVII, no. 4: 80–4.

Aiken, M. and J. Hage. 1971. The organic organization and innovation. *Journal of Sociology* 5: 63–82.

Aldrich, H.E. 1979. *Organizations and Environments*. Englewood Cliffs, NJ: Prentice Hall.

Amabile, T.M. 1979. Effects of external evaluation on artistic creativity. *Journal of Personality and Social Psychology* 37, 2: 221–33.

Amabile, T.M. 1983. *The Social Psychology of Creativity*. New York: Springer Verlag.

Amabile, T.M. 1985. Motivation and creativity: effects of motivational orientation on creative writers. *Journal of Personality and Social Psychology* 48, no. 2: 393–99.

Amabile, T.M. 1988. A model of creativity and innovation in organizations. *Research in Organizational Behavior* 10: 123–167.

Amabile, T.M and S.S. Gryskiewicz. 1991. Creativity in the R&D laboratory. *Technical Report* 30. Greensboro, NC: Center for Creative Leadership.

Benson, C. 1989. Art and the Ordinary. *The ACE Report*. Dublin: ACE Committee.

Bourdieu, P. 1984. *Questions de Sociologie*. Paris: Editions du Minuit.

Burns, T. and G.M. Stalker. 1961. *The Management of Innovation*. London: Tavistock Publications.

Castaner, X. 1997. The tension between artistic leaders and management in arts organizations: The case of the Barcelona Symphony Orchestra. In *From Maestro to Manager: Critical Issues in Arts and Culture Management*, eds. M. Fitzgibbon and A. Kelly. Dublin: Oak Tree Press.

Clancy, P. 1994. *Managing the Cultural Sector*. Dublin: Oak Tree Press.

Cohen, W.M. and D.A. Levinthal. 1990. Absorptive capacity: A new perspective on learning and innovation. *Administrative Science Quarterly* 35: 128–52.

Crane, D. 1976. Reward systems in art, science and religion. *American Behavioral Scientist* 19, no. 6: 719–34.

Csikszentmihalyi, M. 1988. Society, culture and person: A systems view of creativity. In *The Nature of Creativity*, ed. R.J. Sternberg. Cambridge: Cambridge University Press.

Cummings, L. 1965. Organizational climates for creativity. *Academy of Management* 8, no. 3 (September): 220–27.

Cummings, L.L. and M.J. O'Connell. 1978. Organizational innovation: A model and needed research. *Journal of Business Research* 6: 33–50.

Daft, R.L. 1982. Bureaucratic versus nonbureaucratic structure and the process of innovation and change. *Research in the Sociology of Organizations* 1: 129–66.

Damanpour, F. 1991. Organizational innovation: A meta-analysis of effects of determinants and moderators. *Academy of Management Journal* 34, no. 3: 555–90.

Denzin, N.K. 1983. Interpretive interactionism. In *Beyond Method*, ed. G. Morgan. Beverly Hills, CA: Sage.

DiMaggio, P. 1987. Nonprofit Organizations in the production and distribution of culture. In *The Non-Profit Sector: A Research Handbook*, ed. W. Powell. New Haven & London: Yale University Press.

DiMaggio, P. 1991. Constructing an organisational field as a professional project: U.S. Art Museums 1920–1940. In *The New Institutionalism in Organizational*

Analysis, eds. W. Powell and P. DiMaggio. Chicago: University of Chicago Press.

DiMaggio, P. 1992. Nadel's paradox revisited: Relational and cultural aspects of organizational structure. In *Networks and Organizations*, eds. N. Nohina and Eccles. Boston: Harvard University Press.

DiMaggio, P. and P.M. Hirsch. 1976. Production organizations in the arts. *American Behavioral Scientist* 19, no. 6: 735–52.

Donoghue, D. 1983. *The Arts without Mystery*. London: BBC.

Downs, G.W. and L.B. Mohr. 1976. Conceptual issues in the study of innovation. *Administrative Science Quarterly* 21: 700–714.

Eliot, T.S. 1932. Tradition and the individual talent. *Selected Essays*. London: Faber & Faber.

Ettlie, J.E. 1983. Organisational policy and innovation among suppliers to the food processing sector. *Academy of Management Journal* 26, no. 1: 27–44.

Farr, J.L. and C.M. Ford. 1990. Individual Innovation. In *Innovation and Creativity at Work: Psychological and Organizational Strategies*, eds. M.A. West and J.L. Farr. Chichester: John Wiley and Sons.

Faulkner, R. 1983. Orchestra interaction: Communication and authority in an artistic organization. In *Performers and Performances: The social organization of artistic work*, eds. J.B. Kamerman, and R. Martorella. New York: Praeger.

Gibbons, P.T. and Lai Hong Chung. 1995. Defining uncertainty: The implications for strategic management. *IBAR: Irish Business and Administration Research* 16: 17–31.

Glassman, E. 1986. Managing for creativity: Back to basics in R&D. *R&D Management* 16, 2, 175–83.

Goodman, N. 1982. Implementation of the arts. *The Journal of Aesthetics and Art Criticism* XL, no. 3: 281–83.

Goodman, R.A. and L.P. Goodman. 1976. Some management issues in temporary systems: A study of professional development and manpower—the theater case. *Administrative Science Quarterly* 21: 494–501.

Gouldner, A.W. 1958. Towards an analysis of latent social roles. *Administrative Science Quarterly* 2: 444–80.

Grint, K. 1997. *Fuzzy Management: Contemporary Ideas and Practices at Work*. Oxford: Oxford University Press.

Guetzkow, H. 1965. The creative person in organizations. In *The Creative Organization*, ed. G.E. Steiner. Chicago: University of Chicago Press.

Guiot, J.M. 1987. Contribution to the sociological study of theatre companies. In *Economic Efficiency and the Performing Arts*, eds. Grant, Hendon, Owen, and Guiot. Akron, OH: Association for Cultural Economics.

Hage, J. and R. Dewar. 1973. Elite values versus organizational structure in predicting innovation. *Administrative Science Quarterly* 18: 279–90.

Handy, C. 1985. *Understanding Organizations*. Harmondsworth: Penguin.

Hirsch, P.M. 1977. Processing fads and fashions: an organization-set analysis of cultural industry systems. *American Journal of Sociology* 77, no. 4: 639–59.

Janis, I. 1985. Sources of error in strategic decision making. In *Strategic Decision Making in Complex Organisations*, ed. J. Pennings. San Francisco: Jossey-Bass.

Jeffri, J. 1980. *The Emerging Arts, Management, Survival and Growth*. New York: Praeger.

Kanter, R.M. 1983. *The Change Masters*. New York: Simon and Schuster.

Kanter, R.M. 1988. When a thousand flowers bloom: structural, collective and social conditions for innovation in organization. *Research in Organizational Behavior* 10: 169–211.

Kay, J. 1993. *Foundations of Corporate Success*. Oxford: Oxford University Press.

Kets de Vries, M.F.R. 1994. Reaping the whirlwind: Managing creative people. Working paper (8 April 1994), INSEAD.

Kimberly, J.R. 1980. Initiation, innovation and institutionalization in the creation process. In *The Organizational Life Cycle. Issues in the Creation, Transformation and Decline of Organizations*, eds. J.R. Kimberly, R.H. Miles, and Associates. San Francisco: Jossey Bass.

Kimberly, J.R. 1981. Managerial innovation. In *Handbook of Organizational Design*, eds. P.C. Nystrom and W.H. Starbuck. New York: Oxford University Press.

Kimberly, J.R. and M.J. Evanisko. 1981. Organizational innovation: The influence of individual, organizational and contextual factors on hospital adoption of technological and administrative innovations. *Academy of Management Journal* 24, no. 4: 689–713.

King, N. 1990. Innovation at work: the research literature. In *Innovation and Creativity at Work: Psychological and Organizational Strategies*, eds. M.A. West and J.L. Farr. Chichester: John Wiley and Sons.

King, N. 1992. Modelling the innovation process: an empirical comparison of approaches. *Journal of Occupational and Organizational Psychology* 65: 89–100.

King, N. and N. Anderson. 1990. Innovation in working groups. In *Innovation and Creativity at Work: Psychological and Organizational Strategies*, eds. M.A. West and J.L. Farr. Chichester: John Wiley and Sons.

King, N., N. Anderson and M.A. West. 1991. Organizational innovation in the UK: A case study of perceptions and processes. *Work & Stress* 5, no. 4: 331–39.

King, N. and N. Anderson. 1995. *Innovation and Change in Organizations*. London and New York: Routledge.

Koestler, A. 1967. *The Act of Creation*. London: Hutchinson.

Kolb, J.A. 1992. Leadership of creative teams. *The Journal of Creative Behavior* 26, no. 1: 1–9.

Lodahl, T. and S. Mitchell. 1980. Drift in the development of innovative organizations. In *The Organizational Life Cycle: Issues in the Creation, Transformation, and Decline of Organizations*, eds. J.R. Kimberly and R.H. Miles and Associates. San Francisco: Jossey Bass.

Lyon, E. 1974. Work and play: Resource constraints in a small theater. *Urban Life and Culture* 3, no.1: 71–97.

Manz, C.C., D.T. Bastien, T.J. Hostager, and G.L. Shapiro. 1989. Leadership and innovation: A longitudinal process view. In *Research on the Management of Innovation*, eds. A.H. Van de Ven, H.L. Angle, and S.P. Poole. New York: Harper and Row.

Merton, R.K. 1965. The environment of the innovating organization: Some conjectures and proposals. In *The Creative Organization*, ed. G.E. Steiner. Chicago: University of Chicago Press.

Mintzberg, H. 1979. *The Structuring of Organizations*. Englewood Cliffs, NJ: Prentice Hall.

Mintzberg, H. 1983. *Structure in Fives. Designing Effective Organizations*. Engle-
    wood Cliffs, NJ: Prentice Hall.
Mintzberg, H. 1996. The entrepreneurial organization. In *The Strategy Process.*
    Concepts, Contexts, Cases, eds. H. Mintzberg and J.B. Quinn. Englewood
    Cliffs, NJ: Prentice Hall.
Mintzberg, H. and A. McHugh. 1985. Strategy formation in an adhocracy. *Ad-*
    ministrative Science Quarterly 30: 160-97.
Mintzberg, H. and J.B. Quinn. 1991. *The Strategy Process. Concepts, Contexts, Cases*.
    Englewood Cliffs, NJ: Prentice Hall.
Morgan, G. 1986. *Images of Organization*. Newbury Park, CA: Sage.
Murnighan, J.K. and D.E. Conlon. 1991. The dynamics of intense work groups: A
    study of British string quartets. *Administrative Science Quarterly* 36: 165–86.
Nicholson, N. 1990. Organizational innovation in context: culture, interpretation
    and application. In *Innovation and Creativity at Work: Psychological and*
    Organizational Strategies, eds. M.A. West and J.L. Farr. Chichester: John
    Wiley and Sons.
Nicholson, N., A. Rees, and A. Brooks-Rooney. 1990. Strategy, innovation and
    performance. *Journal of Management Studies* 27: 511–34.
Nystrom, H. 1979. *Creativity and Innovation*. Chichester: John Wiley and Sons.
Nystrom, H. 1990. Organizational innovation. In *Innovation and Creativity at*
    Work: Psychological and Organizational Strategies, eds. M.A. West and J.L.
    Farr. Chichester: John Wiley and Sons.
Organ, D.W. and C.N. Greene. 1981. The effects of formalization on professional
    involvement. A compensatory process approach. *Administrative Science*
    Quarterly 26: 237–52.
Ouellette, P.F. and L. Lapierre. 1997. Management boards of arts organizations.
    In *From Maestro to Manager, Critical Issues in Arts & Culture Management*,
    eds. M. Fitzgibbon and A. Kelly. Dublin: Oak Tree Press.
Owen Jones, M. 1996. *Studying Organizational Symbolism: What, How, Why?*
    Qualitative Research Methods 39. Thousand Oaks, CA: Sage.
Payne, R. 1990. The effectiveness of research teams: a review. In *Innovation and*
    Creativity at Work: Psychological and Organizational Strategies, eds. M.A.
    West and J.L. Farr. Chichester: John Wiley and Sons.
Perrow, C. 1970. *Organizational Analysis: A Sociological View*. Belmont, CA:
    Wadsworth.
Peterson, R.A. 1986. From impresario to arts administrator: formal accountabil-
    ity in nonprofit cultural organizations. In *Nonprofit Enterprise in the Arts.*
    Studies in Mission and Constraint, ed. P. DiMaggio. New York: Oxford
    University Press.
Pierce, J.L. and A.L. Delbecq. 1977. Organization structure, individual attitudes
    and innovation. *Academy of Management Review* (January): 27–37.
Powell, W.W. and R. Friedkin. 1983. Political and organizational influences on
    public television programming. *Mass Comunication Review Yearbook*. Bev-
    erly Hills, CA: Sage.
Raelin, J.A. 1985. *The Clash of Cultures. Managers and Professionals*. Boston: Har-
    vard Business School Press.
Roberts, N. 1984. Transforming leadership: Sources, process, consequences.
    Presented at Academy of Management Conference, Boston, August.

Rogers, E.M. 1983. *Diffusion of Innovations*. New York: Free Press.

Schroeder, R., A.H. Van de Ven, G. Scudder, and D. Polley. 1986. Observations leading to a process model of innovations. Discussion Paper No. 48. Minnesota: University of Minnesota Strategic Management Research Center.

Simon, H. 1967. Motivational and emotional controls of cognition. *Psychological Review* 74: 29–39.

Smircich, L. and G. Morgan. 1982. Leadership: the management of meaning. *The Journal of Applied Behavioural Science* 18, no. 3: 257–73.

Staw, Barry. 1990. An evolutionary approach to creativity and innovation. In *Innovation and Creativity at Work: Psychological and Organizational Strategies*, eds. M.A. West and J.L. Farr. Chichester: John Wiley and Sons.

Thompson, V.A. 1965. Bureaucracy and innovation. *Administrative Science Quarterly* 10: 1–20.

Tushman, M. and D. Nadler. 1986. Organizing for innovation, *California Management Review* XXVIII, 3: 74–92.

Van de Ven, A.H. 1986. Central problems in the management of innovation. *Management Science* 32, no. 5: 590–607.

Van de Ven, A.H. and Associates. 1984. The Minnesota innovation research program. Discussion paper no. 10. Strategic Management Research Center, University of Minnesota.

Van de Ven, A.H. and E.M. Rogers. 1988. Innovations and organizations. Critical perspectives. *Communication Research* 15, no. 5: 632–51.

Van de Ven, A.H. and H.L Angle. 1989. An introduction to the Minnesota innovation research program. In *Research on the Management of Innovation: The Minnesota Studies*, eds. A.H. Van de Ven, H.L. Angle and Poole. New York: Harper and Row.

Van de Ven, A.H. and D. Polley. 1992. Learning while innovating. *Organization Science* 3, no. 1: 92–115.

Wallace, J. E. 1995. Organizational and professional commitment in professional and non-professional organizations. *Administrative Science Quarterly* 40: 228–55.

Weber, M. 1956. *Economy and Society: An Outline of Interpretive Sociology*. 1978 ed. Berkeley: University of California Press.

West, M.A. 1990. The social psychology of innovation in groups. In *Innovation and Creativity at Work: Psychological and Organizational Strategies*, eds. M.A. West and J.L. Farr. Chichester: John Wiley and Sons.

Wievel, W. and A. Hunter. 1985. The interorganizational network as a resource: a comparative case study on organizational genesis. *Administrative Science Quarterly* 30: 482–96.

Wilson, D.C. 1992. *A Strategy of Change. Concepts and Controversies in the Management of Change*. London: Routledge.

Wilson, J.Q. 1966. Innovation in organization: notes toward a theory. In *Approaches to Organizational Design*, ed. J.D. Thompson. Pittsburgh: University of Pittsburgh Press.

Wolff, J. 1981. *The Social Production of Art*. London: Macmillan.

Woodman, R.W., J.E. Sawyer, and R.W Griffin. 1993. Toward a theory of organizational creativity. *Academy of Management Review* 18, no. 2: 293–321.

Yukl, G. 1989. Managerial leadership, a review of theory and research. *Journal of Management* 15, no. 2: 251–89.

Zaltman, G., R. Duncan, and J. Holbeck. 1973. *Innovations and Organizations*. New York: John Wiley and Sons.

Zeigler, J.W. 1991. Succession and what's behind it. *Journal of Arts Management and Law* 20 (Winter), no. 4: 57-70.

Zolberg, V.L. 1990. *Constructing a Sociology of the Arts*. Cambridge, MA: Cambridge University Press.

Index

Organ, D.W. and Greene C.N., 25

Organicism, 12–13, 21, 23–24, 26, 35–36, 156–62, 171, 193. *See also* Burns, T. and Stalker, G.M.

Organization, size, age, resources, 27–29

People, management of, 19–21

"Primitive" innovation, 82–85, 172–75. *See also* Druid Theater Company

Professionals, 24–26

Public funding, 2, 163, 192. *See* Arts Council

Reputation, 165–69, 171

Stafford, Maeliosa, 54–55, 57, 62, 64, 72, 76–77, 158

Strategy, 26–27. *See also* Druid Theater Company; Macnas; Opera Theater Company

Structure, 21–24. *See also* Druid Theater Company; Macnas; Opera Theater Company

Theater. *See* Druid Theater Company and Macnas

Theory, of innovation, 9–42

Thompson, V.A., 22–23

Uncertainty, preservation of, 162–165

Van de Ven, Andrew, 9, 12, 191; culture, 31; innovation framework, 13–18, 37–38; institutional processes, 33, 155–56, 165–66, 175; leadership, 29, 169; uncertainty, 35, 162–63

Wallace, J.E., 25–26

Wolff, Janet, social basis of art, 11, 19